HOW TO DEFEAT THE FAR RIGHT

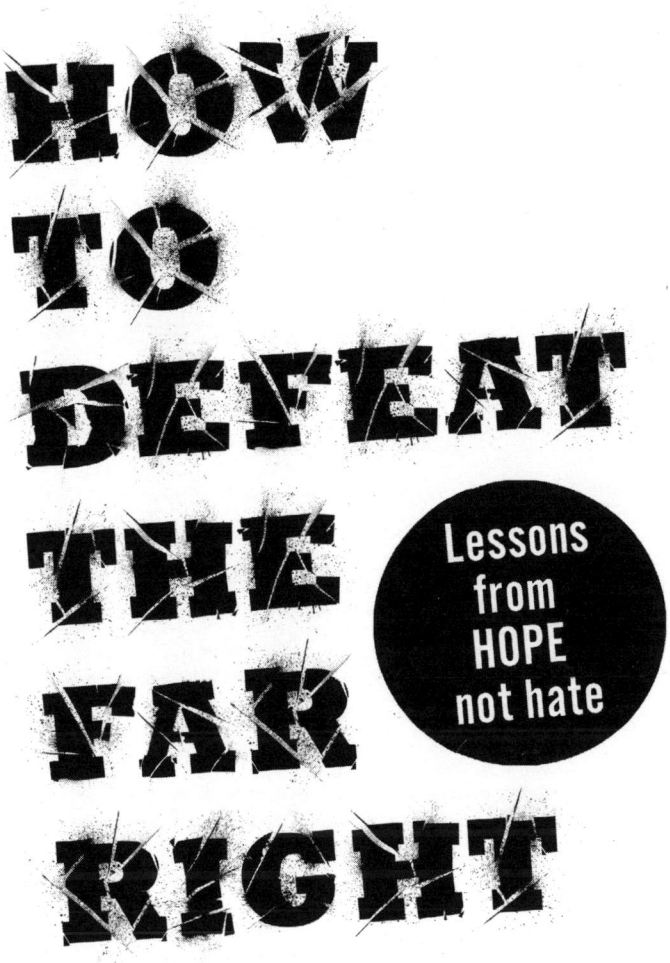

HOW TO DEFEAT THE FAR RIGHT

Lessons from HOPE not hate

NICK LOWLES

Harper North

HarperNorth
A division of
HarperCollins*Publishers*
1 London Bridge Street
London SE1 9GF

www.harpercollins.co.uk

HarperCollins*Publishers*
Macken House, 39/40 Mayor Street Upper
Dublin 1, D01 C9W8, Ireland

First published by HarperCollins*Publishers* 2025

1 3 5 7 9 10 8 6 4 2

© Nick Lowles 2025

Nick Lowles asserts the moral right to
be identified as the author of this work

A catalogue record of this book is
available from the British Library

HB ISBN 978-0-00-877297-0

Printed and bound in the UK using 100%
renewable electricity at CPI Group (UK) Ltd

All rights reserved. No part of this publication may be
reproduced, stored in a retrieval system, or transmitted,
in any form or by any means, electronic, mechanical,
photocopying, recording or otherwise, without the
prior written permission of the publishers.

Without limiting the exclusive rights of any author, contributor
or the publisher of this publication, any unauthorised use of
this publication to train generative artificial intelligence (AI)
technologies is expressly prohibited. HarperCollins also exercise
their rights under Article 4(3) of the Digital Single Market
Directive 2019/790 and expressly reserve this publication
from the text and data mining exception.

This book contains FSC™ certified paper and other controlled
sources to ensure responsible forest management.

For more information visit: www.harpercollins.co.uk/green

Two branches, one tree and a dog

Contents

Prologue 1

1. Eleven Days That Shook Britain 11
2. Local Heroes 23
3. In the Know 43
4. The Battle for Barking and Dagenham 61
5. When Hate Comes to Town 77
6. Tackling Taboo Issues 91
7. Celebrating Modern Britain 107
8. Kippered 123
9. Hate International 137
10. Civic Pride 155
11. Young Angry Men 175
12. Living Together … Well 199
13. Fool's Gold 223
14. Green Shoots 245
15. Power to the People 263
16. Hope 281

Acknowledgements 289
Notes 293

Prologue

'Police! Police!'

Lee can't remember if it was that shout or the heavy feet stomping up the stairs that first alerted him to the intruders in the house. It was shortly after 6 a.m., and he had been in a deep sleep. In what had become normal practice in COVID Britain, Lee had been up late on his computer.

As his shocked parents looked on, horrified and bemused, he was ordered to get out of bed and throw some clothes on. Lee's instinctive reaction was to reach for his phone, but he was ordered, in no uncertain terms, to put it down. Six burly officers in plain clothes and police-issue body armour manhandled him in handcuffs and made him wait while they searched his room before taking him downstairs into a waiting minivan. Lee's mind was racing. He knew why the police were there, but he couldn't quite understand how bad it was for him.

'I was fucking shitting it,' he remembers, now deeply embarrassed. 'I knew I was in deep shit.'

He knew what he had been doing was wrong, but in that moment, as the car snaked slowly through London's rush-hour traffic, he could not remember what specifically he had said and done to find himself in this position. He only knew he had been mixing in things that he shouldn't. To make matters worse, it was his birthday. 'What a way to mark the occasion,' he thought.

Lee was 16 years old, and he had just been arrested for allegedly disseminating terrorist material. He would be held for 11 hours, with officers taking it in turns to shout at him, before being released that evening into the custody of his waiting father.

A few weeks before that fateful morning, Lee had reached out on Instagram to a man who claimed to lead a group called The British Hand. It was a nazi* group that wanted to go beyond talking.

After swapping a handful of messages, Lee was told he would have to go through a vetting process, which turned out to be a few simple questions, like his name and why he wanted to join. From there, Lee was asked to download Telegram, a social messaging app widely used by far-right extremists, and join their group there. He had never heard of Telegram before but excitedly did so. Being in a secret group on an unknown app only increased the excitement for Lee. He was doing something special.

Lee had no idea that the person he was swapping messages with was also just 15.

'He seemed a lot older,' remembers Lee. 'I think during one chat he said he was 17 or something, but for me, at my age, that still seemed really old.'

Within days, Lee was hooked. He would check the private Telegram group several times a day, reading messages that others had posted, occasionally posting himself. There were no more than 20 of them on the group, if that, but this just made it more attractive for the young Lee.

Very quickly, the complaints about immigration, Muslims, the left and political correctness turned to discussions about violence and terrorism. 'I am planning an attack against the Dover coast

---

* In this book, 'Nazi' is a reference to Adolf Hitler's National Socialist German Workers' Party, while 'nazi' refers to post-war and current adherents to some or all of national socialist ideology.

PROLOGUE

where every Muslim and refugee has been given safety if you're interested tell me now,' the group's leader told the members.

Another person on the group was 18-year-old Matthew Cronjager, from Essex. He posted that he wanted to shoot a former friend who had been boasting about sleeping with 'white chicks' and was trying to get hold of a 3D-printed gun or a sawn-off shotgun to kill his teenage target, whom he likened to a 'cockroach'.

Lee felt increasingly emboldened by these conversations, and it was not long before he too was joining in. He had always wanted to join the army, so when discussion turned to infiltrating the armed forces, he quickly volunteered to do it. From there, he told the group, he could give them weapons training.

But then Lee went further. He had seen several references on the internet to the *White Resistance Manual*, an online white-supremacist terrorist handbook written by Axl Hess under the pseudonym Aquilifer in the late nineties or early noughties, which provided advice for making weapons and bombs, and explored the basic tactics of guerrilla warfare. Without a second thought, Lee found a copy online, downloaded it and then shared it in the British Hand group.

Lee knew that merely possessing the handbook had caused others to be convicted, but not for a moment did he think the authorities would be interested in him. 'Why would they be interested in us?' he would later muse. 'We were just a group of kids.'

But at the same time, Lee understood and totally bought into the seriousness of it all. 'I believed it all,' he would later reflect. 'I hated black people. I now hated Jews. I was willing to go all the way.'

Lee's radicalisation had been swift. Literally just a matter of weeks. The COVID lockdown had cut him off from any physical contact with his friends, and he began spending more and more time on the internet. 'Literally, I was on it all the time,' he recalled. 'I would wake up and go on the computer and besides sleep I was on it all the time. I would not even leave the house, go into the garden, I just wouldn't do anything else.'

He even took his meals upstairs so he could eat while online.

His internet usage was already probably more extensive than that of many of his friends when Britain went into lockdown in March 2020, but his shift in thinking and behaviour was still dramatic. Before lockdown, he had dipped in and out of 4chan, an online messaging forum that was increasingly used by extremists, but now he browsed at his leisure. He began following an account on Instagram called 'Black Pilled'. 'Red pilling', a term derived from the film *The Matrix* (1999), was associated with an awakening to a previously hidden reality and was widely adopted by the far right during the 2000s. 'Black pill', however, was first coined by the incel blog Omega Virgin Revolt in 2016 and referred to the perceived futility of fighting against the feminist system. It was considerably more negative and aggressive. While Lee was not interested in the anti-feminist agenda and did not subscribe to the incel – or involuntary celibate, to give it its full name – movement, he increasingly loved the dark side of the page. It mocked, derided and humiliated people. Black people in particular.

In Lee's mind, the dark humour of Black Pilled was a sharp contrast to the seriousness and pomposity of the left. There was no lecturing and none of the continual doomsday predicting, whether it be over climate, democracy or war. It made politics fun, imaginative, engaging.

The murder of George Floyd in Minneapolis by a US police officer on 25 May 2020 was a key turning point in Lee's political development. Up until that point, Lee's core friendship group had been split 50/50 between boys and girls, but Black Lives Matter (BLM) changed all that. 'Most of the girls were doing Blackout Tuesday,' he recalls. 'They were putting black squares up on their Instagram accounts as a sign of solidarity.' Most of the boys, publicly at least, remained silent, and few offered any public support for BLM.

Lee, however, was different. He was angry, and he grew angrier by the day. Why were their lives more important than his? Especially

PROLOGUE

'their' lives. In his mind, his growing dislike of black people now had justification.

As the girls in school, and society at large, aligned themselves with the racial justice movement and condemned structural and institutional racism, Lee was increasingly being drawn in by an alternate reality, consuming more and more racist content and anti-black memes. 'There were memes of black people being ugly, being stupid and being mad.'

'How can you support BLM when you see them for who they really are?' he would think to himself. Unsurprisingly, his friendship group split largely along gender lines. But just as they moved away from him, he was moving away from them: 'I started to build a narrative in my head where I was viewing the world, especially in America, about black people, about left-wing people, as negative. I was disgusted by them.'

The more online content he consumed, the more convinced he was about the righteousness of the arguments. A few lads at school would come up to Lee and privately share their support for his increasingly racist anti-BLM posts on his Instagram account, but most kept clear of him. Lee didn't care. Like many who had been red-pilled, he could now see the truth that was hidden to others, and if anything, it made him feel good. It made him feel special, and he increasingly felt part of an online family of like-minded people. By liking a post or a comment he agreed with, he was joining up with others who felt the same. Writing a comment that was liked by others made him feel he was being accepted and taken seriously.

He found the far right liberating. While the left lectured, the right empowered: 'The left would order you to read this or that book because it was the way to understand the truth. On the right, you were encouraged to read, but as a process of self-empowerment. You were constantly told that "you" would be a better and stronger person for doing so.'

He also became obsessed with 'fashwave', a form of synthwave music that had become popular in fascist circles from the 1990s onwards, giving fascism a cool edge among those who followed it. By July 2020, literally just a few weeks after his 'awakening', Lee was reading and watching more and more extreme content, including conspiratorial content about the Holocaust, polemics about Jewish control and diatribes against black people. It was not long before a vague interest in racist and anti-establishment content gave way to an urge to do more.

'It just made sense,' he later recalled. 'The reality had been shown to me.'

Getting involved and putting his ideas into action became the obvious next move, so when he saw the post from the leader of British Hand, he instantly reached out, wanting to get involved.

'I started to develop a saviour mindset,' he adds:

It made me feel special, unique. I went from 'fuck Antifa, fuck BLM' and I suddenly realised that something more needed to be done and I began identifying more with the right wing. I began to see myself as a fascist. I was also realising that I needed to do more than be online. In that moment, I felt like a partisan preparing to take on the occupier, I was fighting for a cause.

I was the only one who could see the truth. I was the only one willing to do what was necessary. And I was going to do it.

Unbeknown to Lee, though, another person had recently joined the British Hand Telegram group at the same time – Patrik Hermansson, a researcher with the antifascist organisation HOPE not hate, which I have been proud to lead for 20 years, and himself a veteran at offline infiltration. Patrik captured Lee's posts about military training. He was also online when Lee shared the illegal training manual.

Armed with enough clues to identify the leader of British Hand, we decided to go public with the exposure of the group. On Sunday, 13 September, the *Sunday Times*,[1] using our dossier, ran a story about the teenage nazis running a new far-right terrorist group. That

PROLOGUE

same morning, I filled in an online report to counter-terrorist police, alerting them to the group and attaching some of the worst posts.

A week later, the police, who had seemingly been unaware of the group, arrived at Lee's house with a warrant for his arrest.

Lee reached out to HOPE not hate in late 2024 after watching *The Walk-In*, a five-part ITV drama starring Stephen Graham based on the story of how an informant working for HOPE not hate inside the recently proscribed nazi terrorist group National Action (NA) supplied information to his handler Matthew Collins that saved the life of a Labour MP. 'I initially hated you,' Lee told me with a wry grin. 'You got me arrested. You got me convicted.'

'And now?' I asked him, trying to understand why he would reach out to his arch enemy.

After a short pause, he gave me his answer. 'I guess you saved my life and I'm thankful for that.'

We are living in dangerous times. Donald Trump's return to the presidency of the United States in early 2025 has heralded an increasingly authoritarian and far-right government. Trump is threatening to deport millions of people, invade foreign countries, embrace ethnic cleansing in Gaza, destroy public institutions, ignore the judiciary and bring economic chaos to the world. His presence is already emboldening other far-right governments and parties. There are far-right-led governments in Italy, Hungary, the Netherlands and Austria, while National Rally topped the polls in the 2024 French parliamentary elections and the Swedish Democrats came second in the Swedish elections of 2022. In Germany, the hard-line Alternative für Deutschland (AfD), who are so extreme that they are shunned by far-right and populist-right leaders like Marine Le Pen and Nigel Farage, came second in the German federal elections held in late February 2025. Further afield, Israel's Benjamin Netanyahu, India's Narendra Modi, Argentina's Javier Milei and Russia's Vladimir Putin all feel emboldened to continue their crackdowns on opponents and abuse human rights with seeming impunity. Nativist, anti-immigrant and anti-Muslim narratives are increasingly the norm, while action against climate change is being reduced or even reversed.

Britain is not immune to the rise of the far right. Farage's Reform UK received 4.1 million votes in the 2024 General Election and is now polling at levels where Farage could quite feasibly be the next prime minister. In July 2024, Stephen Lennon, better known as Tommy Robinson, founder of the English Defence League (EDL), led a demonstration of almost 40,000 people in central London, while his social media posts reached millions more. In the summer of that year, the UK saw its worst race riots for 100 years, with violent protests in 35 towns and cities, hotels housing migrants set alight and black and brown people violently assaulted. Feeding all of this is a radical-right ecosystem, made up of TV stations, radio shows, podcasts and online influencers. Their daily menu of nativist politics, anti-Muslim rhetoric and conspiracy theories feeds millions of Britons.

The far right is not a monolithic group and comprises the radical right and the extreme right. However, those on the far right share common ideas: chauvinistic nationalism – exceptionalism – of either a race or a country; the belief that the nation – either geographic or racial – is in decay or crisis and that radical action is required to halt or reverse it; and, in some cases, a sense of superiority and a desire for expansionism. The far right feeds off schisms and fault lines in society, and in Britain it is rising at a time when people are reeling from 40 years of deindustrialisation and more recently the cost-of-living crisis and are feeling an intense sense of pessimism about the country's future.

If the state of the world depresses and frightens you, then join the club. I've been fighting fascism now for over 35 years, and I've never known a time like this. The far right is on the ascendency at home and abroad, and clearly what we are collectively doing to oppose it is not enough. But it is precisely at times like this that we need to regroup, take stock of where we are and move forward with a renewed sense of purpose and hope. That is why I've written this book. It analyses where we are and where we need to go. It reflects on what we have done right in the past, what we have done wrong and what we must change to get it right in the future. The book suggests actions for the government, political parties, campaign groups and – most importantly – you.

At times like these, it is easy to hope that someone else does the hard graft that's needed, but the true answer to defeating the far right lives inside all of us. All of us who care about ending poverty, taking action against climate change and opposing racism have the collective power to change society. If we get organised, then we can win. HOPE can triumph over hate.

1

Eleven Days That Shook Britain

As the clock edged towards 8 p.m., the crowds began to grow. A few became a few dozen and then a few hundred. Men, almost all men, and angry too.

'We want our country back!' one shouted. Others soon joined in.

'Allah, Allah, who the fuck is Allah?' rang out. Again, it was repeated by the growing crowd.

The tension on the streets of Southport on that warm July evening was palpable. It had been almost 36 hours since nine-year-old Alice da Silva Aguiar, six-year-old Bebe King and seven-year-old Elsie Dot Stancombe had been stabbed to death at a nearby Taylor Swift-themed dance and yoga event. Eight more children and two adults were also injured in the frenzied attack. Though the police arrested a 17-year-old at the scene, his age and a lack of a confirmed motive meant there was little else the authorities could publicly say.

The outpouring of grief at this despicable act soon turned to anger and rage. By nightfall, an account called the 'European Conservative' had posted on X that 'a migrant stabbed numerous children at a holiday nursery'. Former kickboxing champion and social media influencer Andrew Tate told his three million followers on X, in a post that was viewed over 12 million times, that 'an undocumented migrant decided to go into a Taylor Swift dance class today and stab six little girls'. A largely unknown online news outlet, Channel3Now, which made its money by aggregating crime news and social media posts, claimed the attacker was an asylum seeker who had arrived in the UK on a small boat the previous year and was on an MI6 watch-list.

Presumably referencing some of this disinformation, Farage waded in: 'I just wonder whether the truth is being withheld from us,' he posted on X. 'I don't know the answer to that: I think it's a fair and legitimate question.'

Two social media posts gained local traction. The first was from Eddie Murray, who lived near Southport, who posted on LinkedIn just three hours after the attack:

> My two youngest children went to holiday club this morning in Southport for a day of fun only for a migrant to enter and murder/fatally wound multiple children. My kids are fine. They are shocked and in hysterics, but they are safe. My thoughts are with the other 30 kids and families that are suffering right now.
>
> If there's any time to close the borders completely it's right now! Enough is enough.

The other, again on the afternoon of the murders, was from a new account on the social messaging platform Telegram. It was written by a self-confessed nazi by the name of 'Stimpy' and posted on a channel entitled Southport WakeUp. If the first post conveyed very personal fury at what had just occurred, the second channelled that rage into action. 'Enough is enough. PROTEST, Tuesday 30 July 8pm, St Lukes Road, Southport.'

Perhaps people would have come out on the streets regardless, but St Luke's Road began filling up at the time Stimpy had designated. Perhaps by coincidence, though more likely by design, the meeting point was just metres from the local mosque.

'At about eight o'clock, it started to build,' Ibrahim Hussein, the chairman of the local mosque, told one journalist. 'There were a couple of blokes standing on the other side looking over the fence, and then the two became five and the five became 50 and the 50 became 500. Then the abuse started and the chanting started, you know, the F-words and the C-words and all that.'[1]

People began kicking at the wall on the perimeter of the mosque, and it was not long before it crumbled. Men picked up bricks, some throwing them in the direction of the mosque, while others turned and used them against the police. 'The whole building was shaking [because] of the missiles that they kept throwing,' remembers Hussein. He and the other men inside the building made their way up to his second-floor office, where they locked themselves in.

Outside, the violence was intensifying. The police appeared ill-prepared. Despite a warning in a briefing sent to them by HOPE not hate earlier in the day, they had not considered the mosque a target, so they quickly found themselves on the wrong side of the protesters. Worse still, none of the police were in riot gear, nor were there any officers in riot gear reserve. By the time the police officers had retreated some distance to put on their protective clothing, they had ceded much of the area to the rioters. Police vans were on fire, and the sound of breaking bottles and glasses filled the air.

By the time the violence was eventually brought under control, over 50 police officers had been injured, some with fractures, broken jaws and lost teeth. 'The disrespect toward grieving families and the community is despicable, and I want to reassure residents in Southport that we will have a significantly increased police presence in the town in the coming days,' a Merseyside Police statement read.

The troublemakers, however, were not done. Over the next 10 days, there were outbreaks of disorder in over 25 towns and cities around the country, with some experiencing multiple nights of trouble. While much of the actual violence was spontaneous, there were many people agitating for trouble online.

In a video posted online, Danny Tommo, a key lieutenant of EDL founder Stephen Lennon, called for riots to happen:

HOW TO DEFEAT THE FAR RIGHT

Every city has to go up.
Get prepared. Be ready. We have to.
It has to go off in different cities.
We have to show them we've had enough …
I'm ready to go. I know that a lot of you are. I'm speaking to other people at the moment.
We're ready to go. We are, literally, ready to go …[2]

It seemed that others were thinking the same. A day after the Southport riot, a group of roughly 40 people, some in balaclavas, congregated outside a Holiday Inn in Newton Heath, Manchester. Objects were thrown at police, and asylum seekers at the hotel were verbally abused. That same evening, rioters threw rocks and bottles at police in Hartlepool. Footage circulated online of a black man being set upon in the street and of rioters kicking in the front doors of people's homes. In London, more than 100 were arrested as far-right protesters battled with police outside Downing Street at an 'Enough Is Enough' demonstration. The following night, there was serious disorder in Sunderland – far-right slogans were chanted, and an attempted march on a mosque was blocked by riot police. A car was set ablaze and a Citizens Advice Bureau (CAB) torched. At the same time, over in Liverpool, a few hundred anti-fascists gathered to protect a local mosque from a planned far-right protest.

On the Saturday, there was serious violence in several towns and cities. In Manchester, a mob of a few hundred far-right protesters clashed with police in Piccadilly Gardens, and, again, a lone black man was chased and attacked by an angry mob. Hundreds gathered in Belfast, and an attempt to march on the Belfast Islamic Centre was only thwarted by a strong presence of riot police. Violence and disorder broke out elsewhere, and several immigrant-owned businesses were attacked, including a cafe that was burnt down. Cars were set ablaze, and clashes with police continued into the evening. In Stoke, hundreds of protesters attempted to march on two local mosques but were blocked from doing so by a group of 200 to 300 Muslim men, some wielding bats, who stood in the way. In Hull, a few thousand protesters gathered in Victoria Square for a static demonstration, before some headed off in the direction of temporary migrant accommodation. Police blocked their way, and serious clashes broke out, though not before a car carrying four Kurds was attacked. Shops were set ablaze and others looted in trouble that left 12 police officers injured and 62 people arrested. In Liverpool, the Spellow Hub Library was set alight when 300 people clashed with police after their attempt to reach a mosque was blocked.

Some of the most horrific scenes occurred in Rotherham, where between 700 and 1,000 far-right protesters, some accompanied by small children, gathered outside the Holiday Inn in Manvers, which housed asylum seekers. As windows started to be smashed by bricks, riot police were quickly overwhelmed and retreated, leaving behind terrified hotel residents who could only watch as the protesters set fire to a wheelie bin and pushed it into the hotel. Unsurprisingly, many later reported fearing they were going to die.

That same day, there was also serious trouble in Middlesbrough and Tamworth. In Middlesbrough, a planned protest over the Southport murders quickly turned violent as mobs of masked men – some teenagers – marauded through residential areas, smashing people's windows and targeting vehicles for destruction. Police were pelted with missiles, while the protesters set up a roadblock to check if the drivers were 'white and English'. Down in Tamworth, another hotel housing asylum seekers was set alight, again with residents inside. Racist slogans like 'fuck p***s' and 'get out of England' were sprayed on the wall of the hotel.

On the following Monday, a week after the Southport murders, details of demonstrations at nearly 40 immigration law firms and asylum-support organisations were circulated on the Southport WakeUp Telegram channel, followed by calls to burn down mosques and kill their opponents – me included. The list provoked panic but also saw an estimated 25,000 anti-fascists turning out on counter-demonstrations around the country in a display of solidarity that effectively marked the end of the rioting. In truth, very few, if any, far-right activists turned up at any of these events, but this anti-fascist show of force, accompanied by unusually favourable front pages, changed public discourse, and the far-right's momentum stalled – helped in part by the Southport WakeUp account, which had done so much to initiate the trouble, going silent. Unbeknown to most people at the time, the man behind the account had just been arrested.

Two days before the Southport murders, an estimated 40,000 people had gathered in Trafalgar Square for the latest of Stephen Lennon's video screenings. Lennon had first burst on to the political scene in 2009, when he helped establish and then lead the anti-Muslim street gang, the EDL. Now operating solo, Lennon was, after Farage, the most recognisable and popular figure on the British far right, with a following of hundreds of thousands of die-hard supporters.

In the hot July sunshine, the audience watched *Silenced*, Lennon's latest documentary, which he claimed proved that a Syrian schoolboy, who had arrived in Britain as a refugee fleeing the appalling civil war, was a violent, misogynistic bully. The problem for Lennon was that a libel trial had concluded otherwise, and alongside the £100,000 damages and court costs awarded against him, a High Court Order had been put in place preventing him from repeating these claims. Lennon ignored this order, and despite having been told that he faced contempt of court charges and so a likely prison sentence, he decided to show the feature-length film to his supporters in Trafalgar Square and millions watching online around the world.

Lennon's mood was defiant. His supporters were angry. His politics had evolved since his singular focus on Islam during his EDL days. He now railed against 'illegal' and even legal immigration. He backed COVID-related conspiracies and sympathised with Russia's invasion of Ukraine. Above all, he preached a narrative against a

British government that he believed was stacked against the interests of the white working class, often in favour of minorities and left-wing interest groups.

His social media reach was terrifying. Just on that one single day, Lennon's posts on X, the social media platform he had been allowed back on to by Elon Musk the previous year, were viewed 58 million times. In just the five days that followed the stabbings in Southport, his posts were viewed a staggering 434 million times. Videos with the keyword 'Tommy Robinson' were watched more than 174.8 million times across various platforms over the month that covered his protest and the riots. In the 90 days between 9 May and 6 August, his posts were viewed 1.5 billion times. It's alarming to think that Lennon is liked by 16 per cent of the population according to a 22,500-person poll commissioned by HOPE not hate at the end of 2024, a figure that includes 37 per cent of men between the age of 25 and 34.

Many of his posts were angry, inciting and mobilising. In the immediate aftermath of the Southport murders, Lennon repeatedly called Islam a mental-health issue, shared videos of disorder and encouraged people to join future demonstrations. 'Get there and show your support. People need to rise up.'

Given Lennon's loyal following and considerable reach, it was perhaps unsurprising that chants of 'Oh, Tommy. Tommy, Tommy, Tommy Robinson' were heard at almost all the post-Southport protests.

The post-Southport riots said a lot about the nature and interconnectivity of the far right in Britain today. While there were a few known far-right activists involved in many of the disturbances, they appeared to be there in supporting roles, and the protests themselves were largely spontaneously organised and built through informal networks and friendship groups online.

'In recent years, we have seen the rise of far-right social media personalities who, despite not being part of traditional activist organisations or parties, now have the ability to reach unprecedented numbers of people,' my colleague Joe Mulhall wrote in 2018 – referring to what he has coined the 'post-organisational far right':[3]

> A right-wing alternative media has emerged, stretching from the edges of the mainstream (such as former Trump advisor Steve Bannon's Breitbart News Network), to scores of YouTube vloggers, Twitter accounts and professional media outlets like Rebel Media and InfoWars. This framework allows activists to propagate their views without the need for traditional structures such as a party.

Transformation has largely occurred because of the advance of the internet, which has brought far-right and conspiratorial thinking within the reach of people who previously would have either had to stumble across someone in the far right or seek them out through the post or a meeting. Now people are able to access the far right in their living rooms, bedrooms and on their phones – all away from the prying eyes of respectable society. As people flit around the internet, cherry-picking ideas from here and there, so the link between the individual and the more traditional parties loosens and the appeal of figureheads, like Lennon, grows.

The far right have also been far more successful than the left in using the internet and the vast array of social media platforms that now exist. Whereas once the far right was largely shut out of the mainstream media, often being forced to moderate their public views in order to be allowed a platform, now they have literally built their own media ecosystem, where not only are they no longer censored but, if anything, they can be even more extreme. Just as significantly, many have been able to monetise their activities online, either through crowdsourcing public donations, selling subscriptions or receiving payments from social media companies.

Finally, the riots were further confirmation that the old *cordon sanitaire*, which acted as an unofficial barrier between the respectable conservative right and the traditional far right, now hardly exists, as ideas, narratives and outrage are increasingly shared between the two. While violence continues to be a fault line, their shared hostility towards 'the liberal system' – which they blame for immigration, economic failures and national decline – often glosses over their differences.

If the riots displayed the worst of Britain, they also reflected the best. Across the country, people came together in displays of solidarity, peace and anti-racism. Many local residents in Southport were horrified and disgusted by the way the mosque had been targeted during the riots, and dozens turned up the following morning to help clear up the mess after a plea for help was put online by Norman Wallis, chief executive of Southport Pleasureland. Among the 100 or so people who answered the call were local builders, who lost no time in fixing the mosque's broken wall. Others swept the debris from the surrounding streets, while local shops donated free products, and businesses flung open their doors for people to use as community spaces and places of quiet reflection. A local glazing company offered free windows.

For a community that had already suffered so much with the murder of three of their own, the outpouring of solidarity and community spirit was a sight to behold. It was a mood replicated around the country.

In Sunderland, people came together in response to the Citizens Advice centre being burnt down. Denise Irving, the CAB manager, worked through the night to ensure they were still able to help people, albeit from temporary accommodation in the City Hall. Sharyn Smiles, who worked for Sunderland Area Parent Support, set up a GoFundMe page with a goal of raising £2,000. Having experienced an arson at her own offices the previous year, she knew only too well what a devastating blow it was to any organisation. More importantly, she knew just how important the CAB was to so many people.

'The Citizens Advice is there for all members of our community to use, they have the most amazing team (many of whom are volunteers) and are determined to be back operating ASAP!' she wrote on the GoFundMe page. 'From the bottom of our hearts we ask for the kindness shown to us to be extended to this amazing service.'

Over 700 people donated a total of £23,655. An incredible response. 'It was totally unexpected,' Irving said. 'I still pinch myself because I wouldn't have expected that amount of generosity at all. We're all gobsmacked by it.'

The same community spirit was found in Liverpool, as people reacted to the Spellow Library in Walton being burnt down during the riots there. Writing in the city council newsletter, local resident Angela Cheveau recounted how she went to the library every week when she was young. 'The library was a space of solace and enchantment for me, a place where I could shuffle off my shyness, let my imagination run wild.'

Watching the building being set alight was not just an understandable trauma for her but a devastating cultural blow to the kids still reliant on it. 'I knew the impact that this would have on the local community who depend upon the library as a place of education and knowledge,' she said. 'I thought of the children who would no longer have access to books and the magic they hold.'

Alex McCormick was another local resident horrified by the fire. The following day, she set up a GoFundMe page with the intention of raising £500 towards its clean up and restoration. 'Seeing that a library and community space had been damaged really just broke my heart,' she later told the BBC. 'It made me feel angry.' The response was unbelievable, and by the time the page was closed it had raised over £250,000.

'Seeing people's generosity and people's comments, it goes to show that the good will always outweigh the bad,' McCormick added. 'And people really rally round something good like a library and a community centre. We need those spaces.'

The unbelievable bravery of those who stood up to the rioters was best summed up by the footage of a lone woman in Southport who pushed her way through the angry crowd before holding up a homemade sign in front of them. 'One Race – Human,' it read. 'Hope not hate. Racism not Welcome.'

In response, one woman posted on X: 'Confronting fascists is deeply intimidating even when there's a lot of you. Doing it on your own in the middle of a riot holding up your homemade sign requires a bravery I think not all of us could muster but this woman did it. A legend.'

In January 2025, 18-year-old Axel Rudakubana was jailed for a minimum of 52 years for a 'ferocious' and 'sadistic' knife rampage at the Taylor Swift-themed dance class that had left three girls dead and six other children injured. The court heard, in graphic detail, how the attack took place, his behaviour being described as 'sadistic', according to Deanna Heer KC, the prosecutor. Outside the court, police explained there was no clear motive for his attack, beyond a fascination with death and violence that took him from downloading an al-Qaeda manual, which he used to make ricin, to reading about the IRA. As a consequence, they claimed, they could not define the Southport attack as a 'terrorist incident'. There was no indication to suggest, as Lennon had claimed in the months leading up to the trial, that Rudakubana had converted to Islam.

The police's explanation did little to placate the angry online world. They accused Prime Minister Keir Starmer of deliberately hiding the truth from the British public and even spread the lie that Rudakubana was only in the country because the prime minister had defended his father from accusations that he was wanted for war crimes in Rwanda. The police were dismissed as useless and willing accomplices to Starmer's two-tier policing. A HOPE not hate poll, conducted in March 2025, found that 49 per cent of the British public thought Rudakubana was an Islamist terrorist, with just 16 per cent disagreeing.

2

Local Heroes

Soprano singer Dee Johnson was an unsuspecting hero. Everything about her life up to the point she appeared on television had been about struggle, determination and hardship. The bubbly mum-of-three's life hit a low point after her home was repossessed and she moved to a new area, only to suffer racial abuse.

'I moved into temporary accommodation in South Oxhey. It was bizarre. It was just cold and you were made to feel like an outsider. The teenagers really had a field day with me,' says 33-year-old Dee.

'My children were targeted, I had stones thrown at my windows, dog faeces left outside my door – you name it. My kids were really strong headed and stable within themselves.' Her 11-year-old son was even targeted by an older lad in an attempted hit and run. Dee feared for her children but was determined to stick it out.

When she was first introduced to Gareth Malone, who presented the highly entertaining TV programme *The Choir*, she spoke her mind. 'I met the crew and Gareth, who was the choirmaster, and they didn't want me to just say everything was great. It was a chance to say that this is what it was like for me,' says Dee.

This episode of *The Choir* followed Malone as he worked to create a 500-strong community choir on the South Oxhey estate on the outskirts of north London. The area had been built up in the 1950s as one of several such estates created to rehouse those displaced during the war. Sadly, it quickly declined due to a lack of investment, a failure to update the housing stock and deprivation. In the 2000s, it fell prey to the British National Party (BNP), with the far-right group picking up two of the three local council seats and the larger county council ward.

Dee might have just been one in a choir of 500 others, but the quality of her voice, finely tuned by years of gospel singing, propelled her to the front as a soloist. Her time on the choir certainly changed her wider fortunes too, as she began to form good friendships. She also began to realise that it was only a small minority of kids 'who didn't know better', and their behaviour was not reflective of everyone. 'Just after the show aired, a girl who said she was going to stab my daughter came over and they made their peace,' she told HOPE not hate at the time. 'I've got lovely neighbours. Since the show aired I've had people coming up and saying I can't believe you went through that. A lot come over and say "Hi Dee!" I don't always know who they are.'

Just by chance, the final episode of the show, in which the 500-strong choir performed publicly, was aired in the same week as a council by-election in the South Oxhey ward. The BNP went into the contest in upbeat mood, having won in the area each of the previous three years. However, coming against the backdrop of the pride the community choir had brought to the area, broadcast to millions via Malone's show, and possibly also due to the shame and embarrassment many felt after listening to what Dee had gone through, the BNP vote dropped by half, and their grip on the area was finally broken.

Sue Peters, who joined the choir after seeing it on TV, thought it had been great for the area. 'I've lived here all my life. It's the most positive thing as far as I can remember – it's been absolutely remarkable,' she said.

For Dee, who appeared with her cousins on the first series of *The X Factor*, *The Choir* also raised the area's profile. '*The Choir* was great,' she says, 'There's something else to talk about South Oxhey, not just bad stuff or about the BNP but now Gareth Malone came with *The Choir*. People from Rickmansworth used to say South Oxhey was somewhere they didn't want to go. Then after the show aired they wanted to join the choir. Oh no, we said, now you want to join!' she says, laughing again.

The lessons of South Oxhey's incredible turnaround were far-reaching. People felt better about themselves and so felt more positive about those around them. A sense of community pride had been fostered, and while economic challenges remained unsolved, at least the people could do something about them together.

I remember being inspired by Dee's story. Hearing her talk about the racism she had experienced and yet still finding the strength to sing with 500 local people, some of whom had probably voted BNP, was uplifting and showed us clearly how the answer to many community tensions and problems lay in those very same communities.

In 2001, I was involved in Searchlight, an organisation that publicly operated around a monthly magazine while also having an extensive research operation with a network of informants inside far-right groups. What we were not was a campaigning organisation. However, in the immediate aftermath of the riots in Oldham, Burnley and Bradford in 2001, we quickly felt there was no other anti-fascist organisation that appeared appropriately equipped to take on the new threat.

Regular electioneering was also a new concept for most anti-fascists, for whom 'No Platform' and the dominance of the street had been the main feature of our activity for many years. The main anti-fascist group in existence was the Anti-Nazi League (ANL), which had been reformed in 1991 after the emergence of the BNP in East London. The other dominant anti-fascist group of recent times was Anti-Fascist Action (AFA), with a direct and quite often violent approach that struck fear into fascist groups in the 1980s.

However, as the BNP turned away from the street, so AFA, or more accurately the dominant group within it, Red Action, moved away from anti-fascism and turned to community politics in Hackney and Oxford. The main anti-racist group at the time was Anti-Racist Alliance, which was heavily influenced by Socialist Action and had the patronage of London Mayor Ken Livingstone.

For Searchlight, political campaigning was a totally new concept. We had a small network of key supporters around the country, most of whom helped us with research and had little campaigning experience. Two exceptions were veteran anti-fascist Mike Luft, who had helped set up Oldham United Against Racism (OUAR), and Bradford-based Paul Meszaros. Paul was an old friend of mine from my Sheffield University days, and we had actually become involved in Searchlight together in 1989 after we invited Gerry Gable, the driving force behind the organisation, to speak in Sheffield. Gerry told us the best thing we could do was to get someone inside the local far right, which we did inside of two weeks. Within a few months, we had three people inside across Yorkshire.

Given that both Oldham and Bradford had experienced riots, we were quite well placed to do some leafleting in the 2002 local elections, and our first batch of leaflets was in Oldham, Burnley and Bradford. All followed a similar theme of a swastika being beamed on to the town or city hall, the leaflet carrying a warning that unless people came out to vote, nazis could be running the council. In Sunderland, meanwhile, where the BNP was standing a full slate of 25 candidates, we ran with the headline: 'BNP Leader's Sterilisation Plan Revealed'. The accompanying article explained that the BNP's national organiser was in favour of euthanising disabled people. To hammer home the horror of his views, we likened his policy to that of Nazi wartime scientist Josef Mengele.

While we had played a key role in keeping the BNP out in Oldham and Bradford in the 2002 elections, the far-right party was able to win three council seats in Burnley, its first victory since winning a solitary seat in Millwall, Tower Hamlets, back in 1993.

LOCAL HEROES

The local anti-BNP campaign in Burnley was dominated by the ANL, run by the Socialist Workers Party, which two years later morphed into Unite Against Fascism (UAF) after forging an alliance with Anti-Racist Alliance. The ANL was led by Julie Waterson, a working-class Glaswegian and life-long socialist. While we were politically quite different, our close friendship was born out of being together on the front line. I concentrated on the Oldham campaign while she focused on Burnley, but as we were both staying in Manchester, we would meet most evenings to discuss the current state of play and plan the next day's activities.

Campaigning on the streets of Burnley was much more difficult than Oldham. Despite its pockets of real deprivation, Oldham's proximity to Manchester meant it was more cosmopolitan than Burnley; more people mixed with people from different backgrounds. Burnley's Asian population was also much smaller, and many local whites seemed quite happy to defend the honour of the BNP.

The night before the election, 10 of us met up on the Stoops Estate, one of the most deprived communities in the town, to deliver an open letter from a well-respected local community worker calling on people not to vote BNP. We split into two groups of five and set out, in wet and windy weather, along the rows of small, terraced houses. Julie and I each led a group, though it was not long before I felt I had the rough end of the deal. I had one committed Trotskyist and another hard-line anarchist in my team, and they spent most of the time arguing about the merits of one philosophy over the other. What was worse was they tended to speak to each other rather loudly, sometimes shouting across the road at one another. I dreaded to think what any locals must have thought, and eventually a couple of us had to tell them to stop or leave.

It turned out to be a truly awful evening. In addition to the weather and the descending darkness, we also faced strong hostility from several local people. In all my time campaigning against the BNP, Burnley was the only place where people came out of their houses to challenge me to a fight. I've had angry people before, even BNP supporters telling me where to 'go', but I've never had a man in his 40s, with his partner standing by his side, openly challenge me to a fight there and then. What was worse, this happened on five separate occasions to the two teams during that one single evening. On another occasion, in another part of Burnley, we were actually stopped from leafleting when BNP-supporting kids pelted us with bricks.

Julie and I tried to raise the morale on our return to the community centre, but we were all in a state of shock (to say nothing of being soaked through). In many ways, it was nights like these that really reminded you of the dangers of the politics of hatred espoused by groups such as the BNP – and the importance of winning communities around. These were difficult times, but there were many moments of light relief. The BNP had a huge banner down the side of a disused chimney mill in the town centre. It could clearly be seen by everyone entering the town. One night, a young anti-fascist climbed up the side of the chimney and took down the banner, after which it was taken up on to Rochdale moors and set alight. This proved easier said than done, as it was made of a non-flammable material, so petrol had to be poured over it. The silence of the moors was punctured by a huge fireball lighting up the hillside.

The political establishment was genuinely shocked by the BNP victories in Burnley. Politicians, faith leaders and political commentators lined up to denounce the party. The leader of Burnley Borough Council said he would refuse to work with a 'racist' party such as the BNP, adding: 'It is a disaster. People are waking up this morning asking where this takes us.'[1]

Around the country, the BNP failed to win any of the other 68 wards it was contesting. So, to an extent, winning three councillors on one council enabled the politicians and decision makers to dismiss the BNP gains as a localised problem that could be solved by greater funding and better governance. This strategy was brought into even clearer focus six months later when the BNP won a seat in neighbouring Blackburn. Following these election victories, the government suspended its policy of settling asylum seekers in East Lancashire for fear of provoking a greater local backlash. The BNP was understandably jubilant, and in the run-up to the 2003 elections it campaigned hard on the claim that a vote for the BNP was the only way to stop asylum seekers.

We adopted a much more aggressive strategy with our campaign in Calderdale, West Yorkshire, where a council by-election took place in the Mixenden ward in January 2003. The BNP organiser in Halifax decided to stand in the election. This, we thought, was a gift. He was well known to us as a former football hooligan, convicted thug and a strong supporter of the violent neo-nazi group Combat 18 (C18).* In fact, he even ran a local pro-C18 newsletter, and it was the contents of this that we made the central focus of our election leaflet.

'BNP Candidate Laughs as Child Burns to Death', ran the leaflet headline. We wanted to explain how the candidate used his nazi newsletter to laugh at a local house fire in Halifax in which a child had died. 'Do you really want this sicko as your next councillor in Mixenden?' we ended the leaflet.

At the time, we thought this leaflet was great. Hard-hitting and to the point, like the earlier ones we had produced in Sunderland and Burnley. It was only later, when we actually heard back from the voters, that we realised that we were writing leaflets that made us feel good but had little resonance with the people we were targeting. It wasn't that we were wrong to focus on the candidate's extremist past, but the sensationalism with which we reported it was undoubtedly wrong.

* * *

* Combat 18, which drew its name from the first and eighth letter of the alphabet – AH – for Adolf Hitler, emerged in the early 1990s as a stewards group for the BNP, but quickly evolved into a separate national socialist organisation which openly called for terrorism and a race war against what it claimed was a Jewish-controlled government.

HOW TO DEFEAT THE FAR RIGHT

The BNP was keen to build on its success, and in the 2023 local elections it stood 220 candidates, almost four times as many as the previous year. After our tentative start, we began to divert more resources and time to our campaigning. We were building up networks in areas where we believed the BNP posed a threat, and our material was becoming more targeted.

We continued to work alongside the ANL, but divisions in our respective approaches and tactics were widening. In Oldham, the local ANL group only reluctantly helped distribute our material, while tensions were never far from the surface. In the run-up to the 2002 elections, there was a fierce disagreement between us over the death of 19-year-old Gavin Hopley, who was beaten, stabbed and kicked to death in February 2002. Hopley had been out clubbing with friends in Oldham and in the early hours of the morning had left with two others and looked for a taxi to take them back to their homes in Rochdale. They were not local, and while searching for a taxi they approached a number of cars asking for a lift. Unfortunately, the occupants of one car took exception to the three men and began chasing them. One got away, another was caught and received some minor injuries, but Hopley fell and was set upon. He was robbed and attacked, suffering fatal injuries.

There was nothing in the evidence or subsequent trial to suggest that Hopley was anything but an innocent victim of an appalling attack. Perhaps there was a racial element, perhaps not, but many in Oldham saw it as such, just as they had with Walter Chamberlain, a 76-year-old local pensioner who had been viciously assaulted by a group of Asian men as he walked home from watching rugby the year before. What was indisputable was that it was a gruesome and unprovoked murder that demanded our condemnation. Together with the local anti-racist group, OUAR, we produced an edition of the *Oldhamer* with the simple cover slogan: 'No to racism, no to violence.'

Along with taxi driver Israr Hussain and nurse Debbie Remorozo, who were both murdered in the town, we added the name of Gavin

Hopley. 'All these people were innocent,' our statement read. 'Oldhamers have had enough of the trouble. It is time to say no to the racism, no to the violence and no to the BNP who thrive in a climate of fear.'

Positioning ourselves against all the violence and racism that had scarred the town for so long seemed a perfectly sensible and correct approach to take – but not so for the ANL. The group refused to hand out the leaflet, arguing that it was wrong to add Hopley's name to the list. Just like Walter Chamberlain the year before, when the anti-racist movement was conspicuous by its silence, white victims were deemed not worthy of mention or sympathy.

A key lesson in campaign development is to recognise one's faults and change one's behaviour accordingly, and while we were not involved in the protest outside Burnley town hall for the first council meeting after the BNP had won its three seats, we understood its significance. An ANL protest saw anti-fascist protesters wave placards and shout 'Nazi scum' as the new BNP councillors and their supporters entered the building. Adding to the chaos, flour was thrown over them too.

While I'm sure those protesting felt they were making a legitimate point, the images of the newly elected BNP councillor and 64-year-old grandmother Maureen Stowe covered in flour and clearly scared were counterproductive. Not only did the protesters look like the thugs but anti-democratic ones too. Many local people who spoke to the local newspaper were understandably furious at her treatment.

The final straw in this widening gap with the ANL occurred in the spring of 2003 when the anti-racist movement called for a national demonstration against racism in Manchester city centre, just a week before the local elections. The demonstration cost the sponsors over £200,000 to put on and fewer than 3,000 people attended.

The idea of the march followed the BNP election victory in Burnley the previous year, but we argued that Manchester was not a BNP hotspot, and that demonstrating in a city centre on the final weekend before an election was the last place activists should be.

Instead, we held our own events in our key target areas. The BNP was only going to be defeated in the communities where it was receiving support, not in the multicultural centres of major cities.

Meanwhile, the BNP bandwagon rolled on, with the party gaining 13 new seats in the elections. Seven of these came in Burnley, where boundary changes meant every council seat was up for grabs rather than the usual third. The party took other seats in Calderdale, Stoke-on-Trent, Dudley, Sandwell and Broxbourne. In Burnley, the party averaged 35 per cent in the wards it contested.

With the BNP seemingly on the march, it was clear we needed to have a more sophisticated approach to campaigning against it. Fortunately, help was at hand. We had begun to have discussions with the Joseph Rowntree Reform Trust, who, being based in West Yorkshire, were also worried about the growth of the BNP. They funded some research into better understanding the BNP vote.

The results were fascinating. Communications company Vision 21 surveyed the voters of three council by-elections in areas where the BNP was strong: Mixenden in Calderdale, where the BNP already had one councillor; Lanehead in Burnley, where a vacancy had come up following the resignation of a BNP councillor; and Failsworth East, on the outskirts of Oldham, where the BNP had polled over 30 per cent of the vote in the neighbouring Failsworth West seat a few months earlier.

The research confirmed that the BNP vote was initially a protest vote, representing anger at the mainstream parties, which voters believed had ignored them and were taking them for granted. However, with people having since voted two or three times for the BNP, there was a growing risk they were now positively choosing the far-right party.

The BNP vote was overwhelmingly male, middle-aged to elderly and largely consisted of former Labour voters who had stopped voting for the party some time before. While immigration and asylum seekers came up in conversation in our focus groups, they were found to be proxies for wider discontent. However, it was also clear that many people were still embarrassed to say they had voted BNP. At the same time, while some realised there was something unpleasant about the party, few considered them nazis.

While the research set out to discover who was voting for the BNP and why, a by-product was also understanding who was not voting for the fascist party – and why. By a margin of almost two to one, men were more likely to vote for the BNP than women, but this gender difference did not reflect women being more anti-racist or in favour of multiculturalism than men – it was more that they were generally put off by the BNP's aggressive image and concerned about the tensions and trouble it could bring to local communities and their children. This was especially the case with women between 25 and 55 – those of an age most likely to be mothers.

Conversely, however, many of these same women were put off by traditional anti-BNP and anti-racist slogans and literature. Slogans such as 'Smash the Nazis' and 'Nazi Scum off Our Streets' were equally threatening and aggressive. People preferred positive messages as opposed to negative: they wanted to vote 'for' rather than 'against' something.

Our campaigning was already changing, but the Rowntree-sponsored research helped back our ideas with empirical evidence. Anti-BNP campaigning had to be localised, address local issues and be more imaginative and positive.

Quite by chance, our friends at Philosophy Football, who describe themselves as 'outfitters of intellectual distinction', produced a t-shirt to show opposition to the BNP. A yellow t-shirt, with the words 'HOPE not hate' emblazoned on the front. The 'O' in 'HOPE' was represented by a smiling sun. We loved it. It also encapsulated everything the Vision 21 research had told us.

The HOPE not hate campaign had begun.

The importance of local 'heroes' in fighting the BNP had been clear to us for some time, though we stumbled across it slightly by accident while campaigning in the affluent market town of Clitheroe, in the Ribble Valley. On the surface, it seemed a strange place for the BNP to target. It was a strongly Conservative local authority with one of the highest average incomes in the country. A high proportion of the local population had higher education qualifications, and the local Muslim population numbered just 25 families. Clitheroe was, however, nestled between Blackburn and Burnley. For some locals, the riots in Burnley and perceived ongoing problems in community cohesion in Blackburn created a sense of being under siege. This was compounded by a planning application to extend a house by just over a metre to create a prayer room for the local Muslim population.

A local BNP branch emerged in the town immediately after the party's annual Red, White and Blue festival in nearby Swanley, in August 2002. This, combined with electoral success in Burnley, encouraged local racists and known football hooligans to get active. The BNP immediately latched on to the opposition to the prayer room, a campaign already being championed by the local Conservatives and probably supported by a majority of local opinion.

'25 today, 25,000 tomorrow' was a common refrain heard among those opposed to the application.

After the initial planning application had been turned down, more than 70 BNP supporters attended the planning appeal, which was held just six weeks before the local elections, in which the BNP had decided to stand seven candidates. This was to be the trigger for the formation of a local anti-BNP group, Ribble Valley Against Racism (RVAR).

'All three main political parties were terminally complacent,' local anti-BNP organisers Chris Gathercole and Farouk Shiraz told me when we reflected on the campaign a few years later:

> They all argued that if we all ignored them, the BNP would go away. Opposing them was said to give them the publicity they craved. The implication was that RVAR activity was

irresponsible. Long-established politicians could not believe that the good citizens of Clitheroe would vote for the riff-raff of the town.

They were a really wonderful group of people who simply wanted to stand up to racism. 'To most of us fighting fascism was a new experience,' Farouk added. 'We established links with those who had been resisting the BNP in Burnley and Blackburn. Later we drew on the experience of others from around the country in Oldham, Wigan, Bradford and elsewhere. We learned fast.'

I sat down with Chris and Farouk to map out the election campaign. In addition to explaining the truth about the BNP, we also needed to address the planning application issue head-on. We devised a series of four leaflets, each one following on from the other. Calling the newsletter 'Heart of the Valley', we sought to encapsulate the decency of the local area while also asserting our local identity. To help build brand recognition, the newsletter depicted the famous local viaduct.

The first of the newsletters was headlined 'Stand Up for Decency'. It introduced RVAR and explained its mission. It encouraged people to get involved while alerting them to the BNP threat and more importantly presented the RVAR as mainstream and broad-based. The second took on the planning issue.

In a four-page special, we explained the prayer room proposal, dispelled some of the myths surrounding the plans and Islam more generally, and carried a number of cross-faith endorsements for the right of all religions to worship. 'Some of our supporters had been uncomfortable with the negative approach of denigrating the BNP,' remembered Chris. 'Our mosque leaflet was constructive and low key. It helped to establish RVAR as a responsible group in contrast to the strident, even hysterical, tone of the BNP campaign.'

This leaflet was followed up by a half-page advert in the local newspaper. In a direct rebuke of the BNP campaign pledge – that a vote for the BNP would stop the mosque – the advert explained that the issue was now with the planning inspector, and the local election would have no effect on the outcome.

The third leaflet focused on the violence and trouble the BNP could bring to an area. Entitled 'Life's a Riot with the BNP', it highlighted the role of BNP supporters in the Oldham riots. In this wealthy and conservative area, we knew we could turn the violence associated with the BNP to our advantage.

The BNP was furious with the RVAR campaign. 'Far left fanatics from all over the North West have been bussed in to carry out an illegal campaign,' screamed a BNP leaflet distributed in the last week of the campaign. Our final leaflet, thought out several weeks before, was a perfect rebuttal to the BNP attack. Called 'Vote to Save Clitheroe', with a large picture of the town, it was an open appeal to local people to reject the BNP. More importantly, it carried a number of local endorsers, including the town crier Roland Hailwood. It was undoubtedly one of the most pleasing leaflets I have produced over the years.

There was some amusement in our office as we put a huge image of Roland on the leaflet in his full attire and bell. Roland was arguably the best-known local man in Clitheroe, encapsulating the traditions and respectability of this quaint market town. Several local people, unknown to the RVAR campaign, even put the leaflet up in their windows. It was an important lesson about the significance of local heroes.

When the Mixenden by-election was called again, following the death of a popular Liberal Democrat councillor, we knew we had to take a different approach. As was common during this period, the BNP was playing hard on hostility to asylum seekers. It had produced a leaflet about how these refugees were being given preferential treatment.

The leaflet was then customised to local areas. In Mixenden, the BNP's leaflet claimed that asylum seekers were benefitting ahead of local people in Halifax. Working closely with Sue McMahon, secretary of Calderdale Against Racism, we took the leaflet apart, line by line.

LOCAL HEROES

First, the BNP claimed that local pensioners were having their operations cancelled because of the pressure asylum seekers were placing on the health service. To prove this wrong, Sue contacted the local Primary Care Trust and asked them whether Halifax people were having their operations cancelled. They came back to us describing the claims as 'propaganda'. Next, the BNP claimed that local pensioners were being thrown off doctors' waiting lists ... again, because of asylum seekers. In response, Sue contacted every doctors' surgery in the ward and asked them if they had struck off local pensioners to make way for asylum seekers. They said no and were furious at the BNP claims. The BNP also claimed local care homes for the elderly were being shut only to be reopened as asylum hostels. Sue then contacted all the local care homes, all of which categorically denied any plans to close down.

Again, there was anger at the BNP claims. Finally, the BNP claimed that Halifax post office ran a specific counter dedicated to asylum seekers on Mondays, so we went down with a camera on a Monday morning to prove there was no such thing. Armed with the facts, we now needed someone with more authority to convince local people of the truth. We used the very people the BNP were trying to scare: pensioners. We got a couple of local pensioners to agree to put their names on our leaflet, so it was clear who was calling the BNP to account.

'Don't Scare Our Old Folk', read the headline of our first leaflet, 'Pensioners Speak against the BNP'. The leaflet linked the lies the BNP was telling to the effect they were having on pensioners. 'I read these claims in horror,' Joan, one of our pensioners, was quoted as saying:

> Like all people I worry about our future and I have to say I was almost taken in by the BNP. Now that I have found out that their claims are a pack of lies I am very angry. Life is hard enough for us old folk without the likes of the BNP stirring up trouble with their lies.

The other pensioner, Peggy, agreed: 'Stop scaring us and stop telling lies,' she was quoted as saying.

We followed up with a second leaflet, this time focusing on BNP lies over housing and the post office. We again used local people to speak out. The effectiveness of these leaflets was clear when they were put in front of the two focus groups that had been organised by Vision 21. The reaction of the 'soft' BNP supporters was particularly interesting, as many had initially been regurgitating the same myths about asylum the BNP had been peddling. As they began to read our leaflets, their attitudes started to change.

'If they will lie about this then what else will they lie about?' said one participant. 'I heard that the BNP climbed on a window ledge and put a leaflet though an open window,' said another in growing disgust. A third said that when the BNP had knocked on their door, they 'had done so heavily'. By the end, most of this group said that their view of the BNP had changed, and many were openly against the party. This was a battle of perceptions, and we felt that our leaflets would help change the views of enough people, which, combined with a strong Liberal Democrat campaign, would ensure the BNP was well beaten.

To really cultivate local heroes and make the best use of them, we produced localised newsletters and even tabloid newspapers. The newsletters had mastheads that incorporated something about the area. As mentioned, our Ribble Valley newsletter was called Heart of the Valley and incorporated the aqueduct that runs through Clitheroe. Our Mixenden newsletter was called The Tablet, a play on the Mount Tabor, which made up part of the ward. Above it, we had a trumpeter with 'Speaking Up for Decency' written across a banner.

Some of our inspiration for the localised approach initially came from a local anti-racist group, Wigan and Leigh United Against Racism (WALAR), with whom we worked closely. WALAR was set up in February 2003 when a group of friends came together who were concerned about the rise of the BNP. It quickly expanded, gaining the support of a cross-party, cross-faith, cross-cultural and cross-community organisational alliance, which was also backed by local businesses, trades unions and the council. The key to their success, the organisers would later reflect, lay in the structure of the organisation, its focus and its unity. 'Instead of having a hierarchy, our organisation consisted of a number of important task groups: media, community campaigning, education and sports, music and culture, and finance and fundraising, each of which elected a member to sit on the co-ordinating Steering Group,' they told me at the time. 'Tasks were shared out according to the needs of the campaign.'

The group's biggest achievement was a pre-match launch event at the stadium of Wigan Athletic Football Club, where hundreds of schoolchildren paraded anti-racist banners in front of thousands of cheering spectators. As part of the event, the club, together with other local and national businesses, sponsored a four-page insert in the match programme devoted to the anti-racist message. Over the next few years, we produced several newspapers with WALAR using a variety of local champions and sports stars to spread their anti-racist message. Among the local stars who made comments urging people to reject the BNP were former Wigan Rugby League players, such as Martin Offiah and Shaun Edwards.

But perhaps the most impactful piece we did with a local hero in Wigan was with Lynne Calvert, one of the founders of WALAR, whose life had been saved by a doctor who came to Britain in the 1970s after his family had been expelled from Uganda by Idi Amin. Nine more difficult operations were to follow for Lynne:

> Each time I insisted on seeing Mr Nsamba, because he talked to me personally. He would sit next to me and talk through the scans. He was a middle-aged man, he didn't owe me anything, he could have been like one of those distant surgeons or doctors, but he was really kind. I insisted on seeing him each time after that.

Lynne briefly holds her breath; she doesn't want to take anything for granted, but at the moment she's getting better. 'I can't thank my doctors enough,' she adds. 'Most of them have been black or Asian and they've all been fantastic. It's really nice to feel that they've all been there for me.' She chokes for the first time in our conversation. 'I still get tearful when I think about it.'

We ran Lynne's story in the Wigan edition of a tabloid newspaper we produced ahead of the 2004 European elections. It was one of 29 editions, each localised for a target local authority area or audience. Altogether, 1.7 million newspapers were printed, and it took a heroic effort by hundreds of people to get them out.

Among my favourite editions was Sheffield, where we carried a large feature of local boxing trainer Brendan Ingle, who, in addition to coaching several world champions, helped young boys and girls who were getting into trouble at school. He was a local legend, so getting his endorsement lent credibility to our campaign. The 60,000 copies of the Merseyside paper also carried strong statements from local football legends John Barnes and Pat Nevin, and a war veteran condemned the BNP while remembering his own past during the Second World War. The Stoke edition featured a local community group who took on the BNP after they rubbished the area, while a London Unison edition recounted a positive story of how local east enders, of all races, united together to campaign against low pay.

The numbers of newspapers that had to be distributed meant that much of our campaign effort focused on organising days of action in every place that had a newspaper. Often it required a few. The day of action, where we would ask people to give one morning or afternoon to fight the BNP, became a core tenet of our campaigns. However, while they were the logical way to organise given the task at hand, they came about because our activists were repeatedly being targeted by the BNP and their thuggish friends. Often, as was the case in Oldham and Burnley, this meant people coming out of their houses or people we stumbled across, but occasionally it was far more organised.

LOCAL HEROES

One campaign session in Halifax, in 2003, saw 40 to 50 Leeds hooligans and BNP members mobilise against us one Sunday morning. At the same time, local kids on the estate had been told that we were a pro-paedophile group, so they attacked us with bricks and stones. Refusing to be deterred, we came back a fortnight later, but this time there were over 100 of us. Any opposition quickly melted away, and we never had any problems again.

3

In the Know

'Information is power.' That is what I was told by Gerry Gable, my old boss at Searchlight, and it remains true today. When I first started out in anti-fascism 35 years ago, knowledge was gleaned via human intelligence, gathering information from inside far-right groups. In today's computer age, our information is supplemented by what we can find on the internet, in open and closed forums, and from advanced data analysis.

In the immediate aftermath of the 2001 Oldham riots, with it becoming clear that the former mill town was going to be a major target for the BNP in the following year's local elections, our response was intelligence-led. C18 supporters had been at the core of the group that had 'triggered' the riots, and we had this group heavily infiltrated. The number three in the organisation, Darren Wells, had been supplying top-grade information to us for a couple of years, and as a result we were able to prevent several further potentially violent and incendiary incidents, including stopping two bombing campaigns and providing the information that allowed us to expose the attempts by loyalist paramilitary Stephen Irwin, who led an attack on a pub in Derry that killed six Catholics, to join up with C18.

Darren also played a pivotal role in preventing further trouble in the aftermath of the Oldham riots. In mid-June, a couple of weeks after the riots, C18 tried to disrupt the England and Pakistan cricket match at Manchester's Old Trafford ground. Forty C18 supporters, consisting primarily of football hooligans from Oldham and Everton and a few soldiers from the King's Regiment out of Preston, had planned to run on to the pitch during the match and insert a C18 flag into the middle of the playing wicket in the hope of inciting a violent response from the young Pakistan supporters at the ground. With the test being screened live on Channel 4, the C18 organisers hoped that scenes of a pitched battle in the middle of the wicket would further inflame community tensions far beyond Manchester. However, unfortunately for the gang, we knew of their plans and were able to tip off the authorities, and all 40 men were stopped at the turnstiles and prevented from entering.

While Wells was supplying us excellent information on Oldham C18, his time inside the far right was coming to an end, and this only emphasised the need to get someone in locally. The 2002 local elections were going to be the first electoral test for the BNP of this new world, and we had to be ready.

I began spending two or three days a week in Manchester so I could oversee our work in Oldham, and we almost instantly got some results. Within two months of the General Election, we had three sources of information within Oldham BNP, and there was little happening that we did not know about. We quickly got to know their target areas for the 2002 local elections and the issues they intended to campaign on. More amusingly – for us – we also got sight of their weekly canvass returns, allowing us to build up a picture of their support on the ground. We began to compile files on their leading activists, enabling us to develop profiles on some of their more unsavoury characters.

Within Oldham BNP were many of the very same football hooligans who were also involved in C18 and the small fascist sect the International Third Position. Several others had been convicted for a variety of criminal and anti-social behaviour offences. They included a strong supporter of Northern Irish loyalism who had a conviction for possessing drugs, and another who had once been convicted for sending excreta through the post. Even local BNP organiser Mick Treacy had five convictions for violence, theft and handling stolen goods.

One name that kept cropping up from my meetings with our sources was that of Robert Bennett, or Bob as he was more commonly known to local BNP activists. A stocky, bald-headed man in his mid-50s, Bennett was the party's leafleting organiser. While Treacy was in overall control, it was Bennett who was responsible for getting their material out. Report after report indicated that there was something in Bennett's past that he was keen not to share, as rumours circulated that he was some sort of criminal, but no one seemed to have any details.

We supplemented the information provided by our sources with photographs taken of BNP gatherings, including their monthly branch meeting. Month after month, I would sit in the back of a van, which to the outside world looked like every other builders' van, and, together with a photographer, we would snap away at the BNP supporters arriving for the meeting. Not only would this give us photographs that we could use for the campaign but, from a legal perspective, we could prove people were linked to the BNP.

The July branch meeting, the first to occur since the General Election, was a predictably joyous occasion for the BNP. Almost 100 people packed into the function room of a pub in Hollinwood to hear party leader Nick Griffin triumphantly heralding the election result as just the beginning for Oldham BNP. Midway through his speech, he paused and looked around the room. He asked those who had recently been arrested for their part in the violence that had sparked the riots to stand up. Four men did, with Griffin hailing them as heroes to thunderous applause. All were later convicted for what the judge described as 'triggering the riots'.

Unbeknown to those in the meeting, we had been sitting in the van outside the pub for several hours, meaning we were in place to snap everyone as they arrived. This was no mean feat. With the temperature outside nudging over 32°C, the heat inside the van was almost unbearable. It was so hot that we were both stripped down to our boxer shorts, so when one of the C18 thugs – one of those who would be later convicted for triggering the riots – came up to the back window to peer in, we sat there in complete silence, genuinely fearful. Fortunately for us, the strong one-way glass did its job, and he couldn't see in. Once he was gone, we got back to work, and moments later we managed to get the one and only photo of Bennett, Oldham BNP's man of mystery.

Weeks of painstaking research in local libraries in Manchester and Leeds finally gave us the answer to Bennett's past when we came across local newspaper cuttings alluding to two convictions for armed robbery and one for his involvement in a gang rape. We later learnt Bennett had acquired a total of 47 convictions. It was now clear why he wanted to keep his past hidden.

With the election still several months away, we decided to sit on this information until the last few weeks of the campaign to ensure maximum impact. With our strategy decided, we began to lay the groundwork by producing several local leaflets focusing heavily on the criminality of the local BNP. We handed over details of these criminals to the newspapers, several of which ran prominent stories on their front pages. Treacy, the local BNP organiser, was interviewed on Channel 4 News, a decision he was soon to regret. Predicting Treacy's 'law and order' stance, I had briefed Channel 4's reporter about the Oldham organiser's own criminal convictions. The response could not have been any better. 'If the BNP really cared about law and order, shouldn't it stop people with convictions from standing in elections?' Treacy looked flummoxed, perhaps knowing what the follow-up would be if he simply replied: 'No. If we did that then I wouldn't be able to stand.' He froze, aware he had been trapped.

Oldham BNP entered the elections with real energy and a strong belief that the General Election result would translate into several councillors. Strong canvass returns only reinforced that view. Their excitement quickly evaporated when, two weeks out from the election, the Bennett story dropped, first in the *Sunday Mirror* newspaper and then, that same morning, with our own leafleting session in Hollinwood, one of the areas of strongest BNP support and where Treacy was standing in the election. The following day, we were out again, this time targeting young mothers at school gates.

The leaflet itself was one of the hardest-hitting pieces of literature we had ever produced, and, arguably, it had the greatest impact. I had written it with Martin Salter, who was then the Labour MP for Reading West. Martin had been a long-time supporter of Searchlight and had even attended National Front (NF) meetings back in the 1970s to glean information. He became one of Labour's most effective and ruthless campaigners, and this was reflected in the tone of our leaflet.

'Gang Rapist Leads BNP Election Campaign', screamed the headline. It was direct, if somewhat disturbing. 'If you've recently received a British National Party leaflet through your door the chances are that it might have been delivered by sick rapist Robert Bennett,' it continued. The reader was then told how Bennett had served seven years for his part in the gang rape of two young women.

It ended in chilling fashion. 'The next time the BNP come knocking at your door just remember you might be staring into the eyes of brutal rapist Robert Bennett.'

The leaflet had a devastating impact on the BNP's election campaign. It lifted the morale of our supporters, who until that point had regularly been subjected to abuse, racism and open BNP support on the doorstep. 'We've never had a response from a leaflet like it,' Mike Luft told me at the time:

> People were standing in the street reading the leaflet, even in areas where BNP had been strong.
>
> I think we are seeing a sea change in the town. More people are willing to speak out against the BNP than they were even a few weeks ago.

More importantly, it totally derailed the BNP campaign. 'The BNP didn't know how to respond,' one of our moles told me shortly after. 'Everyone knew that Bennett had a past, but gang rape and armed robbery was a surprise. Treacy didn't know what to do. He rang Griffin in a panic but I think that this just made things worse.'

Rather than holding their hands up, recognising that Bennett's past was damaging and apologising, the BNP went into conspiratorial overdrive. They immediately claimed that Bennett was a Searchlight and Labour Party spy, put into the BNP to derail their election effort. They claimed they were on to Bennett at the time of the *Sunday Mirror* article and had broken links with him several weeks before, even playing down his role within the party.

Matters only got worse for the BNP when it overreacted to a follow-up article in the *Oldham Chronicle*. The local newspaper had come in for criticism from anti-racist activists for being soft on the BNP and claims that it under-reported attacks on Asians while giving considerable coverage to incidents where the victim was white. After the BNP's strong showing in the 2001 General Election, the editorial accepted that Nick Griffin was the legitimate voice of a large section of the white community.

Across the town, the headline on the newspaper stall hoardings read: 'Gang Shame of BNP Chief'. Treacy went ballistic and threatened to sue, leading to an immediate climbdown from the newspaper. Rather than leaving it at that, the BNP targeted the editor himself. 'Rape Shame of Oldham Chronicle Editor', ran a story on its website. Editor Jim Williams was attacked for what was described as his anti-BNP stance, and it repeated its conspiracy theories about Bennett, concluding: 'Perhaps in future, Jim "Lying Beast" Williams will stick to his job – reporting the facts – rather than setting himself up as Oldham's anti-BNP spin-master-in-chief.'

We dutifully printed off the website story and personally handed it over to an enraged Jim Williams. The BNP had just made a new enemy, and a very powerful one at that.

IN THE KNOW

The *Oldham Chronicle*'s editor now had the bit between his teeth. The BNP had showed its true colours, and he was determined to stop it from winning council seats. He went to his board and announced his intention to write a front-page editorial urging the people of Oldham to reject the BNP. The board initially refused his request, with one member even claiming it risked alienating a sizeable chunk of the paper's readership. Williams was incensed and threatened to resign and go public with the board's position if it didn't back him. Faced with a potentially damaging PR disaster, they relented, and the editor got his front page.

'Vote for Oldham, Not the Divisive BNP', ran the headline on the eve of the election, timed for maximum effect. The front-page article was strident in its opposition to the BNP. 'The BNP's reason for existence is racism,' Williams noted. 'It talks of repatriation (though how do you repatriate someone from where they were born?) and it talks of division, barriers and barricades. To that extent a vote for the BNP is a dangerous vote.'

The BNP was not the answer, he said, arguing that they poisoned local communities and encouraged violent confrontations. He ended with a plea: 'The BNP will give nothing to Oldham. It will only take to suit its own racial agenda. So the plea is a simple one – for Oldham's sake vote tomorrow, but for Oldham's sake do not vote for the BNP.'

It was a stinging attack, and on top of our relentless anti-BNP campaign, it was to prove successful. After years of trouble and conflict, the people of Oldham had had enough. The BNP failed to win in any of the wards it was contesting, nor was it able to in subsequent years. Given the riots and the strong BNP vote in the General Election, helping to stop the far-right party from ever winning a council seat in Oldham must go down as one of our greatest achievements, and it was only possible because we had the intelligence to guide our campaign.

* * *

Paul Meszaros was the organiser of Bradford Trades Union Congress's (TUC) anti-fascist committee, which had a proud history of combatting racism and fascism dating back to the NF in the 1970s. He was ably assisted by Lorraine Fitzsimons, who, together with Paul, worked as a community development worker at the Bradford Resource Centre, a place that assisted the community and voluntary sector in the city. They quickly developed a core group of dedicated activists who worked tirelessly, whatever the weather, to spread the anti-BNP message. Among them was Altaf Arif, whose father had been murdered by neo-Nazi British Movement members in the early 1980s.

When the BNP emerged in Bradford in 2001, it was through the Trades Council that people began to organise against it. The riots that scarred the city and highlighted its deep divisions were quickly exploited by the BNP. In the 2001 General Election, the party stood just one candidate, in Bradford, and received only 4.61 per cent of the vote. The following year, the first after the riots, it stood in a single council ward, Eccleshill, where it gained 14.7 per cent (enough to achieve fourth place). It did not take long before the BNP began to crank up its activities. It stood eight candidates in the 2003 local elections, and while none were elected, they polled respectably, coming second in four wards. The anti-fascist campaign, meanwhile, mixed citywide literature with ward-specific leaflets.

In addition to producing leaflets, Paul and his team were also busy undermining the BNP using research, having learnt the importance of intelligence-led campaigning from his days in Sheffield. Paul followed up BNP nomination forms in the 2003 elections and quickly realised that one candidate had clearly falsified his list of nominators. In addition to making a formal complaint, which subsequently led to a conviction, Paul quickly produced a leaflet for the ward the BNP candidate was contesting and got considerable coverage in the local and regional press. But Paul knew that the best information came from inside the ranks of his opponents, so when a call from someone claiming to be inside the BNP came into the Resource Centre where the TUC operated from, he immediately knew to take it seriously.

The caller wanted to remain anonymous and merely wanted to pass on information that a community fun day – which Paul was helping to organise in the eastern part of the city – was going to be attacked by the BNP. After another couple of conversations, the caller identified himself as Andy Sykes and said that he had joined the BNP in the summer of 2001 after receiving a party leaflet through his door on the Eccleshill estate. From there, he attended a BNP meeting, which happened to be the evening before the riots. Andy recalls witnessing BNP leader Nick Griffin in full flow, ratcheting up the tensions with predictions of impending doom. 'He told the audience that we had to defend our communities from Asians coming into the area,' Andy would go on to tell us. 'He said we had to be prepared to fight to protect what was ours.'

Andy quickly became curious about some of the party's claims. He decided to undertake some of his own research and found that most of what the party was saying was untrue. The decision to attack the fun day, which was being held in his local community, was the final straw. 'I was horrified. I told the bloke who asked me that this was a fun day with women and children, and he said that if women wanted to support the TUC they deserved what they got.'

It was a defining moment for Andy. He picked up the phone and rang Paul.

Andy was just what we needed. The all-out local elections of 2004, when boundary changes meant all three positions were up in every ward, coupled with the European elections that were being held on the same day, had loomed large in our planning for quite some time. Here we had an opportunity to not only learn about the BNP's plans but also to use Andy to undermine them. In early 2003, we approached the BBC to suggest they expose the violent intent of the BNP. We told them about Andy and suggested they place a journalist close to him in order to get access to the party's upper echelons. The BBC took up the idea, and one of its journalists, Jason Gwynne, moved to Bradford and joined the party. Jason was an old friend of mine, having worked with me at *The Cook Report* in the mid-1990s and then on the three-part BBC *Hooligans* series in 2002. He was brave, adventurous and a master of undercover work.

Despite our best efforts, the operation with the BBC did not go according to plan. BBC lawyers worried that airing this programme shortly before the elections would break their impartiality rules and so decided to delay its broadcast for a few months.[1] While Andy's information was still useful for directing our campaign, we were unable to make the most of it. The BNP won four council seats and came close to winning several others.

With the 2004 elections approaching, we knew we had to find a story that would undermine the BNP cause. Three months before the elections, we thought we had found it. By this point, Griffin was being accompanied by a personal bodyguard, and that man was Joe Owens, a BNP activist from Liverpool and former kickboxing champion who had convictions for sending letters with razor blades hidden in them and carrying an offensive weapon.[2] Owens had a reputation as a tough man, and we were soon to discover another even more disturbing side to him.

In late February, I was contacted by a journalist friend asking if this was the same Joe Owens who was known as a gangster in Liverpool. So began a six-week investigation into Owens' background, during which we interviewed leading figures of the Liverpool underworld, solicitors and even some former family friends. Everyone seemed to have a story about Owens.

Bit by bit, the story came together. Owens worked the doors in Liverpool and had earned a reputation as a hired-heavy and a hitman. In 1997, he was questioned about the horrific murder of Stephen Cole, a former Liverpool footballer and club doorman. The killing was revenge for the stabbing of one of Owens' close friends and was part of the city's notorious 'door wars', which claimed a number of lives during the mid-to-late 1990s.

According to the prominent Liverpool gangster Charlie Seiga: 'Joey was lucky. Witnesses failed to pick him out in an identification parade.'

Seiga gave a chilling insight into Owens in his autobiography, *Killer*. 'Joey Owens was very different from the rest,' Seiga wrote. 'Although young and in his thirties, he had that sort of "old-school" feel about him. First his manners were impeccable, and the other good asset he possessed was his intelligence. He also showed a lot of respect to his elders.' But Seiga also knew Owens to be a man of extreme violence. 'You could be deceived by Joey's appearance – blue eyes, fair hair, quietly spoken – you just would not be able to dream of what this man was capable of.'

In November 1997, Owens, Seiga and a third man were arrested for the murder of Liverpool gangster George Bromley, who had been shot in the head at close range while visiting Seiga's house, in what local police described as a 'gangland execution'. Owens and Seiga were charged with murder after Owens' fingerprints were found on the newspaper that Bromley was holding at the time of his death. The two men were also charged with threatening to kill Bromley's best friend. Owens was alleged to have said: 'If you don't stop the rumours you'll get three in the head like George.'[3]

Owens' case never made it to court. Days before the trial was due to begin, the main prosecution witness let it be known that he had no intention of giving evidence in court, something Seiga described in his book as 'a small miracle'. With the main witness gone and the men denying the charges, the case was dropped.

The gun used in the Bromley murder was later found in Owens' car when it was stopped by armed police during a thwarted armed robbery of a post office in the Anfield area of Liverpool. Owens, who was on remand at the time, would later claim in his autobiography that he had instructed his lawyer to give his car keys to a friend so he could remove it from a local car park. Unbeknown to him, he later claimed, the friend outsourced the job to three local petty villains, who then used the car for the robbery. Owens denied the gun was his.

We had a further scoop when we found a picture taken at the moment Owens was arrested for the murder of Bromley. A cross-legged Owens sat in the road with his hands on his head, surrounded by half-a-dozen police officers with submachine guns. We splashed the Owens story on the front page of our election tabloid, which had a total print run of over 1.5 million, split into 27 localised editions.

The spring bank holiday was supposed to offer us some long overdue respite from campaigning, and I was back in London having a couple of days off. It was shortly after lunch when I got a call from the commander of the Metropolitan Police's Special Branch. He apologised for ringing on a bank holiday but said that he had an issue he needed to discuss with me urgently and asked if I would come down to Scotland Yard. He refused to discuss it further on the phone, so without any more information I felt perfectly entitled to refuse. He remained insistent, and after I again declined, he rang Gerry Gable and stressed the seriousness of the situation. I eventually relented, and an agreement was made that I would meet one of his officers at my local police station later that afternoon. In a small, pokey room, I was dutifully informed that under the European Human Rights Act there was a duty to inform me that there was a serious and credible threat to my life.

The officer refused to divulge the name of the person behind this threat, though he did say, under questioning from me, that it related to two articles I had recently written. He also suggested that I stay away from the North West for the foreseeable future. He did add, chillingly, that the police had done a risk assessment and had concluded that the person concerned was deemed quite capable of carrying out the threat. Of course, it was all a charade. I knew exactly who the person in question was. I just wanted the young officer to say his name.

IN THE KNOW

I stayed away from Liverpool for the next few years, but when I did eventually go back, four years after receiving the warning from the police, Owens was there to greet me.

There have been too many other examples of when our undercover work helped our campaigning to list here, but a particularly pleasing case was in Barking and Dagenham in 2005. Less than a fortnight after the General Election, Dan Kelley, the BNP's sole councillor in Barking and Dagenham, resigned, claiming ill health. A probably more accurate reason was given in an interview with the local newspaper, where he admitted: 'There's meetings that go right over my head and there's little point in me being there. I'm wasting my time.'

The party's by-election candidate was to be Lawrence Rustem, a surprise choice given that many London BNP activists hated him because of his Turkish roots. He was, however, liked by the party leadership, and it poured resources into the campaign, the highlight of which was a DVD that was distributed to over 1,000 homes in the ward. The slick 15-minute production focused on housing and featured a young mother who claimed she had been on the council waiting list for five years. Her irate father chipped in that while she waited for a home, the Labour council was giving them away to newly arrived African immigrants.

What the BNP had not accounted for was an informer we had at the heart of its campaign. Duncan Robertson had joined the BNP a couple of years prior with the specific desire of undermining its efforts. Duncan had previously been an ANL activist but decided that becoming a mole would have a greater impact in undermining the fascists, so he approached Searchlight with the offer to go inside. Despite ill health, he maintained this role for 10 years until his untimely death in 2013.

A regular BNP activist in Barking and Dagenham, Duncan was able to tell us that the woman on the DVD actually lived in Wood Green, north London, and not Dagenham as she claimed, and the crying baby was not actually hers. We instantly got to work on a hard-hitting leaflet, which carried the headline: 'Gotcha! BNP Caught Lying Again'.

The leaflet was distributed a couple of days before the election and helped have the desired effect, with the BNP polling only 32 per cent of the vote, some way behind Labour, and a drop of 19 per cent from Kelley's winning vote the previous year.

It is now 20 years on, and HOPE not hate is still using intelligence and research at the core of its work. While at any one time we might still receive information from 10 to 15 people inside far-right groups, we are also increasingly using open-source information and more innovative modern research techniques. Research played a pivotal role in preventing Susan Hall, the Conservative Party candidate for the mayor of London, from getting elected. It was a HOPE not hate researcher, Gregory Davis, who uncovered what appeared to be her endorsement of tweets that many considered to be racist and anti-Muslim, a discovery that was to set the whole narrative of the election.[4] Our new Campaigns Director, Georgie Laming, used our research in short online videos that reached over 500,000 people in London during the final few weeks of the campaign. This was complemented by the delivery of over 20,000 leaflets among people identified as probably opposed to Hall's sentiments.[5] Sadiq Khan and the Labour Party used our research in their campaign for London mayor, as did political commentators and media outlets.[6]

If proof was needed that our campaign was successful, it can be found in an analysis of London mayoral polling. In early September, polling suggested that Hall was just 1 per cent behind Khan, but from the moment our research dropped, she slipped further and further behind. People voted for a variety of reasons, but Hall's extremism and character became key defining issues of the campaign.

Our research also helped put Stephen Lennon in prison for contempt of court after he broke a High Court injunction preventing him from repeating the lies he made following his libel case defeat to Syrian schoolboy Jamal Hijazi. Refusing to accept the court verdict, Lennon produced a video repeating the lies, which was released on the internet in early May 2023. HOPE not hate was aware that Lennon was preparing to release this video, so we closely monitored his activities, statements and social media comments. Between early April and mid-June 2023, on either side of the film's release, we identified at least 37 posts on his Telegram and GETTR accounts promoting it. Our investigation also proved that Lennon collaborated with MICE Media, the US-outlet that put out the film and provided new material for it. Following the release, Lennon appeared on podcasts and was interviewed by multiple media outlets. While he has repeatedly claimed to have no knowledge of, or involvement in, the film's release, he praised the airing of it and repeated his libellous claims about Jamal, again breaking the injunction.

The key piece of evidence was that Lennon had shot a new ending for the film, which conclusively proved that he lied when he claimed the film was made two years before and released without his involvement. Gregory Davis identified the hotel where Lennon shot the final scene as being located in Cuba by identifying a 1950s car in the background and tracing a spiral staircase in the reflection of a glass window. My colleague Joe Mulhall then rang the hotel, which confirmed Lennon had stayed there a few weeks before. Armed with all this evidence, we presented an 80-page dossier to the Attorney General's office, and a year later they decided to charge Lennon with contempt of court. Lennon eventually pleaded guilty to what was his third conviction for contempt and was imprisoned for 18 months.

Perhaps most importantly, it was a HOPE not hate researcher who was able to identify one Andrew McIntyre as the person behind the Southport WakeUp Telegram channel, which was one of the main instigators of the riots in the summer of 2024. Amazingly, Gregory tracked down McIntyre's identity through extensive analysis of his online output and his use of the word 'eiy', which we had never come across before.

Seemingly used as a variant spelling of the affirmative 'aye', as opposed to the interrogative 'eh?', McIntyre had used this word across four of the 10 accounts he was operating at the time of the riots. This discovery of a word that is essentially unheard of in British English allowed us to search archived messages from UK-based far-right Telegram chats and identify another 11 accounts belonging to McIntyre, some dating back as far as 2021.

Gregory then began to search for more linguistic clues in McIntyre's writing, soon identifying other distinctive words, such as 'pakki' (an unusual spelling of the racial slur) and 'abaa' (a regional variant of the word 'about'). Neither was unique to McIntyre, but both are used rarely enough that it allowed us to track down other deleted accounts belonging to him. By searching for McIntyre's linguistic tells and cross-referencing them, we uncovered a total of 168 separate social media accounts belonging to McIntyre, 155 of them on Telegram and the remainder on YouTube, TikTok and Twitter.

The vast majority of his Telegram accounts were used for just one or two days at a time, mainly for purposes of harassment. McIntyre would create a so-called 'burner account' to gain access to particular far-right chats and abuse someone or the group as a whole. It was from one of his older accounts that we learnt that McIntyre had referenced himself as living in Bootle, Merseyside, and a photo he had posted of the interior of his car from another account inadvertently revealed a decal sticker showing that the vehicle had been sold at a Skoda retailer in the area.

Most amazingly of all, we were able to locate McIntyre's house by using satellite images on Google Maps to find a large buddleia plant growing from a wall at the rear of the property, which had appeared in a photo he had uploaded three years earlier. We handed a dossier to police on Tuesday, 6 August, and within 48 hours Merseyside Police had assessed our information and arrested 39-year-old

IN THE KNOW

McIntyre. He eventually pleaded guilty and was sentenced to seven and a half years' imprisonment.[7]

4

The Battle for Barking and Dagenham

If there was one campaign that epitomised HOPE not hate and our approach to campaigning, it was the one to defeat the BNP in Barking and Dagenham in 2010. It really was the campaign of campaigns. It was on a scale we had never experienced before, or since for that matter, and its significance and impact were so considerable it is worth retelling in detail.

We first became active in the east London borough in September 2004, when the BNP won their first council seat in the area in a by-election in Goresbrook ward. In the 2005 General Election, the party polled 16.9 per cent, beating their previous highest vote share in Oldham four years before. However, it was in the local elections the following year that the BNP really made their mark, winning 12 council seats with an average vote of 41 per cent in the seats they contested. Fortunately, the BNP only stood 13 candidates that year; if they had stood more, they probably would have already been running the council.

The memory of that election burnt strong inside me. It had begun with a claim by Margaret Hodge, the then-Labour MP for Barking, that eight out of 10 white voters in some of her wards were considering voting BNP. 'They can't get a home for their children, they see black and ethnic minority communities moving in and they are angry,' she said.[1]

She went on to attack the Labour Party leadership for refusing to discuss race and claimed that the 'political class' was scared of the issue. 'The Labour Party hasn't talked to these people,' she said. 'This is a traditional Labour area but they are not used to engaging with us because all we do is put leaflets through doors. Part of the reason they switch to the BNP is they feel no one else is listening to them.'

It was a quiet Easter weekend, but suddenly Hodge had given the media something to talk about. While the BNP had been winning council seats for several years, it was only really with its arrival in London – a few miles from where most of the British press was based – that some in the media appeared interested. Every national newspaper now covered the BNP in detail, with most sending journalists along the District line to ask the people of Barking and Dagenham why they felt the way they did.

Politicians began to brief journalists that the BNP could win 25 per cent in a few wards, and Hodge thought the far-right party could pick up a seat or two. We became increasingly nervous. Within days of Hodge's intervention, the BNP was polling 7 per cent in a national YouGov poll.[2] We watched these events unfold with a growing sense of dread. While Hodge might have simply been relaying her experience on the doorstep, by announcing it so publicly and using it to attack the Labour Party on immigration and for housing policies that reduced the housing stock for local people, it created a narrative that the anti-Labour media were only too eager to exploit.

Four years later, as Griffin and Andrew Brons, the former chairman of the NF, were elected to the European Parliament, the BNP polled more votes than Labour across the borough. The scene was now set for our biggest showdown – stopping the fascist party winning control of the council in the 2010 London elections.

* * *

With the memory of the 2006 election still haunting me, we began planning for this election from the late summer of 2009. We had recently taken on a young but experienced campaigner called Sam Tarry, who fortuitously was from Barking, and while he ran the ground operation, I oversaw the overall campaign strategy and produced our literature. It was a combination that worked well, and before long we had the largest constituency campaign of the General Election. We were supported in our efforts by a close relationship with Dagenham Labour Party, where local MP Jon Cruddas had become a great friend of HOPE not hate. Together with Dagenham Labour, we took over the top floor of the Unite the Union building, situated minutes from Dagenham Dock railway station and on the edge of what was then the huge Ford plant, and split it between us. I moved into our Dagenham office in late January, by which time Sam had things up and running. In addition to the rows of desks, computers and telephones, there were several people hard at work. We were soon joined by Ben Stuttard, Joe Mulhall, Ellie Lowe and Nick Cook.

They were all just out of university or, in Ellie's case, sixth-form college, and had answered an advert to volunteer for our campaign. Ellie said she had wanted to intern 'because it seemed the most important cause at the time':

> This was really my first political involvement and I wanted to be a part of a campaign that I really cared about. I came from just down the road from Barking and Dagenham and the BNP were strong in Thurrock too. HOPE not hate seemed like a step away from the aggressive anti-fascism that I didn't think was for me and gave me an opportunity to get involved.

For Joe, who was to go on to play a key role in HOPE not hate, it was more simple. 'I was unemployed and didn't like fascists,' he said. 'Not much more complex than that, I am afraid.'

All four proved fantastic additions to the team, and without their hard work and commitment we would surely not have achieved what we did. In addition to pounding the streets delivering leaflets in sun, rain and sleet, they helped build and run our days of action, created routes for leafleteers, spoke on our behalf at meetings and put together the databases for our huge direct-mail operation.

Three of the four – Joe, Ben and Ellie – were featured in a two-page *Guardian* newspaper spread on young people getting involved in politics, which was published in the middle of the campaign.[3] Over the course of the piece, they articulated the frustration, disillusionment and disappointment many young people felt towards the Labour Party in the twilight of its government; yet they were still keen on politics and wanted to make a difference. They reflected a great swathe of our supporters. While they were understandably thrilled at the article, those working on the Labour Party campaign were less than impressed.

At the far end of the 'war room', stretching across the back wall, was a huge HOPE not hate banner created for us by the Philosophy Football team. They were great supporters of our work, regularly amplifying our activities and making donations to us too. The banner listed key events in the history of racism and fascism over the years; our positive achievements were highlighted in red, while negative events were written in grey. It provided a fantastic backdrop and placed the HOPE not hate campaign as the latest act in a century of struggle.

Also joining was Caroline Alabi, also from Dagenham, to head up our faith campaign. Building on our experiences in the European elections, where we worked closely with the Bishop of Manchester's office, we knew that mobilising the faith communities would help us turn out the anti-BNP vote. Caroline was a practising Christian and already had a lot of local contacts, so she was ideal for the job. Over the next four months, she used these links to build a solid base within and between the borough's various faith communities. Caroline's work was helped by the fact that Sam's dad was a local vicar, and through him we were able to get more support from other faith leaders.

Campaigning got underway just before Christmas, when we delivered an introductory leaflet in three of our target wards. This was followed in early February with the first of our three tabloid newspapers. Our strategy was simple: to suppress the BNP vote by highlighting its extremism and the incompetence of its local councillors, while mobilising the anti-BNP vote by highlighting the dangers of a BNP council and the threat to community cohesion. While our newspapers carried both messages, the second objective was promoted primarily through our targeted work aimed at those least likely to vote BNP.

Griffin's candidature was a blessing for us. While he hoped his profile would draw the media into Barking and Dagenham, and so create a similar storm to that which had propelled the BNP in 2006, the opposite was true. Research showed that he was less popular among likely BNP voters than local BNP councillors, so our strategy was to highlight just how extreme he was while also casting him as a carpetbagger who had no real interest in the area.

He became the focus of our attack. In our first tabloid election newspaper, we highlighted his absence from the North West since being elected as a member of the European Parliament (MEP) – out of the 24 engagements written up on the BNP website in the six months since his election, only one was in the North West: 'Griffin now says that he wants to be the MP for Barking. Given his record over the past few months, do you really believe he will be there for you?'

To ensure this did not happen, we had to link Griffin to the council fight. The front page of our third newspaper, which went to every property in the borough, depicted him lurking ominously over the town's Civic Centre.

Our message was simple: 'Vote BNP, get Griffin.'

'Imagine Griffin, the man who has praised the Nazis and said the Holocaust didn't happen, taking control of your child's education,' an article inside the paper read. 'Imagine Griffin, the man who still refuses to publish full accounts of his expenses, getting his hands on a multimillion pound council budget. Nick Griffin is not standing in the local elections but he is the one who would be firmly in control if the BNP won.'

The centre pages of the tabloid focused on what a future BNP council would look like and what it would mean for local people. It was a grim picture of a racially motivated council pursuing its ideological goals through local schools, adult and children's services, housing, regeneration and cuts. The edition also carried a survey by the National Union of Teachers (NUT), which had asked its local members about their views on a possible BNP-run council. Almost everyone opposed the idea, with 97 per cent believing it would damage social cohesion in the borough and 75 per cent saying they would consider looking for a job elsewhere.

Linking Griffin to the local council elections was a feature of another leaflet delivered towards the end of the campaign. With a swastika armband placed on Griffin's sleeve, the BNP leader was superimposed in front of a blackboard to convey the message that his extremist views would be taught in local schools if the BNP won control of the council.

Fearing a repeat of 2006, our general approach was to play down the BNP's chances and talk up the divisions within its ranks. We did release one story with a 'Where's Griffin?' line, following the leader's virtual absence from Barking and Dagenham during much of the campaign. At one point, ITV's *London Tonight* news programme ran the 'Where's Griffin?' headline in a package on the Barking and Dagenham contest.

The BNP, by contrast, had an appalling media operation and resorted to poorly judged publicity stunts to attract attention. In early April, the party claimed to have smashed a 'plot' by a party official to kill Griffin, after they had bugged his phone and recorded his conversations. If the BNP thought this would attract favourable attention, they were deluded, as the incident was written up in the press as revealing a violent and divided movement.

In another calamitous move, Griffin then thought it highly amusing to superimpose a jar of Marmite in the corner of the party's political broadcast, in retaliation for Marmite producer Unilever's own TV commercial that depicted two fictitious parties, the Love Party and the Hate Party, the latter allegedly inspired by the BNP. Griffin thought he would get his revenge by making it look as though Marmite was sponsoring the BNP broadcast, but it is hard to think of anything more stupid.[4] Sure enough, within days his party was served notice for breach of copyright.[5]

Our online effort was a key component of our campaign. It raised awareness of the threat, helped us fundraise and, more importantly, mobilised people into activity. As the New Year broke, and in consultation with Blue State Digital (BSD), we decided to let our supporters know about the threat we faced. We reminded people of the horror we all felt when Griffin was elected to the European Parliament and asked them to pledge 'Never Again.' Over 7,000 of our supporters committed to do something in the campaign, ranging from joining an action in one of our key areas to ringing voters via our online phone bank – or even setting up a local HOPE not hate group if one did not already exist.

The underlying strategy was to take our supporters on a journey with us, whether they lived close to one of our target areas or not. Keeping everyone on board, particularly those who lived some distance away from our key areas, was a vital way of making them feel part of the campaign. During our four-month effort, we raised over £100,000 online from more than 8,000 people.

Saturday, 17 April was our big day of action. Sam and our young interns toured London's anti-fascist scene, spoke at trade union meetings and cajoled past and present activists by telephone. Yes, we wanted all of them to come out, but we also wanted them to bring people with them. We were particularly keen to identify 'gatekeepers' – those individuals who could build the day of action through their own networks and, more importantly, organise to bring people there.

The most successful of these was in Hackney, where John Page and his partner Jane Holgate had built an impressive group, Hackney Unites, to turn out the anti-BNP group in successive elections. While the BNP was not a threat in one of the most diverse boroughs in the country, they recognised the importance of turning out the multicultural vote. Sam and I spoke at their meetings, explaining the day of action's importance and our need for their involvement. They duly delivered, providing most of the 80 people who boarded a double-decker bus we had hired to set off from Hackney.

A huge amount of planning had gone into the day. The newspapers arrived on the Thursday morning, two days before our big day, and the four pallets' worth had to be broken up in the car park and then carried, a bundle or two at a time, up the six flights of stairs to the office. They were then broken down again and divided into 'walks', each enough for a couple of hours of leafleting. We cleared some of the furniture to maximise floor space and laid out the bundles across the floor, each with a map and directions on how to get there. With more than 200 people having signed up to leaflet via our email appeals, we knew there would be a good turnout, but as always, we were never totally sure on the real numbers. More in hope than anything, we laid out enough papers to cover 13 of the 17 wards in the borough. At the entrance to our office was a registration table, and then another with HOPE not hate material – magazines, badges and bags – which we'd had made specially for the day. On the far side of the room were tables laden with food, which had been purchased from a local curry house we would often frequent.

It was 10.30 on the Friday evening when everything was complete and I headed home, tingling with expectation. Sam and Nick Cook, one of our interns, remained in the office overnight to guard everything – just in case of attack – and when I returned at 7.30 the next morning, they headed out to shower and change. I was soon joined by Ellie and Caroline, and together we made our final preparations.

The first volunteers began to arrive at 9 a.m., a good 90 minutes before the advertised time. They tended to be local and were keen to get on with the work. They, like everyone else, were amazed at the sight of our transformed base. We would often glance over to see people posing for photographs in front of our huge banner.

The newspapers were going down quickly, and by 10 a.m. it was clear we needed to bundle up the papers for the remaining four wards. Sam, Nick and I would alternate counting out the papers with briefing new arrivals, before sending them on their way. By 10.30 a.m., people were flooding in, some coming under their own steam, while at least 60 had been on the 10.10 a.m. train out from Fenchurch Street – which we had dubbed in our emails the 'HOPE Express'. Queues of activists stretched from our office, down the six flights of stairs and around the side of the building, but despite the 20-minute wait, no one complained.

In addition to the 80 people who also came on the double-decker bus from Camden and Hackney, and the 60 people on the HOPE Express, 26 arrived together from Southwark. Unite and Unison both brought out about 30, and the NUT turned out even more, led by its General Secretary Christine Blower. Smaller groups came from Sussex, Essex and Oxford, and there were even a couple of people from Bristol. We later did a survey of those attending and found that for a third it was their very first political activity.

Caroline and Ellie ran the registration desk and would keep me informed of the numbers coming through. 'We had expected 300 to 400 people,' Caroline would admit later, 'but no one thought we would get over 500.'

In total, 541 people signed in that day. The bundles of newspapers were disappearing at such a rate that by noon we had to break up the 20,000 newspapers we had for the neighbouring borough of Havering and bundle those up too. This was no easy task, as we had no maps and no idea of the ward boundaries, but Nick Cook managed to pull something together at very short notice. Amazingly, by 12.30 p.m. even these had gone out, meaning we had dispatched 92,000 newspapers in just a few hours. The only complaints we had that day were people who arrived late only to find the newspapers had all gone.

At least half the people who turned up returned to our base for a curry lunch, which was dutifully served up by Cruddas and a few of our volunteers. Billy Bragg, who had had an altercation with the BNP's Richard Barnbrook that morning, sang a few songs as a thank you. It was, quite simply, the most amazing day, a view shared by most of the people who had come along.

By the Monday morning, our attention now turned to the next phase of the campaign, which focused on those most likely to be against the BNP. We laboriously went through the electoral register and identified 24,500 black and Asian voters across the borough: 18,000 in the Barking constituency and 6,500 in the Dagenham part of the Dagenham and Rainham constituency. We then broke this down, as best we could, into Muslim, Sikh, Hindu and black African voters, before then hand-delivering personalised letters and accompanying leaflets to them.

Our Muslim leaflet was also distributed at the main mosque in Barking, while our Christian leaflet, which opened out into a poster with 15 local church leaders holding HOPE not hate signs, was given out at several local churches across the borough. On the final Sunday of the campaign, Caroline spoke at six different churches, including one attended by 2,000 people.

Many pensioners in the area had strong memories both of Nazism, from living in London during the Blitz, and of the activities of Oswald Mosley and his Blackshirts. Although they may have been uneasy about immigration, they were also reluctant to vote BNP. To reinforce this concern, we repeatedly highlighted the party's support for Hitler's Nazis and Griffin's well-stated belief that Britain was wrong to go to war with Nazi Germany. A few days before polling day, we delivered a letter by Second World War veteran Kenneth Riley to all the pensioners we could identify in the borough. 'First They Stole My Friends, Now They Steal My Words' was the headline. Riley spoke about how the BNP was the heir of Hitler's Nazis and had outrageously used his own words in a BNP fundraising email. It was a devastating letter and went down really well with local people.

A study of young people across London's boroughs found a surprisingly positive attitude in Barking and Dagenham towards a multicultural society. So with the support of the Public and Commercial Services union, we sent a leaflet to all the area's first-time voters, explaining why the BNP had no answers to the problems facing young people.

The focus of our targeted campaigning was women voters, as our research showed the majority were much more likely to vote against than for the BNP. In early April, we sent out an email to our supporters asking them to fund a 12-page booklet we were producing for women voters. The trade union Unison had agreed to match what we raised, and over the next 24 hours our supporters donated more than £16,000, which was then doubled by Unison, giving us the money to print and post out tens of thousands of booklets to women in our target constituencies.

The booklet was designed and written quite differently from the rest of our campaign materials. It was softer, focused more on the division and fear the BNP brought to local communities than the group's racism or fascism and explained why the BNP's policies were counter to the interests of women. Three of the main articles were written by *Mirror* columnists Fiona Phillips, Coleen Nolan and Ros Wynne-Jones. We illustrated the articles with some of the most unflattering photos of BNP men we could find. Women in 35,000 households across Barking and Dagenham were sent the booklets, accompanied by a letter signed by local GMB Branch Secretary Sandra Vincent, whom we accurately portrayed as a 'hardworking mother of two'.

HOW TO DEFEAT THE FAR RIGHT

The feedback from this booklet was incredible. One woman wrote saying that it not only persuaded her to vote but enabled her to persuade her husband not to support the BNP. Hodge was also full of praise, describing the booklet as the single most important piece of anti-BNP literature distributed during the campaign. But the best reaction was from the BNP itself, which dedicated its entire final leaflet of the campaign to rebutting it. Its response merely repeated our claims and, even better, put our allegations in bold with its rebuttals in ordinary text. The campaign had been going in our direction for a while, and the BNP's response merely confirmed that we were setting the agenda going into polling day.

Of course, HOPE not hate was not alone in opposing the BNP in Barking and Dagenham. UAF had also made the area the focus of its campaigning, though it only operated in Barking and worked closely with Hodge's Labour Party. The two local Labour parties, Barking and Dagenham, and Rainham, also worked hard to combat the BNP, though with quite different campaign strategies. We had been highly critical of Hodge over the years, but to her credit she and her close team had turned their Labour Party into an outward-looking, campaigning organisation. They knocked on doors, spoke to people and piled up the Labour promises. From the autumn of 2009, Margaret took full advantage of Griffin's candidature by organising several quite large days of action in Barking, with Labour activists coming in from across London. Without Griffin on the ballot, Jon Cruddas's campaign material made little mention of the BNP, relying heavily on Jon's popularity and what he had done for local people.

With an abundance of volunteers and growing confidence, we decided to call a second day of action for the bank holiday Monday, just four days before polling. This time, an incredible 385 people turned up. We produced a series of 'Apology' leaflets, customised for our key wards, targeting the appalling performance of BNP councillors over their four years in office. We calculated the allowances they had been paid since 2006 and compared that to the number of meetings they had attended. As housing was the key local issue, we also looked at the number of case referrals each councillor had made to the Housing Department. The results were startling and provided great ammunition for our leaflets. The attendance of BNP councillors was so poor that some were being paid £1,666 for each meeting they attended – and many had not referred a single case.

The outside of the leaflet was left deliberately ambiguous, with HOPE not hate branding, in the hope the reader would open it up out of curiosity. We produced leaflets for the four wards where BNP councillors were standing again but designed a quite different leaflet for Eastbury, where the BNP had selected Jeffrey Marshall as its candidate. Here we focused on his appalling statements on disability, writing on an internet forum following the death of David Cameron's disabled son Ivan: 'We live in a country today which is unhealthily dominated by an excess of sentimentality towards the weak and unproductive. No good will come of it.'

On that one day, we delivered 55,000 leaflets across 11 wards. As a thank you, we held a social in the grounds of a local church. Blessed with more good weather and enjoying good food provided by a number of local restaurants, Eddie Izzard and Billy Bragg entertained the crowd.

With three days remaining, we found ourselves with absolutely no material left, so we were forced to design more leaflets to give to activists who turned up at our campaign headquarters each day to help.

One of the leaflets, which was put out the day before polling, had a bright lightbulb on a black background, with the slogan 'Would the last person out please turn off the light', a play on *The Sun*'s headline against Neil Kinnock in 1992. The leaflet reminded voters of the disaster awaiting them if the BNP won control of the council. Meanwhile, hundreds of our supporters around the country had been ringing voters in Barking and Dagenham through our online telephone canvassing tool.

The BNP went into meltdown in the final week, with its hysterical reaction to our women's booklet reflecting its darkening mood. Tensions were also rising between the two campaigns as BNP members became more hostile and threatening. Obviously irritated by the huge numbers we were turning out, Griffin and a few of his cronies even turned up at our campaign base and began shouting through a megaphone from across the street. It just so happened that a group of activists from the Jewish Council for Racial Equality were with us that day, and while Sam was in the middle of giving them a briefing, they broke away to give the BNP leader a piece of their mind. Surrounding him, they condemned his racism and Holocaust denial. They were soon joined by Caroline, our faith co-ordinator, who stood there just feet away from Griffin, proudly asserting that she was British and there was nothing he or the BNP could do about it. Stunned by this onslaught, he turned and left.

It was shortly after 7 a.m. when I got into the office on election day. I surveyed the piles of envelopes stacked neatly on the tables around our 'war room'. Six months of hard work had come down to this one single day, and, standing alone in our vast HQ, I felt a certain calmness about our election-day plans. I had been growing in confidence in recent days. Laid out on the tables were 6,000 addressed envelopes, one for each of the anti-BNP households we needed to turn out in our nine target wards.

At the entrance to the office was a single table where volunteers had to sign in. If they were coming to help us, then they were led directly to the left; if they were there to join Jon's campaign, then they went right. Some people were happy to help both campaigns, but many more had little desire to do Labour Party work. The sight of volunteer after volunteer heading in our direction, possibly at a rate of eight or nine to one, irritated some on the Labour side and caused enough resentment that words were exchanged.

In total, 176 people turned up to help, a phenomenal effort and a testament to the enthusiasm of our campaign. Billy Bragg appeared once again, and he went out on the doorstep with Matthew Collins, while I stayed with some of our young volunteers to run a surprisingly quiet campaign base. Singer and poet Scroobius Pip put in a stint, as did several mainstream journalists who all wanted to do their bit for the campaign. We even had three 13-year-old boys from Kent who had bunked off from a school trip to London to join us for a couple of hours. When I asked them why they had come, one simply replied that they had followed the campaign online and wanted to be a part of it.

It was nearly 8 p.m. when we made our final push. Teams had been out all day, and in some wards we were now on our third 'knock'. Virtually everyone we spoke to had either voted or intended to vote, so this final session was all about getting those final promises to get to the polls before they closed. With most of our volunteers out, the core team decided to do a final walk together. We had lived and breathed this campaign for months, so it seemed fitting that we all ended it together on the streets. With minutes to go, we were still urging people to run to the polls.

I skipped the election count, deciding to head home to start our live election blog, but it was hard not to feel nervous. We had widely expected Griffin to lose, but I don't think in our wildest dreams we had expected him to lose so badly. He could only finish fourth in the Barking constituency, polling just 14.6 per cent of the vote, down from the 16.9 per cent received by Richard Barnbrook in 2005, while the BNP's Michael Barnbrook polled just 11 per cent in neighbouring Dagenham and Rainham.

It was a humiliating defeat for the BNP leader, and things only got worse for the party with the local (borough) election count the following morning. Despite being up all night, I made my way back over to Barking for the council count the following afternoon. As the stacks of votes piled up, it became clear that the BNP was heading for oblivion. The BNP lost the 12 seats it was defending, by some distance too, and it fell way short in the other wards it was contesting. There was utter jubilation among the successful Labour candidates as the party's 51–0 victory became obvious.

Back at our campaign office, our young interns were following the local election results via the council website, which was being projected on to a white wall. 'Hearing the result was very strange because I hadn't slept for about 36 hours by that point,' says Ellie:

> I had come straight from the election count in Basildon where we'd lost and was feeling very demoralised.
>
> It just felt all very unreal. I think we knew at that point that they weren't taking control of the council, but just as wards like Goresbrook came in with three Labour councillors it felt unbelievable. I remember Joe putting WW2 theme songs on the speakers very loudly for some reason. I guess it also felt nice that the three of us were there together as we'd all started volunteering at the same time and had done it together. It was a great feeling when all the news and social media was celebrating the loss of the BNP and we knew that we'd had a lot to do with that result.

Britain had a new government and was heading into austerity, but many people looked to the defeat of Griffin and the BNP in Barking and Dagenham as a bright spot in a bleak time. For the BNP, the election defeat was the beginning of the end. Their inflated expectations and public boast of victory made their defeat impossible to take. Recriminations led to serious infighting – within a year, Griffin had been deposed as leader, and the party was literally over. HOPE did indeed triumph over hate.

5

When Hate Comes to Town

It was the news that Paul Meszaros and Lorraine Fitzsimons had been dreading. Ever since the EDL had begun their provocative demos across the country, there had been persistent rumours that Bradford would be next. Now, in early July 2010, the news had been confirmed. Their concern was understandable. The last time racists tried to march through the city centre in 2001, a riot had ensued, and 200 Asian men had been sent to prison. The racial fault lines these events opened were exploited by the BNP, and though it had been nine years since those disturbances, the community divisions still hung over the city.

The EDL had been launched in the summer of 2009 as a reaction to a small Islamist protest against a homecoming parade of the Royal Anglian Regiment in Luton a couple of months prior. Standing on the side of the road, a handful of supporters of Muslims Against Crusades (MAC), a rebranding of the infamous group al-Muhajiroun (ALM), had shouted obscenities and waved offensive placards. The British media were outraged, and many of the newspapers carried the protests on their front pages. Also angry were a group of Luton football hooligans. Led by a young 25-year-old football hooligan called Stephen Lennon, they organised themselves as the United People of Luton and held a march in the town a few weeks later, which resulted in 200 people going on a rampage through a predominantly Muslim neighbourhood. After meeting like-minded people in London, many of whom were already involved in the self-styled counter-jihad movement, they decided to turn their local protest group into a national movement. The EDL was born.

Lennon became the group's spokesperson, though fearing media – and so left-wing – scrutiny, he adopted the name of a well-known Luton hooligan, Tommy Robinson, as his *nom de plume*. Despite his young age, Lennon was articulate and confident. He also had a reputation as a fighter and had several convictions for violence along the way.

The EDL's early activities consisted of demonstrations in towns and cities across the country. Their vile anti-Muslim rhetoric and open racism understandably provoked outrage wherever they went, and their protests often ended in violent clashes with the police. HOPE not hate, however, largely ignored them for the first year of their existence. We were gearing up for our fight against the BNP in Barking and Dagenham and didn't really have the capacity – with the exception of taking photos – to do much on the ground. This all changed shortly after the 2010 General Election, when the collapse of the BNP finally gave us some breathing space, and the EDL announced its intention to march in Bradford in what its promotional material called 'the big one'.

Some anti-fascists demanded a counter-demonstration against the EDL, but few, if any, within the city concurred. Even people who would have normally supported such a response understood how delicate the situation was in Bradford. 'The city had still not recovered from the 2001 riots and an EDL demo and counter-EDL demo could well have seen a repeat,' recalls Paul.

The priority for our Bradford team was to stop the EDL march. After news emerged that the EDL wanted to start their march in a predominantly Muslim part of the city before making their way into the city centre, Paul knew it was a race against time to get the demo stopped. The EDL's planned march would have been highly inflammatory, but of course that was the aim of the organisers.

Paul and Lorraine immediately set about discussing options with the local Muslim communities and council leadership, who in turn liaised with the police. It was fortuitous that Alison Rose, the local police commander, had been a Bradford bobby at the time of the 2001 riots, so she was more than keen to play her role. Together, we came up with the idea of organising a petition to show the strength of feeling. It would have been easy for the council to call on the police to apply to the home secretary for a ban, but we were privately advised that the minister was not inclined to ban the protest. Also, we wanted to avoid this being seen as a bureaucratic manoeuvre. By organising a large petition signed by local people, we wanted to demonstrate the strength of public feeling on the issue. Building the petition would also give us the opportunity to talk to people who would not normally consider themselves to be politically engaged.

With a plan agreed, Paul and Lorraine got to work. The following Saturday they erected their HOPE not hate campaign banner in Bradford city centre, something they had done time and time again over the years. 'I arrived thinking this was going to be just another one of those days,' remembers Paul with a wry grin. 'Lots of very apologetic texts and emails but very few people actually turning up.'

This time, he could not have been more wrong. Over the next hour, people came in droves, young and old, white and Asian, all wanting to help stop the EDL coming to Bradford. 'There were 82 people in total, the vast majority had never done anything with us before,' he says. 'It was fantastic. I've never experienced anything like it.'

And this was only the start. Over the next three weeks, more than 200 Bradfordians were involved in collecting an incredible 10,700 signatures from local people. We consciously decided to make it an offline petition, as we wanted the opportunity to talk to people and wanted only Bradfordians to sign it. 'We had people standing inside and outside churches and mosques,' recalls Lorraine. 'People we had never met were ringing and emailing us asking for petition sheets. Shops were putting up posters and I would come across people in the street wearing Bradford Together badges.'

Community activist Richard Dunbar collected 500 signatures by going door-to-door in the predominantly white council estate of Buttershaw. The Bishop of Bradford's office distributed petition sheets and sign-up cards for local churches and came back with almost 1,500 filled in. That all these names were collected over a three-week period at the height of the summer holidays was even more impressive. The strength of feeling of Bradfordians, as demonstrated in the petition, was not lost on the authorities, and they were eventually compelled to act. When West Yorkshire Police finally made the request for a ban, they noted the 'understandable concerns of the community', a direct reference to our campaign.

Opposition to a ban also came from some progressive quarters, with some believing that people should enact 'No Platform' on the streets, while others took a more libertarian freedom-of-speech approach. I had one sharp exchange on Radio 4's *Today* programme with Jamie Bartlett, from the think tank Demos, who argued that 'a bit of trouble was the price of living in a liberal democracy'. I was furious, telling the listeners that it was fine for him to say that from the comfort of his London home, but for the people of Bradford this was something real.

Luckily, however, people power won through, and the home secretary banned the march, though the EDL was still allowed a static protest.

While a counter-protest was organised to oppose the EDL rally, we put our effort into supporting a peace vigil in the city centre the day before the planned protest, believing it allowed us to show our opposition to the EDL without adding to the tensions on the day. To us, counter-demonstrations and street protests were simply a tactic: sometimes to be used, sometimes not. Some argued that our approach 'abandoned' the Muslim community and broke from the time-honoured street resistance traditions of Cable Street, when 200,000 people came out on to the streets to prevent Mosley's Blackshirts from marching through London's East End in October 1936. We believed our approach did quite the opposite. By focusing on stopping the march from going through a predominantly Muslim neighbourhood, we believed we did more to protect the local Muslim community than we would have by being penned in by the police and trading insults or missiles with far-right hooligans.

With the memory of the 2001 riots still fresh in the minds of many, when 200 local Muslims were sent to prison, we decided that our priority was to help de-escalate tensions rather than risking a repeat of those dreadful days 11 years earlier. It always irritated us that the individuals and groups that shouted loudest for street action were very rarely the ones to be arrested. In this, we were supported by some of the young Asian men who had been imprisoned in 2001, who were now intent on warning their younger brothers and relatives not to make the same mistake they did.

From just the petition, we had had successful conversations with 10,700 people in Bradford, and tens of thousands more read the supportive articles in the *Telegraph & Argus* (T&A) newspaper. In our petition, we not only called for a ban but defended and promoted 'our' Bradford – tolerant, multiracial and peaceful. The support from the *T&A* gave us a major boost. It published stories on our campaign for over a fortnight and asked its readers to sign our petition. The *T&A* certainly stuck its neck out, but its bravery was rewarded by an unprecedented response. More than 800 people took the trouble to cut out, sign and post back the petition coupon in the paper – which given that its readership was overwhelmingly white and elderly, clearly reflected the level of concern across the city.

We supported other peaceful initiatives too. A local women's group decorated Bradford city centre in green ribbon, while on the Sunday, the day after the EDL protest, there was a music festival in another part of the city. Even the police offered their support, with many officers wearing armbands made out of the ribbons. Our campaign succeeded in getting the EDL march banned, and in the process it helped develop a new spirit in the city. More importantly, however, the real success of the Bradford Together initiative was how it engaged with local people – real people in real communities.

We were also able to contrast our 'hope' with their 'hate', thanks to the peaceful events held the day before, attended by over 400 people from across the racial and religious divide. Holding up Bradford Together posters, the crowd had sung 'We Shall Overcome' in steely determination. We produced a video pulling together some of the highlights of the campaign and a selection of the hundreds of photographs Bradfordians had sent with the word 'Together'.

The police and council had little interest in giving the EDL a platform, so they put the 700 or so thugs who turned up in the middle of some wasteland in the city centre, surrounded on three sides by a seven-foot wooden wall so it was almost impossible for shoppers to see them. Paul and I watched the far-right protest from the balcony of an overlooking hotel, much to the annoyance of a police surveillance unit who were hoping to use the same balcony for themselves. They tried to make us leave, but we refused to budge, telling them we were there with the permission of the council leader. Muttering under their breaths, they headed for the floor below. It turned out to be one of the most violent EDL protests, with the group's supporters raining down weapons on the police and even fighting among themselves.

The *T&A* featured pictures of local restaurateurs taking trays of curries and samosas to the police station as a thank you for their hard work in protecting local people, a gesture that would have been unthinkable just a few months before.

Harriet Wood, a HOPE not hate supporter from Bradford, summed up the feeling of many when she wrote thanking us for the campaign:

This was a fantastic campaign that was focused directly on the needs of the community affected and not on any ideology. I cannot praise these aims high enough. Much as I agree with notions of 'not surrendering the streets' and 'they shall not pass', I am a Bradfordian who does not wish to see this city become a battleground for a fight nobody here wants. The fight was their aim, therefore the fight is what needed to be thwarted in order to thwart the EDL.

After the EDL protest, the mood within Bradford was best summed up in a front-page editorial in the *T&A*:

They failed miserably to provoke Bradford into the sort of reaction which would have allowed them to brag about the truth of their hate-filled message in the face of trouble-making Muslims. And in their anger and frustration they turned on each other and the police and for all time shattered the self-propagated delusion that they only want to stage peaceful protest.

In their stupidity and their naivety they succeeded in doing exactly the opposite of what they intended: they united the people of Bradford of all colours, creeds, races and religions as one.

Perhaps even more importantly they helped our city to lay some of the ghosts of the riots of 2001. They helped prove that Bradford has moved on, it has grown to a point where it can acknowledge and deal with its differences without the need for confrontation and violence.

In the event, Bradford excelled itself and our great city can lift its head and move on today with the pride it richly deserves.

Racism, whether structural, economic, social or physical, continues to blight the lives of many of Britain's minority communities. Polling of black and minority ethnic (BME) communities in early 2022 found that 28 per cent had experienced racist abuse or violence in the previous 12 months. One in five, 21 per cent, had experienced racial discrimination in the workplace. Two-thirds, 67 per cent, believed that black and Asian people faced discrimination in their everyday lives. The TUC report 'Still Rigged: Racism in the UK Labour Market' found that 'almost one in five BME workers (18 per cent) had to work two or more jobs for financial reasons. Fifteen per cent have worked on a zero-hours contract at some point in the past five years and a similar proportion (13 per cent) have had working hours changed at short notice.'[1]

'Underlying socioeconomic factors like education, unemployment and poverty are clear factors contributing to health inequalities,' noted a report from the British Medical Association. 'However, evidence shows that structural racism leads to people from ethnic minority backgrounds having poorer health outcomes. The impact of COVID-19 on ethnic minority healthcare workers is confirmation of this.'[2]

Despite the clear evidence that people from ethnic minority communities experience racism, discrimination and marginalisation, the far right have created a narrative whereby white people – and particularly white men – are the real victims. This is a narrative that has been around for many years but became more common as a reaction to the BLM movement in response to the murder of George Floyd in the United States. HOPE not hate polling of 20,038 people, conducted in December 2022 and January 2023, found that 30 per cent of people considered themselves disadvantaged in society. While most were younger, poorer and from minority communities, a surprisingly large number of more wealthy people also considered themselves disadvantaged. In fact, 43 per cent of those who had an annual household income of over £100,000 described themselves as such, compared to just 36 per cent whose household income was between £10,000 and £20,000 per year.

As HOPE not hate wrote at the time:

> While most of those who feel disadvantaged are likely to say so because of genuine grievances, for others this feeling speaks to a more general sense of displacement, where they feel that their theoretical status in society is threatened by progressive norms. Framing inequality rooted in entitlement and status has been core to the 'culture war' debates of the last few years, and perceptions of disadvantage are increasingly a determinator for political views.

Our 'Fear & HOPE 2022' report found that those who felt strongly about being disadvantaged in society were also more likely to hold reactionary views on identity. They were more likely to agree that feminism has gone too far and that it makes it harder for men to succeed (48 per cent compared to 33 per cent in total), that British men are not as masculine as they used to be (65 per cent compared to 39 per cent in total), that asylum seekers pose a security threat to British people (62 per cent compared to 45 per cent overall) and to feel more suspicious of Muslims as a result of terror attacks in the UK (60 per cent compared to 43 per cent overall).

The right's 'anti-woke' agenda has weaponised terms like 'white privilege' and 'feminazi' in an attempt to undermine the equalities agenda. This has stirred anger and resentment among some in society, emboldening a view of strict social hierarchies based on identity. While people have always resented others based on a sense of their own precarity in the social order, rapidly deepening inequalities twinned with increasingly reactive politics on the right have resulted in a toxic mix that the far right has found easy to exploit.

When I'm asked for evidence of people like Farage and Reform UK being far right, I refer to their own words. While I'm quick to stress they are not fascists and certainly should not be put in the same category as the likes of Griffin and the BNP, they do fit into our basic definition of far right. In September 2022, in the immediate aftermath of street disturbances between Hindus and Muslims in Leicester, Farage blamed mainstream politicians for the trouble: 'They decided to go down the road of diversity and multiculturalism.' After disturbances in Harehills, Leeds, in July 2024, Farage posted on X: 'The politics of the subcontinent are currently playing out on the streets of Leeds. Don't say I didn't warn you.'[3]

His fellow Reform UK MP Lee Anderson, who, only five months previously, had accused Sadiq Khan of giving London away to Islamists, weighed in too: 'Disgraceful Scenes. Import a third world culture then you get third world behaviour. These animals need locking up for good. They are a product of our spineless namby pamby establishment who have betrayed our great country. I want my country back.'[4]

The editor of the *Yorkshire Evening Post* hit back:

> Armchair experts hundreds of miles away were passing judgement on this great city without a clue of the issues that may or may not have led to the devastating scenes, seeking to capitalise on the pain of Harehills.
>
> Chief among them was Nigel Farage, the leader of Reform UK and MP for Clacton. Mr Farage needs to remember that he is no longer a boorish street preacher but a parliamentarian whose job it is to represent his constituents.[5]

Much of our early community resilience work was done in direct response to threats we faced. We had developed an approach that sought to maximise opposition to hate without further inflaming tensions, while also building from within communities and not imposing our will from the outside, but it was largely trial and error. A few years later, however, we would try to construct a framework for how we approached these things and – possibly more importantly – would seek to share our approach so others could improve their own ability to challenge hate when it arose.

WHEN HATE COMES TO TOWN

In 2019, with our research showing that it was Britain's towns that faced the most serious challenges, our Head of Policy Rosie Carter created the Hopeful Towns project, which set out to 'understand what makes a town resilient in the face of change and tolerant in the face of difference':[6]

> We want to help places across England and Wales to address the range of challenges which this throws up. This will involve providing support at a local level, as well as seeking to influence national policy. Ultimately, this is a proactive approach to community cohesion. We want to address root causes, so as to stop divisive narratives from taking hold. And we want to promote policies which champion the value of towns. We believe that every town matters.

HOPE not hate had long understood that in times of economic hardship, community relations become more fragile, and these hardships could brew resentments and frustrations that could be exploited by those seeking to divide. Immigration and growing diversity had become totemic for the many grievances people were feeling in Britain. We knew that towns were more vulnerable to these conditions, but we also knew that no two towns are the same, and that change depends on both national context and local resilience.

Rosie and her team produced a 152-page report, 'Understanding Community Resilience in Our Towns', which categorised towns into 13 different groups, analysing the key elements and differences of each, and ultimately provided a route map for building resilience in each group.[7]

Highlighting the uniqueness of towns, the report set out our approach:

The only solution is a genuinely place-based approach, which examines the myriad social, economic, cultural and geographical factors at play. This offers a way of crafting policies which recognise the unique circumstances each town is operating in – while also grasping the wider shared challenges that different groups of towns face, and thus offering the capacity to scale up policy interventions.

Towns are not a proxy for 'left behind'. Each has a different geography, population, and history, and not all are feeling the effects of deindustrialisation or geographical isolation.

The project's initial intention was to work in three local authority areas with the aim of bringing together different statutory, voluntary and community groups in order to build a more welcoming climate for new communities. However, the COVID-19 pandemic put an end to that, partly because our team were severely limited in their ability to travel and meet people but also because the priorities of councils instantly changed. Refocusing our work, we established a Towns Network, which over 600 people from councils, national and local community and voluntary groups joined, and we produced several useful 'How To …' guides, held regular seminars and promoted our approach to building community resilience.

At around the same time, in response to growing far-right activity outside hotels and other buildings housing asylum seekers, HOPE not hate also began a project to support the wider migrant and refugee sector to better understand the extent and nature of the threat posed to their work by the far right. We shared intelligence from our monitoring of far-right activity and provided guidance for responding effectively and safely to the challenges posed by the far right.

The importance of this work became clear when hotels and other immigration advice centres came under attack during the riots of 2024. We gave regular updates, provided security briefings and offered advice to worried volunteers and staff. At one point, even the CEO of the Refugee Council turned to HOPE not hate for information about the hotel in Rotherham that was besieged by rioters, after getting nothing from the police.

In the immediate aftermath of the riots, we produced another 'Fear & HOPE' report. While the idea of this came about long before the riots, the disorder gave the report added importance. It just so happened that our polling straddled the riots, so it was interesting – and quite depressing – to see how opinions towards immigration, multiculturalism and Muslims had deteriorated during the riots.

The 'Fear & HOPE' report, entitled 'The Case for Community Resilience',[8] set out our approach to the issue. As my colleague Misbah Malik, who now heads up our community and resilience work, wrote:

> Capitalising off the agenda set in the political mainstream, the far right have sought to refocus divisive discourse to local contexts in order to get a foothold within communities, often to worrying levels of success. Neighbourhood bonds have broken down, communities have become radicalised, and the far right have been able to push their own hateful agenda.

Explaining the far right's political and societal advance through the lens of community resilience, she added:

> Community resilience is the sustained ability of a community to use available resources to respond to, withstand, and recover from adverse situations or disruptive challenges, both natural and man-made, sudden or chronic. It is crucial for sustainable and thriving communities, as it allows for the adaptation and growth of a community during and after periods of hardship.

She then set out the three key pillars of community resilience – social connectedness, resource availability, and agency and empowerment.

Social connectedness means that when community members consider themselves a part of a greater whole, they participate in and feel valued by their community. This fosters a sense of togetherness, relatability and connection, all of which form the basis of informal safety nets and support networks that can be essential in a time of need or when formal mechanisms for support fail.

Resource availability describes how a community with economic security and stability reduces overall vulnerability to the impacts of external stressors by providing a safety net through access to necessary public services that can act as a buffer against economic strain. Having enough additional resources to be able to scale up provision during and after times of hardship is crucial for mitigating and recovering from the negative impacts of adverse situations. This includes governmental, third-sector and community resources.

Agency and empowerment is about individuals within communities having motivation and confidence to actually share social connectedness and resources in order to tangibly build and deploy resilience during periods of hardship, working towards self-sufficiency. Perceptions of community power and agency in decision making are crucial here, as is, ultimately, how people feel about their role in shaping the wider community.

What began as ad hoc responses to hateful marches, seemingly contentious planning applications and racist killings has slowly evolved into a coherent strategy, an approach to community resilience and building community-level cohesion.

6

Tackling Taboo Issues

There are issues on which the progressives and the left really make things hard for themselves. At best, we fail to address issues that are important for ordinary people; at worst, our efforts result in people who should support us turning actively – and angrily – against us. Nowhere has this been truer than on the issue of on-street grooming by gangs. While paedophiles operate in all communities, and the vast majority of those convicted in the UK are white, there is a particular form of paedophilia where groups of men sexually exploit vulnerable young girls, which has led to numerous court cases involving men of Pakistani and Kashmiri origin.

The issue raised its head again in early 2025 when Elon Musk, the world's richest man and owner of X, waded into the subject in spectacular fashion, pummelling Muslim communities and the British government day after day while also aligning himself with Stephen Lennon. We can all complain about Musk's behaviour and express outrage at his pro-Lennon posts, but we partly have ourselves to blame. Collectively, councils, the police, government and local communities have failed to fully address this issue over the last 20 years, and it is this failure that has led us to this point. And it is not as though we were not warned.

I first encountered the issue of on-street grooming back in 2004 when it was to be featured on Channel 4's *Edge of the City* series, a fly-on-the-wall documentary following the work of Bradford social services. One of the episodes focused on an unfolding grooming scandal in Keighley, where up to 65 local girls had been repeatedly raped and sexually exploited by dozens of men. With the programme due to be aired just days before the all-out local and European elections, the broadcaster came under huge pressure from the council, the police and even anti-fascists to delay the film until after polling day. In hindsight, as uncomfortable as this programme would have been given that it was primarily focusing on how the city council and police were not adequately dealing with the issue, delaying the broadcast was politically disastrous, as it allowed the BNP to argue that the authorities were trying to bury news of Muslim grooming gangs. By portraying themselves as the only party willing to discuss the issue, the BNP won four council seats and just missed out on several others.

With the BNP buoyed by its 2004 local election success, it was clear that Keighley was going to be targeted at the next general election. In October, we learnt that Griffin, the party's leader, was to be their candidate there.

Paul, Lorraine and I sat in HOPE not hate's Bradford office to plan our response. Given the furore over the postponement of the film and the political capital gained by the BNP, it was clear that our response had to be different. Having initially supported the decision to delay the programme, we knew we now had to face it head-on. A meeting was arranged with Keighley MP Ann Cryer, who had been raising the issue for several years, and she in turn introduced us to Angela Sinfield, one of the two Keighley mothers who secretly recorded the gangs at work for the Channel 4 documentary. Angela had refused to engage in party politics throughout the whole process, but, after reading a quote from herself on a BNP leaflet, where it was made to look as though she was endorsing them, she was eager to help us.

For the previous five years, Angela's life had been dominated by the turmoil surrounding her daughter Lucy, who was just 12 when she began dating a 29-year-old man, with whom she believed she was in love. It was not long before this relationship turned even more abusive and exploitative, and over a period of a year she was repeatedly abused by several men, including several of her supposed-boyfriend's relatives. 'It starts off in a befriending sort of way to be really nice to these young girls, taking them for rides in their cars, buying them packets of cigarettes, buying them alcohol, buying them gifts and mobile phones because they want to contact them,' recalled Angela:

> My daughter got into it quite bad and began truanting from school on the odd day, then it got where she wasn't coming home from school. She would set off for school at 7.30 in the morning and she would not come home until 11.30 at night absolutely out of her face on either drugs or drink. She ended up going missing for weeks and weeks.

Angela was at her wit's end, and despite pleas to the authorities, nothing was done. The law at the time stated that only the victim could complain, and anything she said to her mother was inadmissible. After 12 months of absolute hell, Angela finally managed to get social services to act, and Lucy was taken into care, where she remained for two years. 'We had to get her away from here,' Angela said.

It was not an easy time for Lucy, as she was moved around the country, largely to get away from her mum. Their relationship quickly deteriorated, with Lucy convinced that her mum was preventing her being with the man she loved – and who, depressingly, she thought was in love with her. By the time I met her in early 2005, she had accepted that her mum was just looking out for her.

'I know she only did it because she loved me,' Lucy told me quietly.

HOW TO DEFEAT THE FAR RIGHT

It was during Angela's battle with social services that Ann Cryer became involved. In May 2002, 14 mothers and one father attended a meeting at her office, and she promised them she would do all she could to help them. While Ann campaigned down in London, the mothers set up Families Against Child Exploitation. Quietly and without any fanfare, Ann was successful in bringing about two changes to the law. Grooming became a recognised criminal offence, and, perhaps more importantly, hearsay – where the girl makes an admission to a third party – could now be considered as evidence.

'We fought for that and got it,' stated Angela proudly.

In 2003, Channel 4 approached Ann about making a programme to highlight the issue, and Angela and another woman agreed to collaborate:

> Me and a friend filmed the programme with Channel 4 over a nine to 12-month period. We agreed to do it because we felt that we were two ordinary working-class women from Keighley who had found themselves in the trap that our daughters had been groomed and felt that we had gone to everybody and nobody was listening.

What should have been a heart-wrenching story of the struggle of two mothers against a system that refused to help became a major national political issue – for all the wrong reasons. The BNP claimed it had been behind the programme, and that its findings would vindicate its stance on immigration and British Muslims in particular.

Angela was furious at the BNP for exploiting their campaign:

> They took four years of my life and my daughter's life and turned it into this campaign that, 'We are doing this, and we are doing the other.' No, you are not. Excuse me, you have not lived that life! We lived that life, we chose to make that documentary because we lived it. We had gone through it.

I mean the truth is a lot of these men are Asian men but I am not racist. It is about criminality.

Lucy was equally furious. 'The BNP have never spoken to me and do not know me, so when they take what has actually happened to me and twist it and turn it to favour them, I think it is disgusting.'

What annoyed the pair more than anything was that the BNP claimed to be alone in speaking out on the issue. 'They are just using it for their own racist agenda,' Angela told us. 'They don't care about us. Griffin has no solutions to solving the issue.'

She compared Griffin's exploitation of their story to the role played by her MP:

> Ann Cryer and her office were the only people who believed in us and stood by us. Everybody else sat in judgement of us, that we were bad parents, that we were bad mothers and that 'there must be something wrong in your family as to why your daughter has got involved in this, et cetera'. I have never been an unfit mother.
>
> Only Ann believed in us and without their help we would not be where we are today.

With the express support of Angela and her daughter, we made them the central focus of our 2005 General Election campaign. We produced 35,000 copies of a tabloid newspaper, one for every door in the constituency, and featured Angela and Lucy's story prominently.

Paul organised a day of action to distribute the newspaper, and 151 people turned out to ensure all the papers went out in one day. The first team went out at 7.30 that morning and targeted the part of the constituency where BNP support was highest. Shortly after 3 p.m., the last team went out. Angela popped in at the beginning of the day to do a couple of media interviews but then had to leave for work. I caught up with her again later on, and she was in jubilant mood, having received several phone calls from local people who had read the newspaper. A few punters in the pub where she worked even raised it with her. They were almost all totally supportive, and there was general anger at how the BNP was trying to latch on to the issue.

The newspaper helped have the desired effect, with Griffin trailing badly in a poor fourth place with just 10 per cent of the vote.

Sadly, the lessons of Keighley were not learnt, and the authorities continued to fail young girls. Many progressives, meanwhile, have continued to either ignore the issue or spend most of their time trying to dismiss the far-right's narrative of Muslim grooming gangs without doing anything to address the issue itself. Each time there was a trial, conviction or even a far-right demo on the issue, some on the left would condemn them for racialising the issue, which of course they were, but in their failure to address the issue itself, they continued to fail the girls and young women being abused.

Over the next few years, more and more grooming scandals were exposed, and each time it was the far right filling the information and political vacuum. Grooming scandals have affected many towns and cities across the north of England and parts of the Midlands. High-profile trials in Newcastle, Huddersfield, Rochdale, Oldham, Bradford, Dewsbury, Rotherham, Telford and Oxford revealed truly horrific tales of abuse and exploitation, but these probably only scratched the surface of the problem. The Jay Report into the grooming scandal in Rotherham, published in 2014, stated that as many as 1,400 girls had been abused by around 300 men. A report into grooming in the Shropshire new town of Telford estimated that 1,000 girls had been abused, and a court case in Oxford suggested 373 girls had been abused. Only a tiny number of the perpetrators have ever been convicted.

Predictably, far-right groups leapt on these horrendous crimes, holding protest after protest across the country – in Rochdale, Telford and Rotherham, to name just a few. In Rotherham alone, there were 15 far-right demonstrations between 2012 and 2015, some organised by the EDL, others by more fringe groups like Britain First and EDL splinter group the Infidels. Most protests never mustered more than a couple of hundred people, some numbered just a few dozen. More recently, former EDL frontman Stephen Lennon produced a five-part documentary series called *Rape of Britain*, with each episode focusing on a different Telford survivor. Four of the videos were first screened at demonstrations in the Shropshire new town, though the overwhelming majority of people attending had come in from out of town.

In May 2013, HOPE not hate and the Islamic Society of Britain (ISB) launched the Community Alliance Against Sexual Exploitation (CAASE) to highlight the continuing problem of on-street grooming by gangs. CAASE was supported by the Muslim Council of Britain, the Christian Forum, Victim Support, the Church of England and the National Association for People Abused in Childhood. With the far right focusing heavily on the growing numbers of arrests and court cases involving grooming gangs, we believed that we had to tackle the issue, rebut myths and offer some real solutions to the problem. Only that way, we argued, could we successfully address an issue that was increasingly dividing communities and whipping up anti-Muslim hatred. More importantly, we needed to focus on the victims of this awful crime, people who were largely forgotten in the political fight that engulfed the issue.

Julie Siddiqi, the then-executive director of the ISB, is one of the most amazing people I have had the pleasure to work with during my HOPE not hate years. Her optimism, drive and resilience have always been an inspiration to me and others. In the face of sometimes intense hostility, often from within the Muslim community itself, she has remained robustly confident in the belief that good will always prevail. In more recent years, many of us might have heard Julie delivering 'Thought for the Day' on Radio 4's *Today* programme. Julie believed it was vital that the Muslim community took an 'overdue' leadership role on this sensitive issue. The initiative was launched in Bradford and was addressed by Keighley mother Angela Sinfield.

CAASE intervened strongly during the Oxford grooming trial, and its robust straight talking, especially from Julie, played a part in preventing the court case becoming more divisive.

In September 2014, following the harrowing report into abuse in Rotherham, which found that 1,400 girls had been abused over a 15-year period, CAASE launched a campaign calling for a new national police unit to be established to tackle the grooming networks across the country, similar to the national football hooligan unit, as well as greater education within schools and faith communities and for local authorities to notify other local authorities when looked-after young people are housed in other parts of the country, something that did not happen at that time and was causing a lot of problems. These were real and tangible ideas to address the issues and stood us apart from many others who were talking about it.

Speaking to the media at the time, Julie remarked: 'There are few crimes more horrific than the sexual exploitation of young women: these girls have been let down by everyone. I have been sickened reading about these cases. There should be no excuse, no hiding place, for those who perpetrate such crimes.'

Of course, it wasn't all plain sailing. While many people in our orbit privately agreed with us, few were willing to go public with their support. The accusation that addressing the grooming was in some way playing into the far-right's narrative or, even worse, being racist or Islamophobic, scared many from speaking out. With a few notable exceptions, many in the Muslim communities shunned us too, with the prevailing attitude being that by talking about the issue they were somehow accepting some responsibility. While I understood this position, I strongly disagreed. On-street grooming by gangs, especially on the scale that had affected some towns, destroyed community relationships and fostered hatred of Muslims. Getting

Muslims to be at the forefront of speaking out against the issue, and even better calling for the guilty to be prosecuted, would have sent a positive message that we were all united against this horrible crime.

While some on the left were quick to condemn the far right for exploiting and racialising the problem, few proactively took on the grooming issue – especially from the perspective of supporting the young women who had been abused. There was often lip-service given to condemning on-street grooming, but this was almost always in the context of attacking the far right for racialising the issue rather than addressing the issue on its own. One person who did speak out consistently and honestly was Rotherham MP Sarah Champion, who repeatedly called out institutions for failing girls and young women and strongly criticised the government for its inaction. Sarah was also quite prepared to question cultural norms, which she argued were allowing grooming to happen and the perpetrators to escape justice. Unsurprisingly, she was widely attacked by some on the left for her views and actions, with them often portraying her as using BNP-type language. However, the people of Rotherham, including many Muslim women, were grateful for her stance.

In fact, the same charge was levelled against me too when I actually got 'uninvited' to a National Union of Students' anti-racism conference for my supposed Islamophobia. My crime, it seemed, was to repeatedly call on the anti-racist movement to do more to condemn on-street grooming by gangs and campaigning against Islamist extremist groups in the UK and abroad.

'It's amusing in its absurdity,' I told the *Guardian* at the time, 'but it does reflect the failure of a small section of the left to understand that we have to confront extremism and intolerance in all its forms.'

But if there was one incident that really highlighted the counter-productive approach of some on the left, it was the response to a group of people from Maltby who joined one of the many EDL protests in Rotherham. One of their daughters had been sexually abused, and in their anger and disgust at the failings of the council and police, they decided as a group to join the demo. Many were initially uncomfortable with aligning themselves with the EDL, especially the former miners who had stood loyal to the union during the miners' strike and the few who had actually joined our campaigning against the BNP in the late 2000s, but in the absence of anyone else speaking out on the issue, they decided to join the protest, albeit walking as a group at the back and leaving a bit of distance between themselves and the other marchers. This nuance was clearly not understood by the counter-protestors, who had gathered in opposition to the demo.

'Nazi scum off our streets,' the UAF protesters shouted.

Many of the Maltby crew, who had travelled the 7 miles into Rotherham on a coach, reacted furiously to being called nazis. They quickened their pace and were soon very much part of the demo. 'If they thought we were nazis, then we might as well act like them,' one of them told Yorkshire HOPE not hate organiser Paul Meszaros, who caught up with them a few days later to better understand their reasons for joining the EDL protest.

They were right to be angry. In not adequately addressing the grooming scandal that had taken place in Rotherham over many years, the council, police and the Labour Party – their party – had failed the girls and their families. And while it is easy for us to say they were wrong to join the EDL demo, the failure of the progressive movement to offer any real alternative protest against grooming meant that the EDL was all there was. And it was our collective failures, and especially the anti-fascist protesters who shouted 'nazi' at them, that pushed them into the hands of the EDL and the far right more generally.

Ignoring a certain issue for fear of how we will be perceived is likely to simply create resentment and a vacuum for our opponents to exploit. More importantly, our silence on the issue was letting down the young people who had already suffered enough at the hands of their abusers.

* * *

TACKLING TABOO ISSUES

If the issue of on-street grooming by gangs has sent some into awkward convulsions, then so has the issue of Islamist extremism and terrorism. Time and again, the same people who can call out the far right for their extremist and hateful ideas remain silent when faced with equally hateful – and at times more violent – acts from Islamist extremists. The argument, pushed by some, goes that in criticising Islamist extremism, you end up playing into the hands of and even legitimising far-right and racist narratives. Coupled with political cowardice and a lack of confidence, this has resulted in the perception that progressives are at best indifferent to Islamist extremism or, at worst, condone it.

Our basic approach should be – just like with on-street grooming gangs – guided by our basic principles of anti-racism and human rights. Of course, that doesn't mean you have to use the exact same tactics as you would against the far right, as our approach has to be guided by what is possible, our capacity and what is most effective.

Over the years, HOPE not hate has repeatedly spoken out and even campaigned against Islamist extremists. Much of our initial focus was on Anjem Choudary's ALM and its various spin-off and splinter groups. In 2010, in the immediate aftermath of the burning of the Union flag on Armistice Day by the ALM splinter group MAC, HOPE not hate went public with our attacks and issued a 'Plague on Both Your Houses' statement.

'We stand opposed to both sides,' I wrote, attacking both MAC and the EDL:

> We oppose the racism and Islamophobia of the EDL just as we oppose the religious bigotry and antisemitism of the MAC. To hear these Islamist extremists publicly deny the Holocaust and call for the formation of a Muslim Waffen SS Division – as they did today – should rightly sicken every anti-fascist just as much as the racist bile spat out by the EDL and English Nationalist Alliance.

Speaking out against Islamist extremism should have been a no-brainer, but any such condemnation would quickly be met by criticism and abuse from some quarters. Depressingly, dealing with Islamic fundamentalism has been difficult for progressives, and all too often there has been an uneasy silence. In a society where Muslims are increasingly vilified, abused and attacked, there is an understandable desire to side with the victims of racism and hatred, to the point where any criticism is seen as giving ground to Islamophobia.

For us, though, it was obvious that speaking out was the right thing to do. 'Islamic fundamentalism ... [and] fascism, are political ideologies and must be dealt with as such,' we said. 'They prey on oppression, poverty and injustice. They both exploit alienation and the alienated and neither can be treated as legitimate or justifiable avenues of discontent.'

We went on to say that there was a symbiotic relationship between the EDL and ALM:

> They need each other to justify their own existence. They are two sides of the same coin and so both must be opposed. Just as we argue that you do not fight one violent extremism with another, so you also do not fight extremism with silence. The anti-fascist movement should be the first to understand this.

Our statement clearly resonated with our supporters. The 'Plague on Both Your Houses' blog was read by over 45,000 people and shared by 2,500 on Facebook. There seemed to be a collective sense of relief that we were finally willing to speak out against all violent extremism. In a subsequent survey, completed by 1,044 people, an astonishing 96 per cent agreed with our approach, while only 24 people, just 2 per cent, opposed it. While, in hindsight, we should have spoken out sooner, we had made a start. And it was from among some British Muslims, who were the ones who suffered most from Islamist extremism, that we were to receive some of our greatest support.

We put our opposition to Islamist extremism into action too. The tabloid newspaper we produced in Tower Hamlets ahead of a planned EDL demo carried scathing attacks on both ALM and Hizb ut-Tahrir, another Islamist group. We put out similar material in Bradford. In Luton, home of both the EDL and ALM, we delivered 20,000 leaflets attacking both.

Joe Mulhall and I have written extensively on the need to face down Islamist extremism, be it against Choudary's ALM network, the appalling attack on the Charlie Hebdo offices in Paris in January 2015, the formation of the Islamic State in Iraq or the numerous terrorist attacks across the UK and Europe. To us, it was not enough to condemn the specific atrocity as it occurred – it was also vital to speak out against the ideology behind it. Islamist terrorism is a gift for the far right. Time and again, trigger events like Islamist terrorist attacks have increased anti-Muslim sentiment in society, have led to surges in support for groups like the EDL and have been followed by violent attacks on Muslims, mosques and community centres. It was imperative that we were forceful in our condemnation of the ideology held by those behind such attacks.

In the editorial to our 'Gateway to Terror' report, which mapped out Choudary's international network, Joe and I wrote a scathing attack on the group and its ideology:

> They seek to impose a system that is intolerant of difference, unaccepting of anyone and anything that fails to conform and that is totally opposed to democracy and free will. All of this is on top of the fact that members of this group, influenced by these hateful ideas, have been involved in the 7/7 bombings and dozens of foiled terrorist plots aimed at killing and maiming innocent people. That's why this report is not only necessary but also 100% in keeping with Britain's long anti-fascist tradition of fighting bigotry and prejudice. This report aims to contribute to that same fight.

* * *

There will always be some who say that HOPE not hate has not done enough on on-street grooming by gangs, left-wing antisemitism or Islamist extremism. And, of course, there might well be an element of truth to that. We took on the grooming issue, but we could undoubtedly have done more. We spoke out against left-wing antisemitism, called for candidates to be withdrawn and even produced manuals and training for activists to better understand the issues, but perhaps we should have been more forceful. We have campaigned around Islamist extremism, though I have absolutely no doubt we could have been more active and more vocal. But all that said, I cannot think of a single national organisation that has been so willing to speak out and, more importantly, campaign on such a broad set of issues and extremisms. Even in the 2024 General Election, HOPE not hate was the only organisation to actually campaign against George Galloway in Rochdale – whose rampant conspiracy theories, anti-immigrant rhetoric, homophobia, strident anti-Zionism and work for Iranian state broadcasters had crossed our agreed red lines – and the seemingly pro-Andrew Tate and, some could argue, misogynist Akhmed Yakoob in Birmingham Ladywood, who claimed he was chosen by Allah to 'challenge the Zionist regime'[1] and in a podcast shortly before the election claimed that Zionists 'control everything now' and that 'Zionism is a fascist ideology.'[2] Yakoob did later apologise for some of his remarks.

Failing to speak out against hate and intolerance, from whichever quarter it comes, is not only morally wrong but politically too. However difficult it might appear, speaking out on politically and culturally sensitive issues only increases our credibility over time.

In early 2025, the government rejected calls for a national inquiry into the grooming scandal, preferring instead to hold up to five local inquiries. While the government claimed that a national inquiry would not get into the specific details that a local inquiry would, this created the impression that the government was covering up the facts that might be unearthed. More dangerously for Labour, the longer it held out from having a national inquiry, the more some working-class communities viewed it as yet another sign that the Labour Party had abandoned them. Seeking to capitalise on this sense of abandonment, Farage announced that Reform would call for such a national inquiry as part of its next general election effort.

Quite predictably, the government was forced to reverse its plans, and in June 2025, following the release of Dame Casey's audit of group-based child sexual exploitation and abuse, it announced a full national inquiry. The government denied this was a U-turn, insisting that they were simply responding to new information – but the media and the public saw it differently.

The government's initial failure to hold a national inquiry was a mistake. Not only has it been forced into a damaging U-turn, so losing any political initiative or capital over the issue, but an inquiry was simply the right thing to do. A society that can't look after its children has failed its first job. Thousands of young girls have been abused in awful conditions, and few have received justice or the ongoing support they deserve. It should be our priority to do right by these girls and women and learn the lessons in the hope that this vile crime is reduced in the future.

7

Celebrating Modern Britain

The Cinnamon Club does a wonderful breakfast. Set in the historic Grade II listed former Westminster Library, it is a top-of-the-range Indian restaurant, a few hundred metres from Parliament. In January 2007, we were still reeling from the shock of the previous May's local election results, but it was here, over a 'full English', that we began to plot our response.

Around the table were Dagenham MP Jon Cruddas, political editor of the *Daily Mirror* Kevin Maguire and Kevin's boss Richard Wallace. I had met Kevin a couple of times over the previous few months and discussed the possibility of the paper supporting the HOPE not hate campaign. He was a big union man and knew many of the people we already worked with. He was also close friends with Jon and Tom Watson, two of the Labour MPs who were facing BNP insurgencies in their constituencies. Richard had a large and dominating personality. His wild, flowing hair hid a slightly ruthless streak that I guess is essential for an editor of a national newspaper. He had been the paper's showbiz editor, but he was a proper Labour man, unlike some of his predecessors. Above all, he hated racism.

At a future HOPE not hate curry night at the Labour Party conference in 2011, Richard would speak proudly of his paper's support for our campaign over the years. 'It is sometimes not fun being a newspaper editor with all the hard decisions and cutbacks you have to make, but our support for HOPE not hate is something that stands out as a great achievement,' he said.

We discussed possible joint activities. To be honest, I can't remember who first suggested a tour of the country ahead of May's local elections, but once the idea was raised it soon gained momentum. We quickly agreed on a positive anti-racist tour that would celebrate modern Britain, taking in many of the main electoral battlegrounds with the BNP on the way. We proposed events on the ground, with the *Mirror* providing celebrities and covering the tour in the newspaper.

Richard initially suggested using a helicopter to get around and literally drop in on local communities. I remember feeling deeply uncomfortable, even embarrassed, with the idea and felt relieved when Kevin voiced concern too. It was the sort of thing politicians did that only reinforced their remoteness from ordinary people. Convinced of his error, Richard then suggested a re-run of the *Daily Mirror*'s highly successful bus tour during the Make Poverty History campaign in 2005. This was more like it, and he agreed to set up a meeting with the coordinator of that campaign, Ros Wynne-Jones.

We finished our fatty fry-up, content we had a plan. Richard reeled off a list of celebrities he thought we could get involved. Even Jon, who had remained fairly quiet during much of the discussion, chipped in with a few names. I returned to our office with the exciting news.

Many considered Ros to be the *Daily Mirror*'s social conscience. She had been a feature writer there for several years but, after the paper's difficulties in the final days of Piers Morgan's tenure, was increasingly given free rein to pursue more socially conscious stories in a bid to rediscover the paper's campaigning tradition. Ros was the perfect partner for us. She genuinely cared about the issues at hand and often went out of her way to help and, if needed, cajole reluctant colleagues into action. Together, we plotted the HOPE not hate bus tour.

The 2006 local elections had vastly expanded our battlefield, with the BNP gaining an additional 33 councillors across the country. While we were fortunate in not having to deal with elections in London, we were now having to operate in many new areas of the country. Our 2007 strategy focused on 50 key wards where we believed the BNP posed a real threat, including 13 in Yorkshire, 11 in the North West, five in Essex and two in the East Midlands. Our main focus, however, was the West Midlands, where there were 19 wards of serious concern. It was here where we were to devote most of our resources.

The HOPE not hate bus tour began its 14-day journey on a cold Saturday morning in March 2007 in Barking and Dagenham, home to the largest group of BNP councillors in the country. 'We want to show what can happen if the BNP threat is not confronted,' said local MP Jon Cruddas, who had one of the 12 BNP councillors in his constituency. We had hired an old 1960s red London bus and decked it out with HOPE not hate branding, plus logos from the *Mirror* newspaper and Amicus, the trade union that was sponsoring the tour. It was basic to say the least. There was no heating to warm us from the open back, and the hard, worn seating offered little protection from the bone-crunching, bumpy ride. And yet there was a basic charm to the bus, which seemed to suit its purpose.

It might have made more sense to use a modern bus or coach, with a travelling speed far exceeding the 38mph that our bus could achieve when going downhill, to say nothing of the comfort, but the bus was eye-catching, iconic and fitted in perfectly with the image we wanted to create. On the bus with Ros and me was the *Mirror*'s photographer, John Ferguson, and filmmaker Gregg McDonald. Joining us the following evening was Gregg's mate Andy Benson – together, they were tasked with producing a short film every evening cataloguing our journey.

From Dagenham, the bus travelled the short distance to Thurrock in Essex, where we were greeted by scores of local people, including dozens of kids. From there, it was up to Northampton for a play about the hardships facing asylum seekers by Banner Theatre. The following morning, dozens of local postmen took a break from their union's annual general meeting to greet the bus, and then it was on to Leicester, where we parked on the famous Golden Mile. We had initially hoped to hold a food festival with Shilpa Shetty, the *Celebrity Big Brother* star, but when she pulled out at the last moment, the festival plans unravelled. But this disappointment was soon forgotten as we arrived in Nottingham to be greeted by 500 screaming schoolchildren and 22 students from the South Nottingham College 'Balls to Poverty' programme. Organising the day was Joe Sargison, their coach and mentor, who had built a fantastic project to take these students on a trip to the 2010 World Cup in South Africa, where they were to coach young township children and give away 7,000 footballs. It was absolute chaos as the kids swarmed around the bus, shouting and screaming excitedly.

Order was only restored when John, the *Mirror*'s photographer, turned a few tricks with a football, assuring us all he could have been a professional.

From Nottingham, the bus moved on to Lincoln, where we were met by the bishop at the amazing cathedral, and from there it was on to the east end of Sheffield and the gym run by Brendan Ingle, a boxing trainer who had coached many world champions but also remained committed to helping the local community. Brendan personified our message of hope, with his gym acting as a magnet for young people who were going off the rails. It was the humbleness of the man and his boxing trainees that really struck us, with Brendan having recently taken the then-world champion Johnny Nelson round to the house of one of his younger boxers who was going off the rails.

Boxers were to be big supporters of our campaign, and our tour visited the Salford boxing gym of Amir Khan, the young Bolton-born boxer and Olympic silver medallist who was only days away from a fight, so we were really pleased he could spare the time to meet us. The gym was a hive of activity, with 15 boxers going through their paces, led by Amir, who was being given an unbelievably high-tempo workout.

'It doesn't matter if you are a different colour or a different race,' he told us. 'Just treat each other with respect.'

'I'm proud to be British. You just have to look at the gym in there. There's English, Jamaicans, me from Pakistan, Indians – we all treat each other with respect. We are part of one big family.'

The bus took a slightly strange route around the country so it could incorporate the West Midlands over the last weekend of March. With dozens of wards at risk in the region and key days of action in Stoke-on-Trent and Sandwell, we felt it important enough to loop back down from the North West.

On a drizzly Friday morning, the bus pulled into Dudley's Market Street, where local man Ade Rollinson, Britain's strongest man and four-time contestant in the World's Strongest Man competition, had agreed to pull the bus for us. To slightly bemused onlookers, Ade harnessed himself up and began pulling the bus through the pedestrianised shopping street.

It was then back on board the bus for the short trip to Birmingham's Victoria Square, where we teamed up with the trade union Unison and delivered several thousand leaflets. Fortuitously, Sugababes were playing at the Birmingham NEC, so they were more than happy for the bus to swing by. They were probably less impressed to meet Ros in a hotel lift the following morning when they were still in their face packs with curlers in their hair.

We were blessed with a glorious blue sky as we arrived in Stoke-on-Trent the following morning. While dozens of local activists delivered our newspapers across the city, the bus headed for a children's fun day in Coalville in the south-east of the city, an area where the BNP had several councillors. More than 200 children enjoyed the day, with attractions such as a DJ school, live music, a steel band, food, face painting and a bouncy castle.

'We have never had anything like this before,' one teenage girl told our filmmaker Gregg. 'Normally kids round here fight each other but today everyone is having a good time and getting on together.'

The chair of the local residents' association was equally ecstatic. While Unison had funded the event, he and his committee had organised it, and their hard work certainly paid off. Interestingly, he told us the area had once been known as the 'United Nations' because of the number of outsiders, particularly from eastern and southern Europe, who moved here after the war to work in the local pits. Today, the BNP was trying to whip up hostility towards newcomers among these descendants of immigrants. The fun day solidified our presence in the area, created good will among the committee and helped spread the HOPE not hate brand. As the fun day wound down, we moved off to a nearby community centre where the political campaigning was being organised in conjunction with the North Staffordshire Campaign Against Racism and Fascism, the longstanding local anti-fascist group. Veteran musician Billy Bragg had very kindly offered us his services for the weekend, playing the first of two gigs for local activists who had been out campaigning. More than 80 people turned up to help, which was probably a record for one of our activities in the city, and we distributed over 15,000 newspapers.

It was an early start on Sunday morning. Sandwell councillor and long-time Searchlight and HOPE not hate supporter Gurinder Josan and I had visited the venue a fortnight before, and it appeared ideal for the day of action. In a large hall, we were able to lay out a dozen tables, each one containing piles of plastic bags stuffed with newspapers. There were 45,000 newspapers divided among the 10 tables, each representing a ward in the borough. As it was a Caribbean centre, lunch was goat curry and rice, but for some reason the cooks had forgotten the vegetarian option, so Gurinder had to ring round local gurdwaras (Sikh temples) to find one that could provide a huge vat of chickpea curry.

As with many of these 'days', we had no idea about the numbers who would turn out – but we were optimistic. The unions had been busily recruiting activists all week, and even the local UAF branch had agreed to mobilise in support. But none of us had expected the 221 people who eventually signed in.

It was an amazing feeling to see so many people pour into the centre. The mood was lifted further by a local steel band playing in the hall as people came to collect their newspapers. Maps and information sheets had been prepared, and an officer from the Transport and General Workers Union (now Unite) ferried groups around in a union minibus. The HOPE not hate bus, initially parked outside, took a group of activists into Great Bridge market, a ward where the BNP had topped the poll with 45 per cent the previous year. As the steel band played, we handed out newspapers and leaflets. The BNP were furious. Its activists viewed Great Bridge as their own, and they initially came out to intimidate our leafleteers, as they had done on numerous occasions in the past, but once they saw our numbers they quickly melted away.

Not all the bus stops went according to plan. In Burnley, a visit to the Stoops and Hargher Clough Community Centre, where a scheme was using cricket to bring local white youngsters together with their Asian counterparts from Stoneyholme and Daneshouse, turned sour when a group of older white youths from the local estate turned up and threatened some of the young Asian kids. White boys being taken away in handcuffs and the Asian boys fleeing in tears was not quite what we intended.

Soap stars provided a mainstay of our bus tours. Over the years, we have visited the sets of *The Bill*, *Coronation Street*, *Emmerdale* and *Hollyoaks* – some several times. In 2007, we visited the set of *Emmerdale*, where Gregg embarrassed us all immensely when he admitted to *Emmerdale* and ex-Page 3 star Linda Lusardi that he was her number-one fan. Bundling the now sheepish Gregg back on to the bus, we continued our tour around Yorkshire.

To make the 2007 event more of a national tour, we also decided to make a trip to Scotland. So, after a wonderful journey through the countryside, we made it up to Glasgow. We were exhausted but exhilarated at the same time. The tour had been a huge success, and we were slightly demob-happy as the bus rolled into Buchanan Street, in the heart of the shopping centre. After 14 days and 1,700 miles, we were making our final stop.

Gregg and Andy were working around the clock to produce a film each day. They slept in shifts, if at all, to hit the deadlines, but even then we often had more for them to do. The *Mirror* was keen to make Glasgow a fitting end to the tour and had arranged for the-then Chancellor of the Exchequer – and soon to be Prime Minister – Gordon Brown to put in an appearance. As a result, there was considerable excitement and support from the crowd. Joining him was Jermaine Jackson, Michael Jackson's brother, who had just rekindled his star appeal in the UK with an appearance on *Celebrity Big Brother*.

Wanting to put on a good show, the *Mirror* asked if Gregg and Andy could produce a film with the best bits of the tour. They had less than 48 hours' notice to complete the task, but they did it, and a fantastic eight-minute film was produced. In addition to the footage they shot along the route, one of them travelled down to London to film a quick interview with Charlie and Craig Reid, from the Scottish band The Proclaimers.

The meeting between Gordon and Jermaine produced one of the most awkward moments on the tour. While a steel band played to the 1,000-strong crowd, the two men got into some small talk on the top deck of the bus. As Gregg had put microphones on the pair, we heard every word from the deck below. There was a long, uncomfortable silence between the two men before Gordon told Jermaine that he had seen him on the telly. Jermaine, perhaps not quite understanding who Gordon was, asked the soon-to-be prime minister how the weather had been during the two-week tour. Obviously not wanting to embarrass the singer, Gordon said it had been ok.

CELEBRATING MODERN BRITAIN

The steel band gave way to the lone Scottish piper, which was the signal for Gordon to speak. 'Let the message go out right across the country,' he said. 'It is HOPE not hate which we support. It is HOPE not hate that will triumph. It is HOPE not hate with the support of the people of Glasgow which we shall take as a message to the whole of the United Kingdom.' With that, the bus tour came to an end.

The tour formed the backbone of an eight-page supplement inside the *Daily Mirror* the day before the election. It was accompanied by an open letter urging readers to shun the BNP. More than 30 celebrities put their name to the letter, among them Amir Khan, John Terry and several other members of the Chelsea football team, plus Sir Alan Sugar, the Olympian Dame Kelly Holmes, actress Meera Syal, chef Jamie Oliver, Richard Branson, musician Beverley Knight, athletics star Denise Lewis OBE and singer Mel B.

The HOPE not hate/*Daily Mirror* bus hit the road again the following year, this time starting in Liverpool with local footballing legend John Barnes, and paid tribute to the murdered black teenager Anthony Walker, whose mother was with us on the bus. The ex-England star, standing shoulder-to-shoulder with Gee Walker, said:

> Whatever racist abuse I went through as a player – bananas thrown on the pitch or whatever it was – is nothing to what this family have been through.
>
> Mrs Walker is an inspiration, finding the strength she has. She has felt the real tragic effect of racism, and no sports player's experience comes near to it.

Anthony, 18, was killed with an ice axe in a racist murder in Liverpool in July 2005. Gee said the HOPE not hate campaign summed up the way she tried to live her life. 'Without hope, I have nothing. If there are people who believe in hate instead of hope, there must be something wrong with them.'

The busy lunchtime crowd was entertained by a local school samba band and other musicians.

Earlier on in the day, the bus met up with two of the players from the Harlem Globetrotters, much to the excitement of Ros, who was taught to spin a ball. Unfortunately, we were all too shy to invite the actor who played Chewbacca in *Star Wars* to join us on the bus when we bumped into him in a lift at City Talk radio.

The highlight for all of us on the tour was a visit to the Hope special-needs school in Wigan. As the bus swung into the school gates, we were greeted by the entire school carrying HOPE not hate banners, flags and hats, which they had made over the previous few weeks. Teacher Fran McCaul said:

> Every pupil has helped make something. Even kids who can't use their hands themselves have been helped to contribute to the flags and posters.
>
> Our ethos at Hope School is that we teach our pupils acceptance and respect for all people, whatever their background, need or ability.

With 170 pupils waving a colourful array of red and yellow flags and banners, the HOPE not hate message came alive. Even the wheels of the children's wheelchairs had been specially decorated with the HOPE sun logo for the day. One excited pupil said: 'I love this bus. It's a very happy bus.'

The school had made a short film of the children making the banners and flags, several of which we were given to take away with us. Towards the end of the tour, we kept our promise to display one of the banners outside Number 10 Downing Street.

There has been a lot of debate over the last few years about identity, how we define ourselves and the values and rules we should all abide by. In the wake of Labour's 1997 election victory, with its promise of Scottish and Welsh devolution, there was a renewed focus on English identity across the political spectrum. Many on the right publicly called for the creation of an English Parliament or, at the very least, allowing only English MPs to vote on matters relating to England. With the widespread belief that the Conservatives would always maintain a majority of seats in England, it was not hard to see why this appealed to them. There were those on the left, such as Billy Bragg and MPs Jon Cruddas and John Denham, who also took up Englishness during this period, attempting to harness radical moments in English history to define a more progressive Englishness. Unfortunately, their attempts to build support for this were largely ignored because many progressives – and indeed the overwhelming proportion of our minority communities – saw Englishness as a narrow and rather exclusive identity, while Britishness was more inclusive. The facts seemed to support this. Repeated polling by HOPE not hate over the years always found that those who identified as English, as opposed to British, tended to be overwhelmingly white and hostile to immigration and multiculturalism.

In February 2011, Prime Minister David Cameron gave a speech to the Munich Security Conference where he advocated what he defined as 'muscular liberalism'.[1] Believing that state multiculturalism was failing and our acceptance of difference was undermining British society and allowing extremism to flourish, he argued for a reset on cohesion.

'Frankly, we need a lot less of the passive tolerance of recent years and much more active, muscular liberalism,' he told the audience, before adding that some Muslim organisations who stood against everything the British public supported received public money and recognition.

'Let's properly judge these organisations,' Cameron continued:

Do they believe in universal human rights – including for women and people of other faiths? Do they believe in equality of all before the law? Do they believe in democracy and the right of people to elect their own government? Do they encourage integration or separatism?

These are the sorts of questions we need to ask. Fail these tests and the presumption should be not to engage with organisations.

In its place, he argued, Britain needed to believe in 'certain values and actively promote them' – by which he meant freedom of speech, freedom of worship, democracy, the rule of law and equal rights. 'To belong here is to believe these things.'

Cameron's speech came under criticism from the centre and left of British politics, not least because it was given on the same day that thousands of EDL supporters were about to march through the streets of Luton, the town where the anti-Muslim group was first created. Referencing our own 'Fear & HOPE' report, David Miliband, Labour's shadow foreign secretary, claimed the prime minister's speech did nothing to offer the sense of economic security that many of those most attracted to extremism actually sought, while Nick Clegg, the deputy prime minister, used a speech in Luton to offer his own rebuke, saying that 'multiculturalism has to be seen as a process by which people respect and communicate with each other, rather than build walls between each other'.[2]

Our own criticism of Cameron's speech was immediate. The speech clearly targeted one community – Muslims – without acknowledging that there were many people across all religious denominations and political affiliations who held conservative religious and political views that could cross Cameron's definition of muscular liberalism. In singling out just one religion, he was othering them in the public's eyes, thus reinforcing the idea that Islam was a problem religion. Additionally, his definition focused solely on social beliefs and norms, and totally ignored economic issues that made many people feel excluded from mainstream society. Economic and political disadvantage, and racial and religious discrimination are huge barriers to people feeling they belong to society – but this was totally ignored. You cannot just order someone to like something; you have to earn that support. As I discuss elsewhere in this book, one explanation for growing dissatisfaction with democracy in the UK is people's belief that the political system is not delivering for them. The answer is not to order them to like democracy, as Cameron set out, but to work to ensure that politics delivers for people. Finally, we were critical of the top-down nature of Cameron's approach: not only was he deciding what British norms were but his views were probably at odds with how many people view belonging.

Identity is fluid and multi-layered. Many of us have several identities at the same time, be they national, regional, local, economic, political or religious. One or more of these identities might be more important to us at any given moment, and what is important to us one week might be less important the next. Likewise, national identities will always be somewhat shallow, as the life of a landed aristocrat or a city worker is a world away from someone who is struggling with a cost-of-living crisis. The reality is that these very same people struggling with the cost-of-living crisis will have an obvious shared identity with others who live with the same stresses. Understanding and accepting these complexities will allow us to better understand people but also to develop strategies to create more cohesive communities.

This is not to say that displays of patriotism are wrong and can't be included, but they have to be authentic and, in part at least, organic. England's success at international football tournaments, Team GB's success in the Olympics or even the huge displays of public solidarity during events such as Band Aid and Make Poverty History can all elicit pride and patriotism, but these will always be moments, and just as quickly as they emerge, so will they disappear. For improvements in shared identity and a sense of unified belonging, people have to really buy into it, and that means wanting it to work.

Polling from HOPE not hate clearly shows that the British public prefer Britain's multicultural society to other options and believe that the government should do more to make it work. When given a choice of four different options to define Britain, 50 per cent of the 22,500 respondents said they supported a multicultural society, where people can celebrate their own traditions while embracing shared British values, and 20 per cent backed a multi-ethnic society, where people prioritise assimilation to British values and identity over their own traditional cultures. A further 15 per cent wanted Britain to be a largely white, Christian country, with 6 per cent wanting us to be solely defined by our ethnic or religious identity.

In the same poll, conducted at the turn of 2024/5, almost three-quarters of people (72 per cent) thought that 'it is the responsibility of Government to improve cohesion between different ethnic and religious communities and reduce tension', with 28 per cent believing it was not. There was also widespread support for local campaigns to promote Britain's diverse and multicultural society and help people from different backgrounds connect, with 50 per cent of Britons backing this and just 12 per cent opposing.

However, almost twice as many people think relations between communities will get worse over the next few years compared to those who think they will get better. This really needs to become a priority for this government, which sadly it is currently not. With Britain's changing demographics, rising far right and the damaging role of social media in spreading lies and division, the government needs to be strong-willed, forceful and confident on this. As our polling shows, it is also what the public demand.

The HOPE not hate bus tours sought to celebrate our local communities and highlight the positive actions and local histories that brought people together. Unfortunately, when we think about extremism, the narrative is often negative. But it is precisely at this moment, when people are divided and scared, that it is even more important to celebrate what brings us together. This might be at a national, regional or even very local level – for it to be believable, it needs to come from the very community that is facing the problems.

CELEBRATING MODERN BRITAIN

All too often, the narrative is one of division and extremism, but up and down the country people get on with their lives together, finding ways to overcome problems and realising they have more in common with one another than they were led to believe. The HOPE not hate/*Daily Mirror* bus tour gave us that opportunity to celebrate the Britain we are and the Britain we want to be. And through the newspaper and with the stars that we met, it promoted a message of HOPE into the homes of millions of people.

In 2024, amid the horrors of the violence and disorder that beset Britain's towns and cities, we saw local people coming together in fantastic displays of solidarity and hope. Whether it was the locals in Southport who helped rebuild the wall around the mosque that was attacked, or local businesses donating supplies for the clean-up, these acts of solidarity were real and authentic. And just like the ethos behind the HOPE not hate bus tour all those years ago, these acts of kindness and solidarity need to be celebrated.

8

Kippered

The 2014 European elections marked the end of one chapter of HOPE not hate – but also the beginning of another. Ridding the North West of Nick Griffin as an MEP was largely overshadowed by the emergence of the United Kingdom Independence Party (UKIP) as a significant political force. There was little time for celebrating.

UKIP had been launched back in 1993. Despite doing well in the 2004 and 2009 European elections, the party had slipped back badly in the intervening years. At the 2010 General Election, UKIP had languished behind the BNP in dozens of parliamentary seats but had been steadily rising in the polls since then. In Farage, it had a charismatic leader who could tap into the anti-politics mood that was increasingly prevalent in British society, and who was not tarnished by the thuggery and nazi imagery that so blighted the BNP. Despite being educated at an elite private school and pursuing an early career as a City trader, the cigarette-smoking, pint-drinking Englishman, who alternated between pinstripe suits and country-gentleman attire, presented himself as a man of the people. And, to a large degree, it was an image that went down well with many voters.

It was in March 2013 that UKIP really burst on to the political stage, when it only just failed to win the Eastleigh parliamentary by-election on a strong anti-immigrant ticket. A few months before, the party had come second with 21.7 per cent of the vote in Rotherham, and a couple of months after Eastleigh it secured 24 per cent in South Shields. In the 2013 county council elections, held on the same day as the South Shields by-election, UKIP averaged 22 per cent in the wards it contested and won 141 new council seats. UKIP had not previously been on our radar, partly because we had enough on our plate with the BNP, but also because it appeared to be a largely single-issue party, and HOPE not hate had no position on the European Union. The Eastleigh by-election changed that. Such was the venom of UKIP's anti-immigrant campaign, featuring outrageous claims that 29 million Bulgarians and Romanians were planning on coming to the UK when immigration restrictions were lifted on the two countries, that some of our supporters demanded we act.

We asked our supporters for their thoughts. More than 3,500 people responded, and a further 1,000 attended almost 60 meetings held around the country to discuss the issue. While there was a general unease about UKIP's anti-immigrant rhetoric, there was also an acceptance that it was not a fascist party, and that Farage was certainly not Nick Griffin. The consensus was that we should expose any racist and anti-immigrant campaigns run by UKIP, and any racist individuals within the party, but not campaign against the party itself.

We agreed to review this decision after six months and wrote to UKIP asking for a meeting to explain our position. This might now appear to have been overly cautious, but at the time we deemed it necessary. Our decision to even consider going after UKIP caused some unease, including from among some of our own funders and supporters. Some thought UKIP were not extreme enough for us to go after, while others, including some anti-fascists, believed that we should stay focused on traditional fascist groups, even if they did not pose the same electoral threat as the BNP.

Perhaps unsurprisingly, UKIP ignored our request for a meeting, and when we came to review the situation again, things had worsened. UKIP was increasing its use of anti-immigrant rhetoric but also, more worryingly, deliberately stoking up public anger through exaggeration and misinformation, making ever more wild claims about the numbers of Bulgarians and Romanians likely to come to Britain when entry restrictions were relaxed on 1 January 2014.

UKIP's turn to the right was confirmed at the party's 2014 spring conference, where Farage made a Powell-esque speech about not recognising modern Britain and the absence of spoken English on his commuter train from Kent to London. The then-political editor of *The Sun*, Tom Newton Dunn, tweeted: 'He's purposely pushed the boat out on foreigner hatred to try to pull in more Labour blue collar, but it sounds ugly. Too BNP.'[1]

With UKIP deliberately whipping up fear and hatred of foreigners, we believed there was little choice but to begin to target the organisation. Although UKIP might not have been openly racist like the BNP, its conscious attempts to vilify and demonise migrants in order to whip up a xenophobic backlash put it within our broader definition of 'far right'.

Taking on UKIP lost us a few supporters and generated many new enemies, especially online, but that was a price we felt was worth paying. What type of anti-racists would we be if we ignored UKIP's quite calculated use of the race card? Interestingly, some of the same people who were advising us not to take on UKIP had, 10 years before, argued that the best approach to the BNP was to ignore them. While we accepted that UKIP was a very different beast from the BNP, we also believed that the same approach to confronting racism applied. Most fundamentally, by ignoring UKIP's racism, we would be guilty of normalising it and abandoning those on the receiving end.

In August 2014, Farage announced his intention to stand in the Kent constituency of South Thanet, where incumbent Conservative MP Laura Sandys was standing down. This contest would become our national priority.

* * *

UKIP went into the 2015 General Election believing its moment had come. It had recently won two by-elections, called after sitting Conservative MPs had defected to the party, and now it not only expected to win several seats in Parliament but privately hoped it would hold the balance of power afterwards. It had been polling an average of 16 to 18 per cent in the months running up to the election, and a series of constituency polls, conducted by Tory billionaire Michael Ashcroft, highlighted the UKIP threat in several local contests. In addition to the two seats UKIP was already holding, these polls put the party six points in the lead in Thurrock, and then between one and three points behind the leading party in several other constituencies.

One of those trumpeting UKIP's supposedly increased sophistication was Nottingham academic Matthew Goodwin, who co-authored *Revolt on the Right* and had been a prominent commentator on the radical right for years. 'This is a party that has learned from the by-elections in the autumn,' he told the *Daily Telegraph* in early March. 'The same person who ran those by-elections in Clacton and Rochester and Strood – which everyone said UKIP could not win – is running the general election and targeted seat campaign.'[2]

Goodwin even predicted that UKIP had four seats 'in the bag', including South Thanet, where Farage was running a sophisticated campaign. He went on to claim that Farage would win by more than many people expected and, in another article, even claimed that the campaign would go down in election history.

Against this growing expectation within UKIP circles, it is perhaps not surprising that we began our campaign against Farage with some trepidation. Our mood was not helped by the UKIP posters that were seemingly ubiquitous in the more deprived estates across the constituency. The party had also bought a large amount of billboard space and was pouring resources into the area to spread its offensive messages about immigrants. In time, of course, this all changed. John Page, our new national organiser, oversaw our campaign on the ground, while I stayed in London producing the leaflets we needed and helping our campaigns elsewhere. In addition to Thanet, we also had campaigns going on in Thurrock, Dudley, Rotherham, Great Yarmouth, Grimsby, and Heywood and Middleton.

Back in Thanet, HOPE not hate supporters took to the streets to target communities where we could turn out the anti-UKIP vote and developed a committed local activist group, many of whom had been involved in our campaigns to keep the BNP out of Barking and Dagenham. We leafleted door-to-door with literature about the NHS, tax policy and economic issues. Each week, we reached thousands of voters across the area, and Farage's support seemed to subside.

Two of my favourite HOPE not hate leaflets were produced for the Thanet campaign. The first was a 'Fat Cat' leaflet, which was literally a cut-out of a cartoon of a fat cat in a pinstriped suit smoking a cigar. Speech bubbles from the happy cat simply said: 'UKIP's tax policies are very fair … to people like me.' Accompanying the amusing and eye-catching leaflet were details about how Farage's party was proposing huge tax cuts for the wealthy. The second leaflet of note carried a fish wearing a shirt, jacket and a UKIP rosette, with the headline: 'Missing in Action'. Farage claimed to be the champion of the British fishing community, but, as our leaflet pointed out, he had missed 41 out of 42 European Parliament Fisheries Committee meetings that he was entitled to attend. The leaflet went on to explain that Farage had missed the three crucial meetings where fishing quotas for each EU member state were decided. 'This failure to engage in these new rules – which will directly affect all British fishermen for years to come – makes a mockery of the claim that UKIP is standing up for the interests of the British fishing industry,' the leaflet concluded.

Imaginative leaflets were also produced for other areas. In Grimsby, our literature mercilessly targeted UKIP candidate Victoria Ayling. She claimed to understand the concerns of local people in some of the most deprived communities in Britain, but we pointed out that she lived in a huge mansion, had been educated at an expensive private school and was in a relationship with a man who had bought the title of 'Baron' on the internet. We also mocked her claims that she had a good knowledge of the fishing community by stating that her experience was limited to selling 'cod liver oil' capsules. In Dudley, we made much of the desire by the UKIP candidate there to reintroduce corporal punishment into schools, while in Yorkshire we superimposed a picture of Farage's face on to an image of Margaret Thatcher, with the title: 'The Nightmare Returns'. In communities that had been decimated under Thatcherism, we prominently reproduced Farage's quote that the former Tory leader was his inspiration. In Oldham, we mocked the UKIP candidate's claim to have been born locally, when in an election in South Manchester the year before he had claimed to have been born there too.

Another significant innovation we introduced in this election was a four-page 'wraparound' we produced for the local free newspaper in Thanet, which focused on the threat UKIP posed to the NHS. Contrasting the contribution that non-British-born staff made to our health services, we highlighted the numerous quotes from leading UKIP officials calling for our beloved NHS to be privatised, and quoted Farage proposing that a private insurance model should replace the current free-to-use funding model. Similar newspaper wraparounds were produced for several other areas where UKIP posed a threat.

A more positive leaflet we distributed across the country was a red card, cut out in the shape of a heart. 'Don't let UKIP break our great love,' ran the words on the front. On the back, we listed a series of quotes from leading UKIP officials calling for the privatisation of the NHS. Polling showed that this message was particularly effective in working-class communities.

By mid-April, just three weeks before the election, Farage was on the back foot and made a national call for support for a weekend of action that turned out to be a poorly attended flop. Despite all the talk of a ground-breaking campaign, UKIP's operation was more akin to that of the BNP, though on a bigger scale. There were lorries, vans and cars driving around, emblazoned in UKIP colours and slogans. There were billboards and adverts in the local newspapers. There were town centre stalls and the obligatory public meeting when Farage was in town. But there was not the type of campaigning we had come to expect from modern political parties, and little apparent targeting. It was loud and visual, and while that creates a stir, it is not always the best way to win elections.

UKIP followed what it described as a 'shock and awe' strategy, whereby it behaved in a manner that was deliberately provocative and hard line in order to generate headlines and appeal to its core following. The strategy was most evidently used during the leaders' debate ahead of the 2015 General Election, when Farage spoke out against overseas HIV sufferers accessing the NHS. 'It was a core vote message. It wasn't to reach out to floating voters,' one senior source told the *Daily Telegraph*. 'We need to mobilise our base and that's what he did.'[3]

The newspaper went on to claim that this issue had been chosen precisely because it would generate such a reaction: 'A UKIP source said Mr Farage had originally intended to warn of the comparatively high proportion of migrants with tuberculosis "but then we realised that HIV drugs are more expensive".'

In South Thanet, Farage also used this strategy when he accused his Labour opponent of being 'anti-white' in a newspaper wrap the party bought. Farage was responding to an interview Will Scobie, the Labour candidate, had given to the *Guardian* to hit back at local gossip suggesting Eastern Europeans had caused a public disturbance in the constituency. Living on the estate where the incident took place, Scobie said that the perpetrators were locals. This proved enough for Farage to use the incident and play the race card, without providing any evidence whatsoever that Scobie's account was wrong.

Despite boasting over 40,000 members, the party lacked activists where it most needed them. Outside of South Thanet, and possibly

Thurrock, most UKIP activities rarely attracted a double-figure audience, and in many of its key targets, the party was, ironically, reliant on hiring gangs of eastern European workers to distribute its material. This lack of planning and activism meant that in Rotherham and Rother Valley, two areas where it had high hopes, UKIP missed the deadline to get letters out to postal voters, who made up 30 to 40 per cent of the total electorate. In Dagenham and Rainham, where UKIP polled 29.8 per cent of the vote, it could have done even better if its campaign had consisted of more than just the candidate and a small group of friends. Even after YouGov had the seat leaning towards UKIP, and with an eight-day bin strike in the run-up to polling day generating huge local anger, the party's lack of activists meant it was unable to capitalise.

As the campaign in Thanet unfolded, it was evident that only the Conservatives could beat Farage, and so our strategy began to shift, with our focus turning towards the more affluent areas of the constituency to shore up the Conservative vote. We talked up the pride of the community and emphasised how useless Farage had been as an MEP, never attending meetings, including those about fishing – an issue he talked incessantly about. We also distributed 10,000 of our national women's booklet targeting women least likely to vote UKIP. Like with the BNP, polling showed that women were less likely to vote UKIP than men.

The real prize came when we got Laura Sandys, the well-respected former MP, to write a direct letter asking electors to choose HOPE over the hateful rhetoric of Farage.

'Being an MP requires complete dedication to your constituents,' she wrote in the letter:

> Your new MP must be passionate about South Thanet. I know what it is like to share your fears, hopes and your sleepless nights when we have to face some really difficult challenges together.
>
> Unfortunately we have UKIP's Nigel Farage here who plays on divisions rather than builds communities. He wants to drive

wedges between us rather than embrace the best values of those in Thanet and Sandwich. If Nigel Farage is elected he will not have the time or be interested in putting you first.

I don't want you to wake up the morning after the election and find you have a part-time representative who only sees South Thanet as a means to an end.

We helped get the letter out to 10,000 women in the areas of the constituency that we thought were more likely to vote Conservative.

In the last week of the campaign, with the election too close to call, Farage spent more of his time campaigning in other seats around the country, at the expense of his own. We, however, never let up, campaigning until the very last minutes of election day. When the result came in, Farage trailed in second place, almost 3,000 votes behind the Conservative Craig MacKinlay.

A dejected Farage accepted defeat – for the seventh time, he had failed to become an MP – and promptly announced his intention to stand down as leader. Of course, he had no intention of really stepping down. Within hours of telling the press he would honour his promise made before the election that he would resign the leadership if he failed to win, he and his close supporters were lobbying the party's executive to ensure his resignation was rejected.

Farage might have failed in his quest to become an MP, but in many ways he emerged as a winner. In a desperate attempt to fend off the UKIP threat, Conservative Party leader David Cameron pledged to hold a referendum on Britain's continued membership of the European Union if he won the General Election. He did win, and, as we all know, a referendum was held in late June 2016.

HOPE not hate did not take a position in the EU referendum campaign, aware that our supporters straddled both sides. A few of us, however, did help set up the small People's Voice campaign, with a particular focus on engaging with working-class women in the north of England. Former Prime Minister Gordon Brown recorded a video from the bombed-out remains of Coventry Cathedral, which was the most watched video of the referendum campaign, with more than four million views across different platforms,[4] and the TUC's then-General Secretary Frances O'Grady produced a video that targeted working women.

While it was important to do what we could, the prospects of a Remain victory were always quite remote. This was in no small part because of the official Stronger In campaign, which was top-down and led by the belief that ordinary citizens would be impressed by 'captains of industry' and people in the City of London telling us that being in the EU was good for Britain. Sadly, most people took a different view, a position that was clear from two focus groups of supposedly undecided women we held in Sheffield a month out from the referendum vote. It was clear from these groups that there was a massive disconnect between how ordinary people saw the EU and how it was seen by the political class more generally, and therefore how the campaign was being run.

Sadly, the referendum campaign was overshadowed by the murder of Labour MP Jo Cox, who was shot outside a library in Batley, West Yorkshire, her hometown and the area she represented in Parliament, a week before the vote. While the gunman, Thomas Mair, refused to answer questions during his police interview, he had a longstanding interest in violent Nazism and terrorism and shouted 'Britain First' as he fired his homemade gun. While we will never know the exact trigger for Mair's actions, the murder took place amid an increasingly xenophobic and anti-immigration campaign by Leave campaigners. A week before Jo's murder, Farage had unveiled his 'Breaking Point' billboard, depicting a long line of migrants walking along a road, resulting in complaints that it was inciting hatred. This followed the official Leave campaign, fronted by Boris Johnson and Michael Gove, running ads claiming that 80 million Turks could come to this country if the UK remained in the EU.[5]

The referendum vote left Britain more divided and polarised than ever. While half the country celebrated, the other half mourned.

Racial violence surged, and many social liberals had nothing but contempt for those who had voted Leave. This proved problematic for us, as we increasingly found those people who had gamely helped us out in the old BNP strongholds like Dagenham, Burnley and Sandwell were now less willing to give up their weekends to positively engage with people they blamed for Brexit.

Another consequence of the vote was the political demise of UKIP. Having achieved its core mission, it now struggled to remain relevant. Farage finally stood down as leader on 4 July 2016, and the baton was handed over to Paul Nuttall, who lacked his predecessor's charisma and political acumen. And so it was no surprise that the party polled fewer than 600,000 votes and won no seats in the 2017 General Election. With the far right posing no real political challenge, HOPE not hate's campaign was considerably smaller. However, the campaigning we did was unquestionably our most targeted to date and pointed to a new level of professionalism and use of data on our part.

By the time of the General Election, we had built up close ties with the polling firm Populus, who had provided the polling and data insight for our 'Fear & HOPE' reports looking at the issues and ideas that brought people in England and Wales together and the ones that pulled them apart. When I went in to see them in early May 2017, just after Theresa May had called a snap election, to discuss a post-election 'Fear & HOPE' report, they showed me their new postcode data project that could estimate political views down to postcode level. Excited, I talked them into selling us data for 15 constituencies where UKIP posed a threat.

If the 2016 European referendum was the chance for those 'left behind' to vent their anger at the political establishment, then the 2017 General Election was the Remainers' revenge. Against all odds, May's Conservative Party lost its majority and was now only in government after being propped up by the Democratic Unionist Party. Labour did unexpectedly well, with party leader Jeremy Corbyn running a strong and human campaign that excited supporters and was in sharp contrast to May's robotic and detached approach.

UKIP, on the other hand, had a disastrous election, polling just 1.8 per cent of the vote, well down on the 12.6 per cent it had achieved in 2015. No wonder that Nuttall, its leader, quit the following day. UKIP was always going to do badly, but it would be wrong to suggest that its poor results reflect a loss of appetite for a radical-right populist party in the UK. Of course, UKIP's poor and bizarre campaign, which placed banning the burqa at its heart, did not help, but in reality the party was on a hiding to nothing from the outset. Farage knew it, which explained his decision not to stand.

The Conservatives called the election so they could gain the majority needed to deliver a 'hard Brexit', so there was always going to be little room for UKIP to play its usual anti-establishment card. On top of that, the referendum result had made former UKIP voters less angry, and many were content to sit this election out. Also, after making a decision not to contest seats with strong pro-Brexit MPs, UKIP only stood 377 candidates. The party went into the election full of bravado, boasting of winning several seats.

It was in Dagenham and Rainham where HOPE not hate made its biggest intervention of the campaign. With UKIP having come second in the 2015 election, polling 30 per cent of the vote, we were concerned that its voters would transfer to the Tory candidate, who was using increasingly tough rhetoric on immigration. Using the postcode data analysis provided to us by Populus, we split the constituency into 29 distinct groups, and over the course of the six-week campaign we delivered different leaflets, letters and online ads to these 29 groups. The data also enabled us to identify where the more economically left-leaning UKIP voter was to be found, on whom we were going to focus our campaign instead of the more culturally conservative UKIP voter, whom we were to ignore.

Building on the success of our imaginative 2015 leaflets, we produced a series of postcards contrasting UKIP's stated priorities with the actual concerns of ordinary people, especially those hit most by austerity and the related deep cuts to local public services. My favourite postcard of this campaign was a cute photo of a fox lurking in a field of long grass. 'Will the fox get it?' ran the wording on the front page.

On the back, we wrote: 'Food prices are rising. Wages are stagnating. Hospital waiting times are getting longer. Life is getting tougher for ordinary people but UKIP want to bring back fox hunting and ban the burqa. UKIP has no answers for the real problems of British people.'

Another postcard carried a photo of a food bank, alongside the wording: 'A record number of working families have used food banks in the past year.' On the back, we wrote: 'Too many working families are struggling to make ends meet in today's Britain. And yet UKIP want to prioritise reintroducing fox hunting, banning the burqa and privatising the NHS.'

Backing up our traditional ground campaign, we undertook our most comprehensive online operation to date, producing Facebook ads targeting key voters in key seats. One objective of our online campaigning was to discourage potential UKIP voters in the party's eight priority constituencies from supporting the party. To do so, we ran a campaign focusing on a selection of issues, including wealth inequality, the NHS, fox hunting, policing and education. To maximise relevance, each ad was hyper-personalised to the constituency.

We observed that the older our audience got, the more they were interested in policing, fox hunting and education. The creative image that appealed most to young people featured a businessman with a cigar and messaging around UKIP supporting the rich, suggesting that unfairness and wealth inequality could be effective messaging strands with this audience.

BSD, the ad agency we used, tested 291 variations of the adverts before deciding on the one they thought would work best. Our most successful ad was an image of police marching in formation, which was probably not surprising given UKIP supporters' core belief in law and order. Once they clicked on the somewhat uncontentious image, they were directed to a page that explained policing cuts in the local area. Although awareness was our goal, we also generated 9,595 clicks through from voters in our target seats to the HOPE not hate website, where potential UKIP voters could read about why they shouldn't vote for the party.

UKIP finished a distant third in Dagenham and Rainham, receiving just 7 per cent of the vote. Amazingly, Labour massively increased its vote to 50 per cent, from 41 per cent in 2015. UKIP was furious with our intervention. 'I believe this is wrong, unfair and amounts to cheating!' UKIP candidate Peter Harris told the *Daily Express*. 'It is time HNH came clean and admits they are the left-wing attack dogs of the Labour Party! I will be making a formal complaint to Electoral Services and the Electoral Commission asking them to carry out a thorough investigation.'[6]

If any formal complaint was made, we certainly heard nothing about it, and the campaign was not challenged by the Electoral Commission.

HOPE not hate has continued to use advanced data in our election campaigns and used another data company to build our own postcode model, this one even more advanced, with more than 100 economic, cultural, political and attitudinal views layered in.

In the 2024 General Election, we used our updated postcode software to help prevent George Galloway from retaining his seat in Rochdale. Over the course of the six-week campaign, we delivered 24,000 leaflets and letters to households that our data suggested had residents who disliked Galloway's views. Like in Dagenham and Rainham a few years before, we split the constituency up into several distinct groups and delivered different messages into homes in each. Just like UKIP, Galloway cried foul, producing a video declaring that we were breaking the law. Of course, he was talking nonsense and was just trying to explain to his supporters why he had been out-organised and out-campaigned.

9

Hate International

'I want to invite, right now, onto the stage the man behind Brexit, and a man who led, brilliantly, the United Kingdom Independence Party in this fight and won despite all the odds, despite all the horrible name-calling, despite so many obstacles. Ladies and gentlemen, Mr Nigel Farage.'

It was 25 August 2016, just two months after Britain had voted to leave the European Union. Republican presidential candidate Donald Trump vacated the rostrum to make way for the then-leader of UKIP.

'Well, thank you and good evening, Mississippi,' Nigel Farage began:[1]

I come to you from the United Kingdom with a message of hope and a message of optimism. It's a message that says that if the little people, the real people, if the ordinary decent people are prepared to stand up and fight for what they believe in we can overcome the big banks, we can overcome the multinationals. And we did it. We made June 23rd Independence Day, when we smashed the establishment. And we did it.

They did everything they could to demoralise our campaign. On the day of the vote itself, that morning, they put us 10 points behind. And actually they were all wrong. They were wrong because what the Brexit campaign did was reach those people who've been let down by modern global corporatism. We reached those people. We reached those people who have never voted in their lives but who thought that by coming out and voting for Brexit they could take back control of their lives, take back control of their borders and get back their pride and self-respect.

Folks, the message is clear, the parallels are there. There are millions of ordinary Americans who have been let down, had a bad time, feel the political class in Washington are detached from them. Feel that so many of their representatives are politically correct parts of that liberal media elite. They feel that people aren't standing up for them and they've already actually given up on the whole electoral process and I think you have a fantastic opportunity here with this campaign. You can go out, you can beat the pollsters, you can beat the commentators, you can beat Washington and you will do it by doing what we did with Brexit in Britain.

Politics was changing across the globe, and the old order was under strain like never before. Globalisation might have opened up new markets around the world, but it had also allowed large corporations to shift production to cheaper countries while also opening our own domestic markets to cheaper imports. Though consumers got cheaper products, old industries contracted, and the communities in which they were based became increasingly forgotten and left behind. The financial crash of 2008 saddled countries with huge debts as banks were bailed out, and ordinary people paid the price through austerity. When more than a million people began their long journeys to Europe in the summer of 2015, simmering anger and resentment erupted. European countries re-erected their borders, the British voted to leave the European Union and, in November 2016, Trump was elected president of the United States.

* * *

HATE INTERNATIONAL

I was brought up to believe that internationalism should always be a central part of the anti-fascist mindset. When I first became active in Searchlight back in the early 1990s, we had a European editor who was instrumental in setting up a research network that spanned the continent. After the Berlin Wall came down in 1989, he helped create an anti-fascist network within Germany and, as the nazi violence grew, even planned for the eventuality of moving the leadership of this movement to Norway if the situation on the ground got too bad. I also got involved in our international work, albeit on a much more limited basis. I worked closely with the late Swedish journalist Stieg Larsson, now better remembered for his *Millennium* crime trilogy, to undermine and expose C18, which was hugely influential in Scandinavia. In 1994, I worked with German anti-fascists to stop an international friendly between Germany and England on the anniversary of Hitler's birthday in Berlin's Olympic stadium after we learnt of plans by German and British nazis to use the occasion to attack the city's Turkish community. Two years later, in 1996, I exposed how European far-right mercenaries, many of whom had fought for Croatia in the Balkans conflict, were being recruited by South African nazis to destabilise the new Mandela government in the hope of sparking a civil war.

For the far right, by contrast, despite gains at the ballot box, their own nationalism limited their ability to work together.

This began to change after 2001, when a new transnational movement first began to emerge. Self-defined as the counter-jihad movement, it saw Islam as an expansionist religion and an inherent threat to Western civilisation. While some of the ideological founders of this movement, such as Bat Ye'or, emerged as early as the late 1980s, it was only after the 9/11 terrorist attacks on the US and the subsequent war on terror that these ideas really became widespread on the far right.

The counter-jihad movement is a broad network encompassing neo-conservatives, Christian evangelicals, Jewish extremists, racists, football hooligans, nationalists, right-wing populists and some former leftists. Some are hard-line in their views, others less so. Some are openly racist, others not so. Few have anything more than a minority following in the religious or political traditions they claim to represent. The movement's adherents rarely distinguish between Muslims, Islam and radical Islamists, believing that all three are one and the same. The Islamists, the counter-jihadists argue, are being aided and abetted by gullible liberals, who, through their advancement of multiculturalism, immigration and political correctness, are allowing Muslims into Europe and failing to deal with the consequences once they are here.

We believe that a critique of Islam is perfectly acceptable, as it should be of all religions, but what marks the counter-jihad movement out is that in the name of opposing Islamist extremism, generalisations are made about an entire faith. Many fail to differentiate between the actions of a few and those of the vast majority of Muslims who also reject the extremists. What's more, the logical conclusion of many of the counter-jihadist thinkers is of conflict between the Christian West and Islam, and for some this is eagerly anticipated because they believe it is only through the removal of Muslims from Europe that the problem can be eradicated. And with governments perceived as either too weak to acknowledge the problem or as complicit in its growth, it has to be left to the movement itself to raise the alarm.

In July 2011, far-right activist Anders Breivik killed 77 people in Norway. Eight people died as a result of a bomb he left in a van outside a government building; another 69 were killed during a mass shooting at a Workers' Youth League summer camp on the island of Utøya. Breivik claimed he was striking back at those he held responsible for allowing Muslims into Norway, but at the same time he hoped his actions would spark violent reactions or copycat actions. He was immersed in and inspired by the counter-jihad movement, and his 1,500-page manifesto, which he released on the day of his attacks, referenced hundreds of articles and speeches by leading counter-jihad figures. The counter-jihad world rushed to distance themselves from him, but it was their ideas that inspired Breivik, and, for those with the most hard-line positions, his actions were the logical conclusion of their belief in the need for a violent confrontation with Islam.

While the counter-jihad movement has ebbed and flowed over the years, the central plank of its philosophy – that the very future of Western civilisation is under threat from Islam, mass migration and liberalism – has become increasingly dominant on the global far right. It also became a unifier, with elements of this philosophy becoming apparent within traditional far-right and populist-right political parties and authoritarian leaders in central and eastern Europe, as well as in the US conservative right and the Catholic right. While each took and used slightly different elements of the counter-jihadist ideology to explain their worldviews and drive their activity, the shared concepts of the threat overcame the self-interest of nationalism and created an internationalism on the far right of politics that had previously been lacking.

In 2016, a young Swedish student called Patrik Hermansson approached HOPE not hate with a request to get involved. Though now studying in London, Patrik had been active with Expo, our sister organisation in Sweden, for whom he often took photos of nazi protests and demonstrations. While we were always on the lookout for new photographers, my colleague Joe Mulhall immediately thought that Patrik could be put to greater use. After a couple of conversations, Patrik was set to go undercover. Over the next 18 months, Patrik travelled through British, European and later American far-right circles. From the backrooms of pubs with Britain's elite fascist groups to American alt-right leaders with links to the Trump administration, Patrik's journey graphically highlighted the growing internationalisation of the far right and its increasing proximity to power.

He initially joined the London Forum, the UK's leading, and probably only, nazi discussion group at the time, just ahead of the

HOW TO DEFEAT THE FAR RIGHT

US Presidential Election in November 2016. While the Forum had been running for several years, it was the rise of Trump – and the alt-right that supported him – that saw a surge of interest in its activities, with interest from many people who were younger and more engaged with the internet than the traditional Forum attendees. As Patrik noted after infiltrating the organisation:

> The alt-right, an assembly of older far-right ideas which see white men in particular as victims and use online activism to disseminate its message, grew into one of the largest far-right movements in decades. They made far-right ideas more palpable and made them more attractive to young men. For the London Forum it was an opportunity they could not miss.

New business cards were made, and some of the old stalwarts even began referring to themselves as alt-right. To cope with the surge of interest, Patrik was asked to vet each new recruit. 'During the interviews I heard how men of different backgrounds felt that Trump's victory, alongside Brexit and the rise of alt-right, had made it feel like these extreme ideas had become more normal,' he recalled. 'As one prospect told me, it felt like "our side is winning". The stigma of being a far-right activist had dropped.'

After gaining the confidence of the Forum's leaders, Patrik was quickly introduced to a wider network of meetups and activists that spanned Europe and the US. He attended pagan ceremonies, drank mead from horns and sat next to some of the most prominent far-right thinkers in the world at fancy dinners in London. Having told people from the outset that he was studying for a master's in London, he then announced his need to travel to the United States for his research, and his new political friends quickly put him in touch with leading figures in the increasingly influential alt-right over there. One was Greg Johnson, a secretive white nationalist activist from the West Coast. He invited Patrik to attend a conference he was organising in Seattle. Patrik probably got more than he expected, as Johnson messaged him while at the airport saying someone had become ill and asked if Patrik could do the keynote speech.

The audience assembled in front of Patrik was younger, and many were armed. 'No one spoke in cagey terms about violence or hate, it was all out in the open,' Patrik reported back. 'I attended a barbeque with armed nazis in Seattle that same evening, and over the following weeks I met with the notorious Jared Taylor at his house in Virginia.'

Patrik finished his infiltration by attending the infamous Charlottesville demonstration in August 2017, where thousands of white nationalists from across the US marched in defence of statues and other symbols remembering the country's racist past. In an ensuing clash between white nationalists and anti-fascists, a young anti-fascist activist called Heather Heyer was killed after being hit by a car driven into the anti-fascist crowd by James Alex Fields. Patrik, who was only metres away from this confrontation, decided to call it a day.

In September 2017, a few weeks after Trump had seemingly defended the white racist protestors, we released Patrik's story in the *New York Times* along with an accompanying film.[2] Frustratingly, while this film was shown in many countries across Europe, it was never aired in the UK, with broadcasters being concerned that we had done our own undercover filming and so had not met the strict risk assessment and legal signoff they were forced to adopt. That aside, the operation was an amazing success, as it blew the lid off an increasingly confident and well-financed international far right who were taking full advantage of Trump's election victory.

To coincide with the release of Patrik's undercover story, HOPE not hate produced a report into the international alt-right movement. This report was, at least in the UK, the most comprehensive analysis and investigation into the far-right movement that was piggy-backing and influencing Trump's rise to power. Called 'The International Alternative Right: From Charlottesville to the White House', it merged Patrik's information with that gleaned from two of our other researchers who went inside the same networks at the same time. Our research team later combined their knowledge to produce a book on the alt-right, which was published by Routledge.[3]

Over the summer of 2015, an estimated 1.3 million people entered Europe from Asia and Africa, the most in a single year since the end of the Second World War. While the EU initially tried to organise a fair distribution of migrants across Europe, this quickly fell apart as right-wing national governments and domestic pressures led countries to put national interests above European solidarity. Right-wing governments in Hungary, Poland and the Czech Republic used the crisis to double down on existing anti-immigrant rhetoric, introducing new draconian legislation to further criminalise migrants and clamp down on the media. Far-right parties in Western Europe framed their election campaigns around the dangers migrants posed. Even moderate governments closed their borders, built fences and warned migrants they would be sent back if they crossed national borders. In the UK, the memory of the migrant crisis, as best immortalised by Farage's Breaking Point poster, played a significant role in the referendum on membership of the EU.

One pan-European far-right activist group, Generation Identity (GI), also sought to make political capital out of the surge in migration. But for GI, closing the borders and limiting the flow of migrants was not enough. Central to their far-right ideology was the belief in the Great Replacement theory: the idea the white populations of Europe were being demographically and culturally replaced by non-white peoples through mass migration, demographic growth and a corresponding drop in the birth rate of white Europeans. For GI and other extreme far-right groups, the answer was 'remigration' – the idea that the non-white populations of Europe should be returned to their countries of origin.

In the summer of 2017, the international Identitarian Network, to which GI was central, launched its Defend Europe mission, gaining headlines all over the world. Their plan was to get a ship, sail into the Mediterranean and hinder refugee rescue missions, which the far right increasingly blamed for enabling migration into Europe. Over a four-month period, HOPE not hate set about disrupting their plans, with amazing success. The short battle against Defend Europe was a glimpse into the future of what fascism and anti-fascism would increasingly look like. The Identitarians were an international network of activists drawn from across Europe, raising support and money from far-right people all over the world.

For us, it was clear that effective anti-fascism no longer simply required us to know the enemy in our street, community or even our country but rather to understand that the threat was international and act globally. Facing an increasingly transnational far right that operated largely online, we knew the battlefield had fundamentally changed and that new tools were required to fight it. This wasn't about producing newspapers, leaflets or placards – it was about using satellites, pressuring multinational tech companies, shaping media narratives, and building new levels of international cooperation and support on social media.

In May 2017, we broke the story that three members of Génération Identitaire, the French GI group, accompanied by the Canadian alt-right journalist Lauren Southern, had been detained by the Italian coast guard after using a small boat to try to block a vessel operated by the non-governmental organisation (NGO) SOS Méditerranée. We then uncovered that Defend Europe had raised enough money to charter a ship, the *C-Star*, which was currently docked in Djibouti in East Africa. We exposed the owner of the ship as a convicted fraudster who had been sentenced to two-and-a-half years in jail.[4] At the same time, we also launched a successful campaign calling on the *Daily Mail* not to publish sympathetic articles written by Katie Hopkins, who had recently used her *Sun* column to seemingly demonise migrants and mock those who had drowned.

Believing that the best way to disrupt GI's plans was to make it difficult for their boat to operate in the Mediterranean, we contacted the Egyptian and Suez Canal authorities to raise our concerns about the ship being allowed access to their ports. GI would later blame HOPE not hate for stalling their vessel in the Red Sea. More bad news followed when US-based fundraising website Patreon removed users linked to Defend Europe, after lobbying from HOPE not hate. Worse was to beset GI, as no sooner was *C-Star* released from its detention in Suez and allowed to enter the Mediterranean than it was again detained after docking in the Turkish Cypriot port of Famagusta. However, on 31 July, after weeks of costly delays, Defend Europe activists finally managed to board the ship and begin their anti-refugee 'mission' in the Mediterranean in earnest.

With the mission underway, August started with HOPE not hate revealing the real identity of key Defend Europe supporter and propagandist Peter Sweden (real name Peter Imanuelsen). We had long been worried about the state of the *C-Star* and its fitness to carry out the dangerous Defend Europe mission, so, after speaking to numerous maritime experts, we drew up a formal complaint and successfully requested an immediate inspection known as a Port State Control Inspection. The vessel was classified 'Priority 1', meaning next time it entered a European port it would be stopped and inspected again.

The final straw for Defend Europe came on 17 August, when an alliance of NGOs, both local and international, including HOPE not hate, managed to get *C-Star* banned from Maltese ports. Hampered by a lack of port facilities and fearing an inspection of the ship, GI announced the end of their mission, having achieved none of their stated goals. Worse was to come for GI after HOPE not hate successfully infiltrated the group on multiple occasions, forcing GI to close its UK operation altogether. Adding to their woes, the group's leader was banned from the UK, we exposed two activists as serving members of the Royal Navy[5] – one of whom was imminently to become a sonar engineer on a nuclear submarine – and the resulting recriminations forced the European leaders of GI to expel the British branch from the international network.

HOPE not hate's work had resulted in the complete destruction of GI UK.

For a man who has emerged as such an important part of the radical-right ecosystem, Sir Paul Marshall has kept a surprisingly low profile. Despite being a co-owner of GB News and the founder of Unherd, little was publicly known about Marshall other than his past involvement in the Liberal Democrats, that he had been a pro-Brexit donor to the Conservative Party under Boris Johnson and that he was a board member of the Ark Schools academy chain. That was until the HOPE not hate research team got to work. In February 2024, one of our researchers revealed that Marshall was 'liking' and 'reposting' racist, Islamophobic and homophobic content from an anonymous X/Twitter account he ran, and also discovered that in September 2023, Marshall had set his X account to 'Protected' mode, which meant that only those who already followed his account could view his activity, and he could choose whether to accept any new followers. He then removed any identifying information from the profile and changed the username to @areopagus123, which matched the name of a company he had set up in 2021, Areopagus Ventures, which seemed to derive from Marshall's interest in *Areopagitica*, John Milton's polemic in defence of free speech.

Marshall increasingly endorsed posts from extreme Islamophobic and anti-migrant activists, including notorious hate accounts such as the Britain First Deputy Leader Ashlea Simon, American anti-Muslim campaigner Amy Mek and the shady Italian anti-migration account Radio Genoa. Among the posts 'liked' by Marshall were extremist declarations that bordered on calls to violence, including one that declared it was 'a matter of time before civil war starts in Europe. The native European population is losing patience with the fake refugee invaders.'

In January 2024, he 'liked' another that warned: 'If we want European civilization to survive not just close the borders but start mass expulsions immediately. We don't stand a chance unless we start that process very soon.'

HOPE not hate broke the story with *The News Agents* podcast.[6] It instantly got picked up by other mainstream media outlets and has since been raised in Parliament. While *The News Agents* went on to pick up the 2024 Scoop of the Year award for its special edition of the podcast, the public exposé of Marshall's views had little detrimental impact on his business and political interests. Even though Marshall was forced off the board at the Ark academies, he was publicly backed in the Commons by the then-Communities Minister Michael Gove, and following that year's election, the Labour government saw no grounds on which to prevent him from acquiring the *Spectator* magazine and appointing Gove as the new editor.

But it is Marshall's involvement in the Alliance for Responsible Citizenship, or ARC as it is more commonly known, that is probably most consequential.[7] ARC has become arguably the most important global conservative conference in the world, attracting between 4,000 and 5,000 people to its three-day event. ARC was created in June 2023, and its conference in February 2025 saw Mike Johnson, Speaker of the United States House of Representatives, speak alongside former Australian Prime Ministers Tony Abbott and John Howard, UK Conservative Party leader Kemi Badenoch and Reform UK leader Nigel Farage. There were a host of historians, academics and journalists, among them were Sir Niall Ferguson, Bjørn Lomborg, Konstantin Kisin and Ayaan Hirsi Ali. Opening the event was Baroness Philippa Stroud and co-hosting was Canadian author Dr Jordan B. Peterson.

That so many leading figures on the international right are so keen to speak at ARC is testament to the event's importance and the platform it provides even to those not directly in the room. In an interview with the *Sydney Morning Herald*, former Australian Deputy Prime Minister John Anderson, who helped shape the initial ARC conference, described the group's emergence as a response to a 'civilisational' moment in which the Western world 'is plagued by self-doubt and confusion' regarding its values and beliefs. Anderson said the goal of ARC was to 'regroup, and put forward a positive agenda' by providing a better narrative than one of inevitable doom and decline.

In a narrative similar to that deployed by the counter-jihad movement 10 to 15 years previously, a central theme running through many of the speeches at ARC is the idea that Western civilisation is facing an existential threat, though their enemies go beyond Islam to also encompass liberalism and the growing geopolitical threat of China.

Company records show that Marshall is one of ARC's two directors, along with Dubai-based investment management group Legatum, founded by Christopher Chandler. Legatum is, alongside Marshall, co-owner of GB News.

Eight years after Patrik went undercover for us in the alt-right, a young journalist called Harry Shukman reached out for advice and support for a project he had been planning for a while. For several months, Harry had been running a small independent blog on the far right, but now he wanted to go inside. Over the next 15 months, Harry moved seamlessly through a number of far-right groups until he found himself at the heart of the international world of scientific racism, which is the belief that there are meaningful and measurable differences between 'races', especially in terms of intelligence.

A discredited pseudoscientific theory of genetic superiority of some ethnic groups over others, race science – or 'scientific racism' – had quietly been rehabilitated through a complex and inter-connecting global web of scientists, journals, podcasts and conferences. At the heart of Harry's infiltration, which later formed the central plank of a Bafta-nominated film about HOPE not hate, *Undercover: Exposing the Far Right*,[8] was the Human Diversity Foundation (HDF), a million-dollar race science company largely continuing the work of the Pioneer Fund,[9] perhaps the most notorious financial backer of the intellectual far right. Created in 1937, the US-based group distributed Nazi propaganda and developed close ties to the Third Reich. After the Second World War, tainted by the horrors of Nazi Germany, the Pioneer Fund operated in the shadows, funding race scientists and eugenicists, enabling them to publish papers seeking proof that black people were less intelligent than white people. Some of them were academics, such as Richard Lynn, a psychology professor at the University of Ulster, who aspired to 'have a go at the rehabilitation of eugenics'. Another recipient of Pioneer funding was Jared Taylor, the white nationalist leader of American Renaissance, who has said: 'When blacks are left entirely to their own devices, Western civilization – any kind of civilization – disappears.'[10]

By the early 2000s, the Pioneer Fund appeared to have disappeared, but Harry's investigation led him to discover that it had in fact morphed into HDF, run by Danish 'race science' researcher Emil Kirkegaard, private school- and Cambridge-educated writer Matt Frost and Erik Ahrens, a social media advisor for the German far-right party AfD. Pretending to be a potential investor, Harry won the three men's confidence, was given copies of their business plan and ultimately discovered that the group's key funder was Andrew Conru, a wealthy tech entrepreneur who had initially made his money by founding Adult Friend Finder.

While Conru later claimed to HOPE not hate that he had no idea of the real work of HDF and publicly claimed he was withdrawing support, he has in fact made several previous donations to other elements of the race science movement. During subsequent research with journalists at the *Guardian*, who ran Harry's story over several days, it was revealed that Conru had given $50,000 to Bryan Pesta,[11] a former recipient of Pioneer money who is now part of HDF's underground research team, and had given an undisclosed sum to Simon Webb to publish a 2021 book, *The Equalitarian Dogma: Why Ideology and Not Science Dominates Debate on Ethnicity and Race in the Modern World*, which references race scientists like J. Philippe Rushton.[12]

Conru is not the only US tech entrepreneur who takes an interest in eugenics and race science. Harry's undercover investigation also brought him into contact with PolygenX, a company offering parents a science-fiction-like service: screening which IVF embryos will have the highest IQ. Our research charted the support for eugenics and connections to far-right activism of leading figures within the company. While the company strenuously denied the allegations, both *Guardian* and HOPE not hate lawyers felt comfortable enough with the evidence for us to publish the story. Jonathan Anomaly, one of PolygenX's key employees, said on Louise Perry's podcast in June 2023: 'There's big demand for it among the wealthy already and among the well-connected in Silicon Valley.'

To Harry, in October 2023, Anomaly went further, boasting of having a three-hour lunch with Elon Musk in Austin, Texas, where they discussed the polygenic screening of embryos. 'He thinks it's cool,' Anomaly said of the encounter, which took place six weeks earlier. 'I know he supports us.'

Two other prominent Silicon Valley tech billionaires who were also interested in this world were Peter Thiel, the former CEO of PayPal, who met with several key people behind HDF, including flying Kirkegaard out for a one-hour meeting to discuss his work. He has also met with Anomaly.[13] The other is Marc Andreessen, general partner of Silicon Valley venture capital firm Andreessen Horowitz, who was a paying subscriber to race-science YouTuber Edward Dutton,[14] a key part of the HDF network.[15] While there was no indication that Thiel or Andreessen funded or were even aware of the far-right politics of those behind HDF, that they interacted at all indicates the growing interest in eugenics among sections of the right-wing Silicon Valley world.

It is also interesting to note that Musk, Thiel and Andreessen are three of the biggest backers of J. D. Vance, now the vice president of the United States.

* * *

HOW TO DEFEAT THE FAR RIGHT

I would never have thought I would ever utter these words, but the progressive movement needs to take a leaf out of the far-right playbook. Despite the progressive side of politics supposedly being the internationalists, it is the right, and particularly the far right, that are more internationalist in outlook and organisation. They have built an ideology that transcends borders and are better at sharing ideas, people and money. Supporting this is a vast and growing far-right ecosystem than spans TV stations, newspapers, podcasts, Substacks, YouTube videos and online content on supportive platforms like X.

A victory for one is quickly viewed as a victory for all, and the momentum rolls forward to the next contest. The progressive lane of politics has simply nothing that compares. Progressives need to learn from the right – and we need to learn quickly. Where is our shared learning from the campaign strategies that worked well in the 2023 Polish General Election, when the progressive Civic Coalition defeated the ruling Law and Justice Party, but failed to stop the far-right AfD from securing second place in the 2024 German federal elections? Where is our equivalent to the ARC conference where we can share and develop the ideas to keep the forces of hate at bay? Where is our shared ideological defence of liberal democracy that we can use collectively to counter those who claim that extreme measures are required to defend Christian-Judea civilisation? Where is the space for practitioners, activists and policy makers to meet to discuss how we prevent another repeat of a migrant crisis having the same political fallout as it did in 2015?

While it is perhaps understandable that we are all swamped with trying to hold back the charge of the far right in our own individual countries to have much capacity to think beyond our own borders, our mindset does need to change. Not only can we better learn from our own successes and defeats in each country, but with far-right international networks becoming increasingly influential, it is often the case that their weaknesses might be found beyond our national borders. Some elements of the progressive world, such as the climate movement, are better at organising and coordinating internationally, but the same cannot be said for the anti-fascist world or even the migration world. Unless we change our approach, and change it quickly, we will continue to be at a disadvantage.

10

Civic Pride

One of the key lessons we have learnt from the HOPE not hate campaign is that you have to earn the right to be heard. Too many political activists preach at others, telling them what they should do and how to do it. At best, you will continue to be ignored; at worst, people will double down on the attitudes or behaviour you objected to in the first place. You can earn trust by simply spending time in an area, understanding why people are doing what they are doing or thinking what they are thinking, showing you genuinely care about their needs and involving them in the decision making.

Earning the right to be heard requires humility, empathy and a lot of hard graft.

I learnt the importance of this approach through my good friends Paul and Lorraine in Bradford. As trained community development workers, they understood better than most the social and economic pressures many communities face and the corresponding allure of the far right. They also understood that the far-right's slogans, promises and scapegoating were never going to turn these communities around, but they knew that us just saying this was often likely to fall on deaf ears. We had to – quite literally – prove it.

Faced with the BNP's growing support across Keighley in 2004 off the back of the grooming scandal, Paul and Lorraine knew they had to do something different from what they and the wider anti-fascist movement had done before. While they obviously had to address the grooming issue head-on, the problems in Keighley were far deeper than just that one issue. It was an area of high deprivation, and many people believed the BNP line that they were losing out because they were white and that Muslim communities were receiving more funding. The grooming scandal only reinforced their suspicions or even dislike of Muslim people.

As we saw time and again, there was a kernel of truth to their claims, though not because of racial bias as they alleged. Rather, in those days local government funding was allocated by determining levels of deprivation across Lower Super Output Areas (LSOAs) (approx. 1,500 homes), so a particularly deprived Output Area (approx. 160 homes) surrounded by slightly less deprived communities would see the overall level of deprivation level out and therefore possibly be overlooked for funding. With predominately British-Muslim areas of Bradford having higher levels of average deprivation, funding understandably went there first. These explanations meant nothing to the people in the poorer communities of Keighley, where there was considerable support for the BNP.

Undertaking a community-development approach, Paul and Lorraine reached out to and met with community groups, the voluntary sector, local faith leaders and businesses. They also changed how they talked about these areas. They were no longer described as 'BNP estates', as we might have lazily referred to them in the past, but rather as communities vulnerable to BNP lies. Gradually, through dozens of one-to-one conversations, we began to arm people with the confidence and arguments to defeat the BNP.

With our new partners in local faith groups and businesses, we launched 'Keighley Together' as an initiative to bring local people together around an anti-racist agenda but also to call for investment and council support in the area. The launch event, attended by dozens of local people holding up huge white letters that read 'Keighley Together', was covered extensively by the local and regional media. The profile of Keighley Together was particularly important for its success. It did not look like the usual left-wing campaign, as alongside the churches and voluntary sector groups it was a mobilisation of civil society from within the very communities at risk. It was owned by local people, and this was crucial for taking on the BNP. Keighley Together posters quickly began to spring up in windows across the area, helping to change the atmosphere from one of hatred and racism to one of hope and togetherness. Paul and Lorraine's work did not end there. We worked alongside local residents to support them in devising a funding bid to Bradford council for a physical community centre.

The results of our community development work were evident in the May 2005 General Election campaign. In a town where we could previously only have counted on half a dozen activists, at least 65 local people came out to deliver our election newspaper. More importantly, the people of Keighley heavily rejected Griffin and the politics of hate, with the BNP trailing in fourth with just 10 per cent of the vote. Clearly, our approach of taking on the grooming issue head-on was crucial, but to even get to the point where local people would listen to us was a consequence of the hard work we put into the area. It would have been easy to enter the election campaign at the last minute with a leaflet exposing Griffin's racist and fascist views, but this risked being ignored by local people who were angry at both the grooming scandal and high levels of deprivation.

However strong the forces of hatred may appear, we demonstrated that there is always a majority, though often silent and scared, who will stand up for hope if given the option.

The lessons of Keighley helped shape our response to a strong BNP election result in the Friar Park ward in Sandwell in 2006. The BNP had never previously stood in the ward and despite literally doing no campaigning at all still polled 34 per cent in the election. Coupled with a strong BNP showing in several other wards across the borough

– up to 45 per cent in some – this caused panic among the local Labour Party. There were calls for us to do some anti-racist work on the Friar Park estate, which according to the most recent census was 98 per cent white British and struggling with high levels of deprivation. I discouraged this approach and instead sat down with one of the local councillors, Simon Hackett; together, we came up with the idea of starting a community newsletter, which we hoped could act as the heartbeat and voice of local people. Once established as part of the local community, we figured it could address racism and other social issues.

Building on Paul and Lorraine's work in Keighley, and the notion that we could not ask for the support of local people without doing something to help them first, we also drew inspiration from a community newsletter from Golborne, a small town in the borough of Wigan, that I had been given by one of our supporters there. The newsletter had very quickly established itself as the 'voice' of the local area and so had become a trusted source of information. I sent copies of the Golborne newsletter to Simon, and after he discussed it with some of his local colleagues, we agreed that we should follow this approach on the Friar Park estate.

In addition to his work as a local councillor, Simon's day job was working for local MP Tom Watson, and between them they developed the newsletter idea further. They got some funding for the first couple of editions and recruited someone to work with a local Sure Start centre to help put it together. Who better to involve in putting together a community newsletter than young mums? More than any other group, they were invested in bringing their kids up in a safe and friendly community. They also had strong opinions about what people wanted but were generally outside the usual corridors of decision making. What began as a slightly tatty photocopied newsletter became a glossy 16-page magazine with interesting local stories celebrating local people and sports clubs that had done well, promoting local health services that were generally under-used and hosting competitions like the best-dressed house at Christmas.

The newsletter soon became a trusted local voice and was a simple and effective way of spreading an anti-racist message without seeming to ram anything down anyone's throat. Simon then secured funding for a community fun day, which was held for the following few summers and brought local people together in a positive way. The fun day also provided us with the opportunity to bring dance groups and sports clubs from more diverse parts of the borough into the area as part of a subtle anti-racist strategy.

When the BNP stood in Friar Park again the following year, their vote dropped by half.

Down in London, another group of anti-fascists were responding to the growth of the BNP with a similarly community-focused approach. Called Hackney Unites, the group grew out of a local trade union response to the electoral rise of the BNP, who, in addition to becoming the official opposition on Barking and Dagenham Council, were winning councillors in the London boroughs of Redbridge, Havering and Bexley. While Hackney Unites was formed by local trade unions, it quickly evolved into a strong and inclusive community-organising project.

The group's first important action was to persuade the local free newspaper not to take a BNP advert ahead of the London Assembly elections in May 2008. With less than a week to stop the advert going in, the group dismissed the idea of a protest and petition as ineffective and instead looked at the one constituency that had real power in the newspaper operation – the newsagents who distributed the paper. 'Realising that the majority of newsagents in Hackney came from ethnic minority communities, and knowing they would share our horror at the prospect of the BNP establishing a base, we asked our supporters to visit their own newsagent and take in a leaflet explaining our opposition and a sheet which the newsagent could fax over to the publisher,' Hackney Unites co-organiser John Page remembered.

The fax to the newspaper offices was simple, even blunt. 'If you run the BNP advert, cancel my order for your paper.' More than 100 newsagents signed up, and under such local opposition, the newspaper relented and refused to run the BNP advert.

Emboldened by this victory, Hackney Unites continued to grow, producing a regular tabloid with a distribution of 50,000 copies across the borough, holding local community meetings and campaigning on issues important to local people. Hackney Unites became a community coalition for social justice, and a community conference held six months later was attended by 30 organisations and over 400 people.

At the heart of a successful, vibrant and strong local community are the relationships that bind people together. It might be the community centres and clubs where people socialise, it might be the collective things we do together or it could be the activities and sports we participate in. All these things are generally defined as social capital. The problem is that these bonds are weakening, nowhere more so than in the very communities that have seen the greatest economic upheaval and deindustrialisation over the last few decades, leaving these places increasingly susceptible to extremist narratives. Not only have the main workplaces gone – and in many former coal, steel or fishing towns, these were often the reason the town developed in the first place – but so too has much of the community infrastructure that came with them, be it the local unions, the working men's clubs or the vibrancy of the high street.

The working men's clubs offered more than just a place for local people to drink; they were often the heartbeat of a local community. 'Clubs are places we can belong,' Kirsty McNeill, now the MP for Midlothian, wrote in the Co-operative Party pamphlet *Community Britain*.[1] 'Being rooted in a membership model they provide a microcosm of what a more co-operative economy and society could be.' Membership of the Club & Institute Union, the central co-op supporting the clubs' movement, now numbers one million. Fifty years ago, it was seven million.

CIVIC PRIDE

There are so many other indicators of declining social capital, some resulting from changes to our community infrastructure, others down to our own behaviour. Over 20,000 pubs have closed since 1980, and live music venues are diminishing fast, with 10 per cent closing their doors permanently in 2023 alone. 'Rising costs, shifting habits, and post-pandemic pressures are accelerating the decline of nightclubs, live music venues, and pubs, leaving cultural and economic voids in towns and cities across the UK,' wrote the architecture website Building Design.[2] It predicts that, at the current rate of closures, all major nightclubs could vanish by 2029.

Deep cuts to council budgets and 15 years of austerity have had a huge impact on the decline of social capital. According to Fields in Trust,[3] over 800 playgrounds have closed since 2013. Almost a third of children under nine (31 per cent) now have to walk more than 10 minutes to get to their nearest playground. At a time when NHS data shows that 28 per cent of two- to 15-year-olds were either overweight or obese, 279 school playing fields were sold off between 2010 and 2023. However, this pales into insignificance compared to the 10,000 sold off under the 1979–97 Conservative governments. Data from the Local Government Association showed that local authorities have seen their central government grants decline by £24 billion in real terms since 2010, devastating local services and funding for community and voluntary organisations. Combined with a sharp reduction in donations during the pandemic and subsequent cost-of-living crisis, this has forced many charities to scale back their work or close altogether.

In addition to funding, our lifestyle options have also reduced the time we spend with one another. According to Ofcom,[4] the average adult spends four hours and 20 minutes online a day, rising to six hours for those aged 18–24. More people are staying at home rather than going to the pub. As of November 2024, 68 per cent of households have a subscription to an online streaming service, while those going to the cinema fell from a worldwide high of 1.6 billion in 1946 to 176 million in 2024. The nature of work has also changed for the worse, with smaller workplaces and offices replacing large factories, and workplaces where people could interact in a way that they were unlikely to in any other aspect of their lives outside school. This has reduced the opportunities to mix with people from different cultures, religions and ethnicities.

COVID and the cost-of-living crisis saw people cutting back on social and leisure activities. Research from the Carnegie Trust found a third of people said they had reduced the time they spent with friends, while a quarter said the same about family.[5] Additionally, half said that the cost-of-living crisis had limited their ability to participate in leisure activities, such as eating out or going to the cinema.

In 2020, HOPE not hate set up the Hopeful Towns project to understand what makes a town resilient in the face of change and tolerant in the face of difference. Run by Rosie Carter, who had started as a community organiser in Dudley for us several years before, this project sought to support towns across England and Wales and to address the range of challenges in local communities by providing support at a local level, as well as seeking to influence national policy. The project built on several years of work Rosie had done at HOPE not hate, from numerous iterations of the 'Fear & HOPE' reports, the seminal 'Fear, HOPE and Loss' report – which sought to better understand the drivers of hate at a local community level – and the National Conversation, an initiative she ran in collaboration with British Future to seek a consensus on immigration.

Rosie was supported in this project by Chris Castle and Chris Farley, and it produced several important reports. We published 'The Town Index', an extensive inventory of the UK's towns, bringing together well over 100 data variables for all 862 towns across England and Wales to create 14 'clusters', each representing a set of resilience challenges faced by some towns but not by others.[6] We released 'Building Back Resilient',[7] which looked at how the COVID-19 pandemic increased the risk of social divisions in some communities, and 'Loss on the Terraces' explored the role of football clubs in holding together local identities and the human cost of the financial crisis facing the game.[8]

The team established the Towns Network, which was joined by over 600 practitioners, to disseminate information and share good practice, and produced a series of resources to support local authorities and community groups in writing successful bids, using the media more effectively and making the most of empty spaces. Building stronger and happier communities and increasing social credit were fundamental elements in improving community cohesion.

Local community initiatives can also bring people and communities together. The Himmah project in Nottingham is a social justice organisation with a mission to tackle food poverty, racism and educational inequalities in the city. In addition to organising the largest food bank in Nottingham, it also runs cooking classes, a community garden and the Salaam Shalom Soup Kitchen, which brings Muslim and Jewish people together to serve 140 hot meals every Wednesday evening for those in need. It has also formed a partnership with Phoenix FC, a local football club based in the centre of a large, white working-class council estate.

'We started up a conversation with the club and explained how we had the capacity to deliver 60–70 food parcels a week in the area,' remembers Sajid, the director of Himmah. Each parcel has enough food for three meals a day for seven days. The club manager told Sajid that he needn't look any further than the kids who came to play football there, many of whom did not have enough money to buy boots or kit. A relationship was established, assumptions challenged and friendships made, and before long people from Himmah and Phoenix began attending each other's events.

Twenty-three years after I walked the streets of the Stoops estate in Burnley delivering a letter from local community activists urging local people not to vote for the BNP, I was back, visiting the person who had penned that original letter. Over six feet tall and with broad, strong shoulders, Chris Keene is an imposing and fearless figure. He probably needs to be, given that he is a die-hard Leeds fan living in the town of one of their key rivals. He still runs the Stoops and Hargher Clough Community Centre, but these days he does so as a volunteer. The lack of funding means that the centre is only operational because Chris and an ageing group of dedicated volunteers give up their time, including a couple who do amazing work on finance, administration and essential building repairs.

In addition to his youth and community work, Chris is a committed anti-racist, and over the years he has run numerous excellent initiatives using sport and music to bring people of different ethnicities together. More recently, the centre brought together white and British-Asian mothers to create a giant quilt with images celebrating diversity. This activity is running alongside a family theatre event, a world music night and a school-based writer in residence project.

The community centre serves the Stoops estate, the most deprived area of Burnley and the 17th most deprived – out of 32,000 Output Areas – in the country. 'It's an intensely deprived community,' Chris tells me over a cup of tea. 'Whenever people talk about a recession or talk about a cost-of-living crisis – well, people who live in our community are always experiencing a cost-of-living crisis. It never goes away. Trickle-down economics doesn't work around here.'

The issues on the Stoops estate mirror those of Burnley itself. When I came here shortly after the riots, I was shocked to see so many houses boarded up. A *Guardian* article written in November 2001, titled 'Ghost Town',[9] noted that more than 5,000 homes in Burnley, 10 per cent of the total housing stock, were empty. In some parts of the town, there were literally entire streets where every house had metal boards covering the doorways. It was said that houses were on sale for £2,000 each, though even these lower prices were not enough to persuade people to move in. In fact, most of those who could, left the town. Even today, with many of the empty houses demolished and other parts of the town regenerated, Burnley, according to Which?, still has the cheapest housing of any town in the country.

CIVIC PRIDE

Historically, Burnley was built on the wool and later cotton industries, so much so that by the 1930s, 70 per cent of adults employed in the town worked in the cotton mills, and the town produced the largest quantities of cotton anywhere in the world. The cotton industry was complemented by the opening of a coalmine, and a network of canals and railways transported both to the domestic and international market. The Second World War heralded the decline of the textile industry and its replacement with engineering, and for many the post-war years were a boom time. Highly skilled, well-paid jobs were matched by success for Burnley FC, with the club winning the First Division title in the 1959/60 season and being runners-up two years later, when they also got to the FA Cup Final. In a clear boost for local pride, Burnley won the Lancashire Cup five out of six years between 1959 and 1966.

But the good times were not to last. By the early 1990s, engineering jobs began to decline, fast. In 1992, the engineering company BEP, which supplied Rolls Royce, among others, closed. This was followed in 1997 with the closure of Prestige, which made high-quality knives, forks and spoons, and then in 2002, the closure of the Michelin plant and the loss of 452 jobs. What new jobs came were largely unskilled and certainly lower paid. Shop Direct opened a call centre in the town, employing 300 people, and the site of the Prestige factory was used for a Sainsbury's supermarket. Economic decline was mirrored by Burnley FC's dismal performance, with the club slipping down all four divisions. Only a last-day win of the 1986/7 season against Leyton Orient prevented Burnley dropping out of the league altogether.

The collapse of engineering affected Stoops too. A stone's throw from the community centre were three factories that closed in the 2000s, Kirkstall Gears, Mullards (Philips), which made TV tubes before the invention of flatscreens and Lucas Aerospace plant, which supplied reheat jet pipes for use on the McDonnell Douglas Phantom F-4 jet fighters and car parts for Rolls Royce – it closed in 1987 with the loss of 800 jobs, many of which had been held by people who lived in the surrounding community. It was not until 2015 that the land on which the factory once sat was redeveloped.

When Chris talks about 'our' community, he's not exaggerating. He lives in the area and has been linked to the Stoops and Hargher Clough Community Centre for over 30 years, the last 15 as an unpaid volunteer. For Chris, it's personal.

The BNP might be a distant memory in the terraced streets of the Stoops estate, but the anger and disaffection they once exploited have not disappeared; nor have the underlying problems. Chris, who has been a community and youth worker for over 40 years, has seen it all. While the factories are long gone and new houses have been built on their land, economic and social problems persist. 'The area is stigmatised,' he says:

> If I think back to when we had regeneration funding, we set up, among other things, a wage subsidy project, because employers were prejudiced against people with a particular postcode. This provided employers with £500 when they took someone on with a BB11 4 or BB11 5 postcode. Then for the first six months the employer would get 50 per cent of the wage costs subsidised by this project, and for the second six months it was 25 per cent. If they still employed the person after 12 months they would get another £500 bonus.
>
> For the three years the project was in place, the number of local people employed in this community increased, but as soon as the wage subsidy was withdrawn the numbers employed dropped.

The area also suffers from huge health inequality, made worse by structural problems. There is not a single doctor's surgery in the ward, with the closest being on the other side of a motorway or in the town centre. A health clinic was built nearby, which was supposed to house a number of health services but is now largely empty due to a lack of investment. It once housed a two-day-per-week eye clinic for the local community, but when the grant to the provider was withdrawn, they quickly left. With only 40 per cent of households in the area having a car, many local residents are forced to make multiple bus journeys to get to appointments or receive treatment at hospitals and health centres across Lancashire. A late-running bus or a missed connection often means people losing their place and going to the back of the queue.

Under the Conservative administration, which took control of Lancashire County Council in 2017, most of the youth clubs were closed and the numbers of youth workers reduced to the bare minimum. In Burnley, that has meant the loss of three of the four youth clubs and 80 per cent of youth workers. 'The only youth club that is left is The Zone, in Burnley town centre, which offers a very limited range of services and isn't neighbourhood-based. You need to be where young people are, where the most vulnerable who are in need of support are.'

Chris rues the lack of contact between vulnerable young people and professionals. 'All these interventions on issues like racism, sexism, homophobia, all the things that you want to address, this work simply isn't being done now.'

This is a particularly acute issue on the Stoops estate. 'Persistent absence in this community is 28 per cent,' Chris tells me, up from 8 to 10 per cent in the pre-COVID days. Schools have tried everything to address this, but the figures remain stubbornly high:

> So those vulnerable young people the youth workers would traditionally identify, make contact with, engage with and then try to encourage them to come into buildings like this and engage with trained workers, such as the teenage sexual health project and anti-racist projects. All of those things that address behaviour these young people begin to display, well, that's all gone.

Filling the void are the criminal gangs, who use the young kids to carry and sell drugs and commit burglaries.

I catch the train out of Burnley with mixed emotions. On the one hand, I'm in awe of what Chris and his fellow volunteers do and have done over so many years to amazing effect, but at the same time I'm angry that many of the social ills we as a society like to complain about have been partly caused by cuts to services and staff. There are people like Chris doing amazing work in communities up and down the country, but it is a disgrace that it is left to volunteers to do this work. The last question I asked him was what kept him awake at night. As a project that now has to scrimp and save just to keep the lights on and can no longer afford to take local kids from the Stoops estate out on day trips to the Blackpool lights or Chester Zoo, I was expecting him to say money. But it was not.

'I'm 68 in a couple of months,' he told me quietly, 'and my colleagues are in their mid-70s. What happens when we go? Who will keep this place open? We're working with some younger volunteers to enable them to pick up the torch, but they're largely overwhelmed with the financial pressures of day-to-day life.'

He fears that without proper financial support, the building is likely to close, and with it the final bit of social capital on the estate.

Surely, as one of the wealthiest countries in the world, we can do better than this.

After years of fighting the BNP, Paul wanted to use the space provided by their demise to do something different. 'We were getting better and better at fighting the far right, but we were still fire-fighting and it was frustrating,' he told me. 'All our focus was on elections, and while it was important to stop far-right parties from winning, we were not changing anything on the ground':

> I just thought that this is precisely the period where we should be doing the sort of slow grind work of building trust in those communities and offering better solutions to the questions that

they had in a way that wasn't dependent on election timetables. So it just seemed to be a gift that we'd got this time. We don't know when the far right is going to pose an electoral threat again, but when they do we will be able to remind people what we have done alongside them over the years.

In the early autumn of 2016, three months after Labour MP Jo Cox was murdered by a far-right sympathiser, Paul and his team organised a community fun day in Bradford's Centenary Square, in the heart of the city centre. Hundreds of people enjoyed an array of food from the various communities in the city while listening to music, poems and dance. It was a dazzling display of colour, tastes and sounds. But, for Paul, it was not enough. While the event achieved its purpose, he was conscious there were few local white working-class people there, especially those from some of the city's more deprived communities. He decided to flip the work on its head. 'I realised that instead of trying to get people to come to town, we needed to go to where they were,' he would later tell me.

Paul organised a meeting up on the Buttershaw estate, one of the city's poorest, to gauge interest. Alongside local faith leaders and the police, one of those attending was Andy Walsh, who ran the Sandale Community Hub on the estate. Paul had grand ideas about what they could do, including a project to help train local young people in research skills to measure things about the local community that were often ignored in official statistics. All that was put on hold as COVID struck, and the project, like everything else, went into deep freeze.

COVID actually proved to be the making of the project: 'The value of the project and the value of our joint work with Andy really came to fruition.' While the authorities struggled to get anything organised for the most vulnerable, Paul joined up with Andy and his community service to help local people. 'We organised a "knock it up, knock a door", but you run,' laughs Paul, remembering how people had to leave food on the doorstep to avoid direct contact.

'We were delivering food parcels to every house where we knew there were children every day, and hot meals for the elderly and others who could not get out of their homes.'

The HOPE not hate team printed a letter that was hand-delivered to every home on the estate advertising the services available. In addition to what went to people's homes, HOPE not hate supporters donated over £8,000, which allowed Andy to transform a room in the community centre into a food bank – which continues to operate to this day. They also organised regular phone-in sessions, where volunteers could ring elderly people living on their own to have a chat and make sure they were all right. The project was so successful that the council soon diverted the delivery of its own support to this part of Bradford through the community centre.

Once COVID restrictions ended, Paul went back to putting on local community fun days to provide young families with entertainment for their kids in the summer holidays but also to introduce different communities, cultures and cuisines to local people. 'The first event we did was Buttershaw by the Beach,' Paul remembers. 'Many people around here don't have the money to go on expensive foreign holidays or even more expensive British holidays, so we thought we would bring the beach to them.' Almost 1,500 people attended. Two years later, at an event held at Bradford Park Avenue, home of the city's second football club, almost 4,000 attended. Each event was preceded by an eight- or 12-page community newspaper, which allowed us to both advertise the event and highlight positive local stories, encouraging participation in local sports clubs and voluntary groups and promoting local services that people were entitled to.

When I ask Paul about how he measures success, he pauses:

If you're looking for me to provide statistics that racism was 7.3 and now it's 4.1, well, I can't do that. I don't know how anyone could do that. I'm sure that racism still is a massive problem up there, and presumably there will be an above-average predilection to vote for the far right than in other places. But anecdotally, I can answer it.

My favourite story comes from one of the Buttershaw community events. There were two old fellas at one of these events, and me and Andy had both overheard them saying, 'We're not bothering. We only hear there's that foreign muck', as they passed a stall where Syrian refugees had cooked this amazing food. These people had never seen a falafel in their life.

But later on in the day they got lured in. When I passed the stall as I was going for a break these same two blokes were chatting to the Syrian refugees. They were there standing around all drinking black Kurdish tea together and getting on like a house on fire.

I hope it's not just naivety, but I hope that they may have learned something that day and the next time that they get a leaflet, whether it's from Reform or someone else, they might just think differently.

In 2025, Paul organised his most ambitious initiative yet to tie in with Bradford's City of Culture status. While the official organisers were putting on high-end culture in the city centre, Paul organised another community fun day, but this time at Odsal Stadium, home of the Bradford Bulls rugby league club with a crowd of 10,000 people. A number of smaller feeder events were held across the city, in both white British and British Muslim areas, which saw young people link up with local artists to produce murals on the theme of modern Bradford and anti-racism. In addition to this, kids from across the city came from their own neighbourhoods to form a huge procession before walking into the big event at the Odsal Stadium.

The ethos behind Paul's work, and that best describes our approach to community organising, is the admission that Bradford is a deeply divided city, where communities live parallel lives and don't mix or even have much to do with one another. From this starting point, our work is about breaking down these barriers in small, incremental ways. 'It's not the events themselves that are central, though of course they are important, but it is always the building of the events that were in a way more important,' says Paul:

> I'd like to think that what we are doing is a qualitative step forward, whereby we're bringing far more people together and far more people from different backgrounds together. We want to be at the centre of the drive for building social cohesion in the city.
>
> We are trying to get people, especially the kids, to think about what it means to be a Bradfordian. To us it's about place and it's about civic pride, because we know wherever we've worked, whether it's been in Oldham or Bradford, or wherever that is where there's problems with civic pride, that creates almost like a vacuum that the far right can feed off. So sense of place and pride in place is really important.

'To move forward, we need to be honest about where we are now,' adds Paul:

> It's about people. And how damaging is it when you've got white kids in this city who are embarrassed to say [they are] from Bradford? Take kids in Bradford East, your family goes on holiday, everyone's got the new football shirt on. They've got Leeds shirts on, because they don't want to be from Bradford. If people ask them where they're from, they say Leeds, because they're embarrassed, because they know if they said Bradford, they're going to get a load of racist fucking rubbish thrown at them.

In response to the appalling violent disorder that spread to over 25 towns and cities following the murder of three young girls at a Southport dance studio in the summer of 2024, HOPE not hate wrote a submission to the Cohesion Commission, which had been established to devise a new approach to community cohesion. At the core of our submission was building resilient communities. 'Resilient communities have the sustained ability to use available resources to withstand, and recover from adverse situations or disruptive challenges, both natural and man-made, sudden or chronic,' wrote Misbah Malik, who now heads our community team. 'Resilience is crucial for sustainable and thriving communities, as it allows for the adaptation and growth of a community during and after periods of hardship.'

Misbah went on to explain that more resilient communities are better able to use their social, economic and political capital and resources to overcome the challenges they face: 'Resilient communities are able to reject this divisive rhetoric, turning towards and leaning on each other during times of stress rather than turning away from each other.'

It is long-term work in building more cohesive communities with the skills and resources to respond to challenges, tensions and trigger-events when they occur that is vitally needed. This must happen on a community level by councils, voluntary and community groups and campaign groups like HOPE not hate, but it must also be driven and supported at a national level too, and this requires both funding and a change in mindset. The government and the civil service need to learn to devolve power and funding, not just down to local councils but to the very groups and people doing the work on the ground. It is local people, at the heart of every community, who have most to lose when things go wrong. And it is local people who have most to gain when our communities are stronger and more resilient.

HOPE not hate is spending an ever-increasing amount of its time on building social capital and community resilience. We intend to expand our Bradford work to other communities vulnerable to far-right rhetoric and division, combining local community development and organising with the production of community newspapers to help spread our message and encourage community participation. At the same time, we have embarked on a new project to build community events in several of the towns and cities impacted by the recent riots, and a few others that did not see disorder last summer but are still vulnerable to the far right. Working with local community groups, we are putting on fun days, holding events, offering resilience training and producing local newspapers. Our slogan for this campaign is: 'When HOPE comes to town'.

11

Young Angry Men

Ask any parent, especially one with teenage boys, and they will share their anxieties over what their child is viewing on the internet and to whom they might be chatting online. In fact, these concerns spread far beyond the family home, with teachers, counter-terrorist police and even Home Office ministers expressing their alarm to us at the rise of extremism, particularly aggressive misogyny, among teenagers and young men. The issue was graphically depicted in the Stephen Graham Netflix drama *Adolescence*, in which a 13-year-old boy stabs a schoolgirl to death who had been mocking him on social media.

Keir Starmer told the makers of *Adolescence* that it was 'really hard to watch', as he hosted a Downing Street meeting to discuss the influence of toxic material online. He added that it shone a light 'on misogyny, on online content, and this sense of children, particularly boys, getting drawn in to this world'. The BBC described it as sparking 'a national conversation about the impact of social media and "manosphere" influencers'.[1] The *Big Issue* said it highlighted the 'buildup of misogynistic ideas as Jamie is radicalised'.[2]

While most people found the drama deeply troubling, few commentators or politicians offered any real solutions to the problems it depicted.

* * *

Young men have long had a reputation for being unruly, getting involved in gangs and causing trouble. From the Hooligan Boys of Lambeth in the 1870s, to the early disorder at football games in the 1880s; from the Teddy Boys in the fifties to the seaside town battles between mods and rockers in the sixties; from the skinheads in the seventies to the football hooligans in more recent times. Young men have also had a long history of racist violence in Britain too. Police reports from the 1919 race riots in Liverpool recount how 'a well organised gang consisting principally of youths and young men, soldiers and sailors, ages of most of them ranging from 18 to 30 years … commenced savagely attacking, beating and stabbing every negro they could find in the street',[3] while Geoff Pearson's essay '"Paki-Bashing" in a North East Lancashire Cotton Town' recounts the racist attacks on recent arrivals from Pakistan in Accrington in 1964.[4] More recently, the NF launched a youth wing in 1978, with membership restricted to 14- and 15-year-olds, and then launched *Bulldog*, which glorified racist violence among football fans. At roughly the same time, first Rock Against Communism and later Blood & Honour mobilised young racist skinheads around music, while the British Movement's Honour Guard put racist thugs on the street.

All the same, what is happening to some of our young people appears quite different now from what has gone on before. Young people are much more likely to be radicalised at home than on the streets, transnational movements are increasingly replacing national – and nationalist – organisations, middle-class kids have entered a previously working-class world, misogyny and anti-feminism are increasingly replacing traditional racism and the levels of violence are becoming ever more extreme.

Improvements in gender equality, and the feminist campaigns driving them forward, have been met by opposition and resistance from many men, especially online. We have seen women, especially women in the public eye, being targeted, abused, vilified, violently attacked and even killed. Aggressive misogyny is becoming increasingly common in classrooms, and an anti-feminist theme runs through much of the far-right's rhetoric. What we now define as the manosphere is a loose collection of websites, forums, blogs and vlogs concerned with men's issues and masculinity, oriented around an opposition to feminism and, within certain spheres, an embrace of extreme misogyny. At its heart is the belief that feminism is more about contempt for men than it is gender equality.

According to HOPE not hate's Simon Murdoch, writing in 2019, 'the often deeply conspiratorial worldview of the manosphere is crystallised by the manosphere's use of the "red pill" term: a metaphor for the process of awakening to the truth of some aspect of reality that has supposedly been hidden by progressives and elites'.[5] While the term first emerged at the turn of the century, it only came to common usage a decade later with the rise of the alt-right and in particular with the creation of the 'r/TheRedPill' subforum of the popular forum site Reddit.com in 2012.

In the UK, the issue of aggressive misogyny and online radicalisation really came to the public's attention in the summer of 2022 when the American-born but Luton-raised Andrew Tate emerged as one of the world's most prominent social media influencers. His videos had been watched a total of 11 billion times on TikTok alone, and his name was the second most searched for term on Google, with only Donald Trump above him. A former world kickboxing champion, Tate has inspired a generation of young men with his aggressive machismo, his negative and even violent views towards women and his glorification of wealth and money making. An old-time friend of Stephen Lennon, Tate's politics, adoption of conspiracy theories about a global cabal out to rule people's lives, violent misogyny and obscene love of money encapsulate the shifting dangers of extremism highlighted in our polling and policy work.

Tate's profile and reach are quite staggering. A poll of 18- to 24-year-olds commissioned by HOPE not hate in January 2023 found 97 per cent had heard of him, with 26 per cent having a positive view of him and 30 per cent having a negative view. When it came to just males, 46 per cent liked him and only 25 per cent disliked him.[6] The figures were even more startling among 16- to 17-year-old males. Here, 54 per cent liked him, while just 18 per cent did not. His appeal was broad, with more Muslim boys liking him than their white counterparts. A larger polling of 22,500 people, conducted by HOPE not hate in December 2024, found that 81 per cent of Britons had heard of Tate, with 12 per cent liking him and 44 per cent disliking him.

In the summer of 2022, as the media began writing articles about Tate, HOPE not hate decided to act. Our research team produced a dossier setting out his history and beliefs. Our education team were able to take the research and use it to inform safeguarding leads and other teachers of the risk Tate posed to young people and run teacher training on the issue, and our campaigns team called for Tate to be removed from social media platforms. We do not call for the de-platforming of figures lightly, and we understand that social media is an important space for debate and disagreement. However, Tate's aggressive misogyny, including glorification of rape, posed such a risk to impressionable young people that we had to act.

Our campaign was a great success, and within a matter of days, YouTube, TikTok, Instagram, Facebook and Twitter had removed his accounts.[7] While Tate moved his operation to alternative and less-regulated platforms like Rumble, his removal from mainstream platforms made it harder for ordinary people to reach and share. Perhaps just as importantly, it shone a light on the problem of misogyny – which of course did not start or end with Andrew Tate.

Gradually, Tate was later reinstated to most of the platforms, and despite numerous allegations of rape, human trafficking and assault, he continues to inspire and provoke. The conviction of Kyle Clifford for the murders of Carol, Louise and Hannah Hunt at their home in Bushey, Hertfordshire, in July 2024 and the rape of Louise Hunt during the attack sadly highlighted the growing problem of violent misogyny and the influence of Tate. Prosecutors at Cambridge Crown Court said Clifford's actions were fuelled by the 'violent misogyny promoted' by Tate, even listening to his podcast on the day before the attack.

HOPE not hate launched its education work in 2015, and eight years on we had become the second-largest provider of anti-prejudice training in schools, after Show Racism the Red Card. We used data from our Fear & HOPE reports to target schools in communities that were most susceptible to far-right narratives, with a particular focus on the smaller communities and towns in East Anglia and the East Midlands. Leading our work was Owen Jones, a young organiser who first got involved with HOPE not hate in the 2009 European elections when he was a student union officer at Leicester University. He went on to become our Midlands organiser and did some amazing community organising in Dudley.

The highlight of our first year's work was a course run for seven- to 14-year-olds in conjunction with Colchester United Football Club, linking our message of inclusivity and tolerance with football. Within a year, we were engaging with 12,779 pupils, had created 216 HOPE not hate School Ambassadors and had visited 63 schools. We began to broaden our work, offering students a more holistic understanding of how discrimination manifested itself and was maintained through prejudice and inequality.

We also ran training sessions for teachers, advising them on the far right and helping them to identify the signs of radicalisation. A particularly pleasing part of our work was the feedback that came from the young people themselves, with four out of five describing the training in positive terms.

The Education Unit really came of age in 2018. We expanded the scope of our work to deliver a robust syllabus around prejudice and discrimination, with several standalone workshops that interlinked to provide schools with a dynamic offering rather than just one-off sessions. Using our research team's work, we began delivering lessons on the manosphere. By the following year, in addition to doubling the number of teachers we trained, our Education Unit had become known as a leader in the field of informal education, and our materials were made available for download on the Department for Education's website. In 2021, we published *Signs of Hate*, a resource for teachers and other public sector workers to learn about and develop the skills to spot far-right terms, symbols and codes. We posted a copy of this book to safeguarding leads in every secondary school in England and Wales.

The scale of the problem in schools was clear from a poll of over 4,000 teachers we undertook in February 2024. Almost seven in 10 teachers had heard 'hateful language' in the first term of that school year, with 36 per cent having heard pupils mention 'extreme individuals' and 18 per cent witnessing their pupils 'encouraging or endorsing the targeting of specific groups'. Four in five teachers had seen some form of prejudice from pupils in the same period, with 61 per cent seeing homophobia, 55 per cent racism and 41 per cent aggressive misogyny.[8]

In light of the increasing number of teenagers becoming involved in far-right extremism and terrorism, we conducted a review of our education work in 2024. We decided to scale back the scope of what we were delivering in schools and focus more narrowly on youth radicalisation, and hateful and harmful views.

Despite the depressing feedback from teachers, young people in the UK remain overwhelmingly progressive, tolerant, open-minded and anti-racist. In the 2024 General Election, YouGov estimates that only 9 per cent of 18- to 24-year-olds voted for Reform, far fewer than the 41 per cent and 18 per cent who backed Labour and the Greens respectively.[9] Our own polling has consistently shown that young people have more progressive views than older people. This is not to say that some young people do not hold reactionary and prejudiced views, but these people are in a clear minority. This can be explained by young people having other priorities and experiencing different economic stresses than older people, but also because of changing demographics, with almost a quarter of those under 25 being from an ethnic minority background. This has meant young people are more likely to interact with people from other ethnic and religious groups than older people.

This is in sharp contrast to the situation in several other European countries, where the young are increasingly voting for far-right parties. In the 2025 German federal elections, 21 per cent of 18- to 24-year-olds and 23 per cent of 25- to 34-year-olds voted for the far-right AfD, compared to just 10 per cent of those over 70 years of age. In France, 33 per cent of 18- to 24-year-olds voted for Marine Le Pen's National Rally in the national elections of 2024. With young people also backing parties of the left, the main losers in both countries were centrist parties.

The situation is starting to change in the UK, with our latest polling showing 15 per cent support for Reform among 18- to 24-year-olds, though this is in line with the doubling of support for the party since the General Election. While young people as a whole remain progressive and more tolerant than older people, there is a clear and growing group who not only have increasingly right-wing views but probably because of the internet and the role of social media influencers also have a shared identity, language and focus. In the summer of 2020, at the height of the BLM movement, our educators began hearing young people in different parts of the country raising the issue of how homeless British veterans were being left without help on the street. At first, we could not understand why the same issue was being discussed in schools so far apart until we learnt that it had been raised by a popular right-wing YouTuber a few days before.

We are also witnessing a growing gender gap between the attitudes of young men and young women. Among 18- to 24-year-olds, 18 per cent of men say they would now vote Reform, compared with 7 per cent of women in the same age group. Almost twice as many young men as women think immigration has had a negative impact on their local community, while almost half of young men (47 per cent) agree that 'feminism has gone too far and makes it harder for men to succeed', compared to just 19 per cent of young women. Perhaps unsurprisingly, young men are twice as likely as young women to like Tommy Robinson.[10]

In a study of 2,040 young people, conducted in the summer of 2024, HOPE not hate found a growing group of young people with reactionary and hateful attitudes. Report author Anki Deo, who now runs our data and insight team, noted that:

> an escalation of culture wars around issues like trans rights and #MeToo, a mainstreaming of conspiracy theories post-COVID-19 and the explosion of online misinformation resulting from a lack of responsibility shown by social media companies has emoted reactionary responses and deepened divides not just amongst young people, but across the whole of society. All of this is happening against a backdrop of political and economic instability.

The poll findings highlighted the increasing complexity of young people's political views, with many young people holding progressive views on some issues and reactionary views on others, possibly reflecting how they accessed and consumed content in the social media age. 'Hateful attitudes do not exist in isolation: stereotypes, debates around identity and conspiracy theories are frequent in media, political discourse,' Anki noted:

> This content has never been more accessible than it is now due to its prevalence and popularity online. Young people today have been raised with technology and the internet, with social media companies competing for their attention and advertisers for their custom. Technologies are changing and advancing at a pace that makes it hard for adults working with young children to keep up with. The long-term impact of extensive social media use in young people is still yet to be seen.[11]

* * *

The internet has obviously transformed how we do politics and consume news, probably more so for young people. Far-right content, which was once the preserve of smoked-filled pubs, boring newspapers and long-winded speeches, is now available in a format that is both accessible and watchable. An increasing number of young people get their news almost entirely from social media platforms, where far-right content is glorified, conspiracy theories are common, immigrants are linked to violence and progressives are mocked. What were once complex political theories, such as the Great Replacement, which states that Western elites are conspiring to undermine or 'replace' the political power and culture of white people living in Western countries, or Eurabia, a conspiracy theory that claims there is a determined plot for the Islamic takeover of Europe, are now distilled and spread in 30-second videos. Few far-right activists will have read the works of the French novelist Renaud Camus on the Great Replacement or Bat Ye'or's book *Eurabia*, but many will know enough to align themselves with these books and the ideas within them.

Social media companies must take some responsibility for the growing attraction and accessibility of far-right narratives for young people. 'Algorithms on social media platforms also play a role in reinforcing radical ideologies,' claims Vision of Humanity in an article on youth radicalisation: 'Young users engaging with extremist content are frequently exposed to more of the same, creating echo chambers where radical views are normalised.'[12] A 2024 study by academics at University College London, the University of Kent and the Association of School and College Leaders found that social media algorithms amplify extreme content, which helps normalise harmful ideologies for young people. In an algorithmic modelling study, the report 'found a fourfold increase in the level of misogynistic content in the "For You" page of TikTok accounts over just five days on the platform'.[13]

The internet has also transformed the class nature of the British far right. Unlike many other European countries, Britain has not had a recent tradition of intellectual fascism. While there has been the odd exception, the vast majority of people who have been active in the far right, certainly since the 1970s, have come from working-class backgrounds. Perhaps this is not too surprising given Britain's drinking and fighting culture and how this has influenced the social movements that have long fed the far right, such as the skinhead and football hooligan sub-cultures. As the internet's influence has grown, so has the importance of these youth sub-cultures waned, resulting in a growing number of more middle-class and affluent young people being drawn into the far right.

One only has to compare those centrally involved in the nazi terror group C18 in the 1990s to those involved in NA and its spin-offs to see the changing class make-up of the far right. Those involved in C18 were almost exclusively from working-class backgrounds, with many also involved in the football hooligan scene and petty criminality. By contrast, many of those who have been convicted of terrorism in more recent years come from quite affluent backgrounds. There was Harry Vaughan, the son of a senior House of Lords clerk who attended an exclusive London boys' school. Then there was Luke Hunter, convicted of seven terror-related offences, including encouragement of terrorism, in 2020,[14] whose father was a former senior counter-terrorism officer and mother a top executive with Johnson & Johnson.[15] The father of Andrew Dymock, the leader of the nazi Satanist group the Sonnenkrieg Division, is a professor of dentistry at Bristol University. There are numerous other examples.

An important moment in the development of a radicalised far-right culture among young men in the UK came following the 2017 terrorist attacks in London and Manchester, which led to the formation of the Football Lads Alliance and a march through London attended by 50,000 people, and then their reaction to the growth of the BLM movement, which emerged in the immediate aftermath of the death of George Floyd in Minneapolis in late May 2020. While most Britons were supportive of calls for solidarity and addressing racism, discrimination and racial inequality, a sizeable minority were not. Among them were many young men. The visual symbolism of the statue of Bristol slave trader Edward Colston being thrown into the River Avon delighted those disgusted by slavery but repulsed others. This sense of outrage was heightened further when the statue of Winston Churchill in Parliament Square was daubed with graffiti. While of course it was quite possible to support calls for racial equality while also being sickened by the Churchill statue being attacked, in the polarised world of social media, this desecration of our history was seen as an attack on British history and Britishness. Across the country, large groups of football hooligans met up to 'defend our monuments', while in London, the Democratic Football Lads Alliance, a spin-off from the Football Lads Alliance, called a protest in central London that resulted in widespread violent clashes with police. And it was not just the far right attempting to derail the conversation.

The supposed battle of statues quickly became the most significant fault line in the culture wars. While no one of significance publicly called for these statues to be desecrated, the issue was used day after day in the right-wing media to attack the left and the movement for racial equality.

A year later, the Conservative government tried to weaponise the culture wars in the face of a right-wing backlash against footballers taking the knee ahead of games to highlight the issue of racism. At the start of the European Championships, which were taking place in the UK, Home Secretary Priti Patel refused to condemn fans who booed players for taking the knee and described the footballers' actions as 'gesture politics'.[16] There was an immediate backlash against her comments, helped by the success of the England team, with 59 per cent believing she was wrong to make them, including 49 per cent of Conservative voters. However, a significant minority of people, including 33 per cent of men, agreed with her.

There will be some who will argue that the growth in reactionary attitudes among young males is a consequence of white supremacy being challenged by women and minority communities, and it therefore needs to be confronted and not appeased. While there might be an element of truth to that, it is not a full explanation. There are different groups of white males, some who are doing very well in society and others who are not. Those who are not doing well feel increasingly disadvantaged and disengaged from the political system and believe their identity is being ignored or even attacked.

A report produced by the Education Select Committee and published in 2021 set out the problem well, explaining how white working-class children do far worse at school, even when compared to others in the same economic situation.[17] Statistics for white working-class boys are even more stark.

Matthew Goodwin, giving evidence to the cross-party Education Committee, claimed that the national conversation over the past decade had become 'much more consumed with other groups', and disadvantaged white families felt they were not afforded the same recognition, respect and esteem as others. The writer Kenan Malik disagreed. 'The problems that white, working-class children face have little to do with being white and much to do with being working class,' he wrote in response to Goodwin's intervention:

> The status deficit felt by many white, working-class communities is real. The cause, though, isn't 'other groups' grabbing the attention, but an array of economic, social and political changes – the transformation of the labour market, the weakening of trade unions, the savaging of public services, Labour's shift away from its traditional constituencies – that have upended the social standing of the working class.
>
> We need to stop thinking about the problems faced by the 'white working class' in terms of its whiteness and look upon class in a non-racialised sense.[18]

Lee Elliot Major and Emily Briant have critiqued the education system in their book *Equity in Education: Levelling the Playing Field of Learning*, which blames a mindset in education that treats working-class children as 'inferior' and requires them to become 'middle-class clones' in order to succeed in school. They argue that it is not just a question of other groups moving ahead, but white working-class children, especially boys, falling behind.

Failing in education, and being told their culture is inferior, makes young men increasingly susceptible to voices telling them to be proud of who they are – and this helps explain the appeal of Andrew Tate. While the media primarily focuses on Tate's misogyny, his popularity is far broader and centres largely on male assertiveness and an unabashed glorification of wealth. Likewise, support for Stephen Lennon is about more than just his views on Muslims or immigration. Lennon has cleverly tapped into his supporters' broader sense of victimhood and disadvantage, and people see his struggles as theirs. He literally fights for them at a time when they feel no one else does.

Young people's increasing involvement in the far right has been even more pronounced in loose networks that are formed online and on social media platforms. 'Groups are usually started as small chat groups on popular chat app Telegram or gaming adjacent platforms like Discord by people as young as 15,' my colleague Patrik Hermansson wrote in HOPE not hate's report on youth radicalisation 'Plugged In But Disconnected':

> It is a worrying trend that has been aided by an increasingly social media-centred way of organising in the wider far right.
>
> The groups have used Instagram and TikTok to reach out to new potential members and to promote their activities, which usually include offline activism such as stickering and flyering, as well as graffiti, physical training activity and banner drops over bridges.[19]

The groups tend not to be around long, but they act as a window for young people to engage with the broader far-right world: 'The groups have provided stepping stones into the movement and educated the members in far-right activism. Members of groups have later attended far-right demonstrations and some are involved in terror-related criminal cases.'

A growing number of teenage boys are becoming attracted to nazi terrorism and extreme violence, with 31 teenagers being convicted of terror-related offences in 2022 alone. While changes to terrorist legislation and police enforcement account for the explosion of convictions, it still remains true that more young people are dabbling in violent far-right extremism than before. What's even more alarming is that many are revelling in gratuitous violence, sexual mutilation, indecent images of children and nazi Satanism.

Harry Vaughan, the son of a clerk at the House of Lords, as mentioned earlier, was convicted of 14 terror offences in 2020 and admitted further crimes including possession of indecent images of children, as well as videos of young boys being raped. Despite the severity of his offences, Vaughan was only given a suspended prison sentence, with the judge telling him that the shame of being arrested and the trial was punishment enough. There was also the case of Jack Reed from Durham, who was convicted of plotting a terrorist attack and unrelated child sexual offences. He told police that he raped a young girl in an attempt to desensitise himself before embarking on a terror campaign. Reed was just 13 at the time of his arrest. The common thread linking Reed, Vaughan and a number of others convicted of terrorist offences and found to be in possession of sexual images of children was involvement in nazi Satanism, principally the Order of Nine Angles (O9A). Formed in the late 1960s, the O9A is arguably the world's most extreme Satanist group and has been linked to murders, sexual assaults and paedophilia across Europe and North America.

One of O9A's most popular channels on the social media platform Telegram was called 'RapeWaffen'.[20] The conversation in this channel glorified sexual violence and encouraged using it as a political weapon. Young O9A supporters in the UK were also consciously sent child sexual abuse images by the group's leader in the US as a way to prove they were outside the norms of society. While the O9A are at the very extreme end of the nazi movement, their propaganda has been widely circulated among young far-right activists since the emergence of youth-led nazi groups in the 2010s.

O9A have operated under different guises. In the UK, O9A followers have been involved in NA and later the Sonnenkrieg Division. In the US, the O9A operated as the Tempel ov Blood and largely controlled the nazi terrorist group the Atomwaffen Division, whose members killed several people. Among them was Devon Arthur, the group's co-founder, who killed two other Atomwaffen members; Sam Woodward, who killed a gay, Jewish US university student in California; and Nicholas Giampa, who shot his girlfriend's parents in 2017, after they forbade her to date him because of his nazi views. More recently, O9A has re-emerged with a heavy influence on the online network called '764' that revels in violence and suffering for its own sake and operates across hundreds of online chat rooms in Europe and North America. In 2024, two British teenagers linked to the group were convicted under terrorism legislation, and at least two others have been arrested. A Swedish chapter took on the slogan 'No Lives Matter.'[21]

The emergence of 764 highlights another increasingly common global trend, whereby a growing number of young people appear driven not by ideology but by a desire for extreme violence. In the United States, this has become the most common form of domestic terrorism in the last few years, leading the FBI to deploy a new term to describe it – Nihilistic Violent Extremism (NVE).

According to the FBI, NVE refers to 'individuals who engage in criminal conduct within the United States and abroad, in furtherance of political, social, or religious goals that derive primarily from a hatred of society at large and a desire to bring about its collapse by sowing indiscriminate chaos, destruction, and social instability'.

HOW TO DEFEAT THE FAR RIGHT

In her book *Black Pill: How I Witnessed the Darkest Corners of the Internet Come to Life, Poison Society, and Capture American Politics*, the CNN journalist Elle Reeve describes how people on platforms like 4chan deal in explicit nihilism. 'The black pill,' she writes,

> is a dark but gleeful nihilism: the system is corrupt, and its collapse is inevitable. There is no hope. Times are bad and they're going to get worse. You swallow the black pill and accept the end is coming.
>
> You start searching for evidence to prove to yourself that you're correct, and it's easy to find … The hardships and a heartbreak you've faced can now be explained as the inevitability of a sweeping historical force.

The horrific murder of three young girls at a dance studio in Southport appears to fit into this category. Rudakubana appeared fascinated with extreme violence, and just as he downloaded al-Qaeda manuals he also searched for information on the IRA and other terrorist organisations. The same could probably be said of Nicholas Prosper, the 19-year-old who was sentenced to 49 years' imprisonment for murdering three members of his family in Luton in 2024. Prosper had planned to go and kill people at a local school and told police on his arrest that he wanted to be known as the most famous school-shooter of the twenty-first century.

Over the years, I have met about 200 people who have been in the far right. Some have come to HOPE not hate out of remorse, while others have offered to sell us information. Some want to unburden themselves from what they've done and then walk away, while others are keen for their story to be a warning to others. When I watched *Adolescence*, I immediately thought of James Crow, a young man now in his late 20s, who for several years was active in the far-right group Britain First. James is not your run-of-the-mill extremist. He is quietly spoken, lacks confidence and is clearly sensitive. It seems hard to imagine him active in a group surrounded by aggressive racism. James has cerebral palsy and, largely because of this, was badly bullied at school. Day in, day out, for several years, he was picked on by a gang at school. He reported what was going on to teachers, but nothing changed. He became more and more isolated, playing hours of video games alone until he eventually built a replica of his secondary school on the popular computer game Minecraft, using it to plan a knife attack on his bullies and on the teachers he felt had ignored him.

He went to school one day with the intention of carrying out his planned attack, but fortunately he was too scared to go through with it. He took the kitchen knife back home and quietly put it back in the drawer.

At about the time he was leaving school, James became friends with someone who displayed clearly racist views. James began to copy his newfound friend's behaviour. Within a short space of time, James ended up contacting Britain First, a far-right group whose members were attracting headlines by filming themselves entering mosques and walking through areas with a large Muslim presence in order to intimidate local communities. For the next three years, James was a Britain First activist, travelling around the country attending meetings and leafleting sessions. The trigger for his decision to leave the far right came when he travelled to Calais, France, and saw first-hand the appalling conditions many migrants were experiencing and listened to their stories about the lives they had left behind to risk trying to cross the English Channel. Suddenly, James' hate was replaced by empathy. He turned his back on Britain First and approached anti-fascists with his story in the hope he could deter others.

Time and again, far-right activists have told me about incidents in their childhood that helped put them on the path to extremism. I've heard repeated stories of the bullied becoming the bully. As with James, the far right offer a chance to reverse one's own situation, to finally feel superior and to assert power over – and instil fear in – others.

Social isolation is another key driver for extremism. In the summer of 2017, Robbie Mullen's life turned upside-down when he reported to HOPE not hate's Matthew Collins that one of his friends was planning to kill Labour MP Rosie Cooper. Robbie was a key activist in the nazi group NA, which the home secretary had proscribed as a terrorist group a few months before and ordered to disband. Of course, the group never did disband, and every week Mullen and his fellow NA members would meet up to train, plot and plan.

For the 22-year-old from Runcorn, who had left school at 14 shortly after the death of his father, NA quickly became a family, one that he was missing. Being involved in NA was exciting and gave him the sense of belonging he lacked.

The ban changed things for Robbie. As the talk turned to violence and terrorism, he became scared. Fearing his future was jail or death, he reached out to Matthew at HOPE not hate for help to get out of the far right. Matthew had himself been a nazi as a teenager and could empathise with Robbie's story. The initial plan was to debrief Robbie and literally empty his mind of everything he knew about NA. A few weeks after reaching out, Robbie reported to Matthew that Jack Renshaw, a former BNP youth activist who had emerged as a significant figure within NA, was planning to kill his local MP as well as a female police officer who was investigating him for a racist speech he had given 15 months before, and that he hoped the police would kill him. Robbie instantly knew he had to tell us about Renshaw's plan, not least because it was only days away from happening. He knew that doing this meant his life was never going to be the same again. Renshaw eventually pleaded guilty to attempting to murder the MP and the police officer. What Robbie did not know at the time he passed on the details of the plot was that Renshaw was facing additional charges of grooming minors. It appears that the fear of going to prison for this and being known throughout the movement as a sex offender had propelled Renshaw to come up with the murder plot.

While Robbie's story is exceptional in many ways, the sense of social isolation and boredom that drove him into the far right in the first place is sadly all too common. Likewise, while Renshaw's murder plot was highly extreme and unusual, there are several features about his story that we have found increasingly commonplace in recent years. His hatred of MPs – women MPs especially – is often found among the violent far right. The far right used to view women as homemakers and mothers. Today, they often despise women and consider them the target of sexual violence. The threat of rape has increasingly been used as a political weapon in extreme far-right propaganda.

With a growing number of young people being drawn into extreme far-right violence, the focus of the authorities is understandably on stopping acts of terrorism and extreme violence, but more must be done to divert young people from getting to this stage in the first place. It is essential that social media companies are held accountable for their role in introducing young people to extreme violence, misogyny and far-right ideas through their algorithms, and there must be no watering down of regulation under pressure from the US. The school environment is another place for interacting with vulnerable young people, but as our research and polling graphically shows, teachers are over-stretched, schools are under-resourced and a significant number of young people are excluded from or are skipping school. In years gone by, some of these young people might have been picked up by youth workers – but they, and the youth clubs they worked in, are now few and far between.

While dealing with violent extremism and terrorism will require a law enforcement response, it is also important not just to rely on top-down solutions. When Prime Minister Starmer says that he and others have no solutions to the online misogyny highlighted in *Adolescence*, we could and should be involving the young people themselves. Young people are best placed to respond to youth extremism, and it has been from among them that successful counter-cultures have emerged. In much the same way that Rock Against

Racism used music to mobilise a generation against the NF in the late 1970s, and projects like Kick It Out and Show Racism the Red Card have used football to spread anti-racism, the answer to misogynistic and far-right ideas must come from young people themselves. That might involve us supporting them with funding and opportunities, or it might just be leaving them to be themselves.

In the centre of Hull, perhaps 100 metres from the main shopping street, there is something very rare. The Warren is a 1,500 square-metre youth centre, hosting a digital hub, recording studios, rehearsal rooms and a mini studio. It provides mental health services, counselling and a complementary therapy service for young people. It provides employment services and skills support, free food for all its users and a kitchen where young people can learn to cook. On the roof of the three-storey building, there is a rooftop sensory garden, and there is space for young people just to chill out, to sit there until they are ready to engage.

'We're also an Arts Council England national portfolio organisation, which means that the art and music produced by the young people at The Warren is deemed to be of as much national importance as something produced by the Royal Shakespeare Company,' says JJ Tatten, The Warren's CEO.

While JJ might be the CEO, The Warren is actually run by the young people themselves through a fortnightly parliament and various sub-committees that derive from it. Established in 1983, the centre recently received £1.9 million from the Youth Investment Fund, and it was the young people themselves who decided on the changes they wanted and helped create the bid.

Youth clubs are an increasingly rare sight in Britain's urban landscape. Research released in 2024 by the trade union Unison found that 1,243 council-run youth centres across England and Wales were closed between 2010 and 2023, and 42 per cent of local authorities had no council-run youth centre in their area by the end of 2022/3.[22] The problem doesn't stop at the closure of buildings. The YMCA in

England and Wales estimates that 4,500 youth work jobs have been lost since 2010, with 600 going in London alone, and without the jobs there has been a sharp reduction in universities offering youth work courses.[23] In total, the YMCA estimates a 73 per cent drop in funding for youth services between 2010 and 2024.[24]

Unison warned that these cuts 'have left vulnerable youngsters across some of Britain's most-deprived communities isolated and exposed to a rising tide of mental health challenges, anti-social behaviour, drugs, gangs, knife crime and child sexual exploitation'.

Back at The Warren, JJ is under no illusion about the pressures young people face today:

> I'm in my late 50s and I think I've probably got more in common with my grandfather's generation than I do with young people now, because they are growing up in a fundamentally different world where the advent of social media and technology is a significant factor in their lives.
>
> It's actually made them more disconnected, not more connected. Algorithms have pushed people into tribes. Now you think of the youth sub-cultures of the past, the skinheads, mods and others, these tribes used to come together in the youth club. They would be in a youth centre, there would be music on but they would have to take their turn when things were played. But now these tribes are set apart and the tribes are more driven by hate and a pursuit of blame for how they feel, are what have been created in the absence of coming together. Young people are more separated than they ever were before.

There has been a move to bring youth workers into schools and even A&E departments as part of a broader provision to support young people, but JJ thinks this goes against the core principles of youth work:

What young people need is their own space to be together, so young people can come together, encountering different outlooks, different attitudes, different races, different ethnicities, different genders, all of that.

It is in this environment that young people can explore and understand differences:

You can't hate somebody you come to like, you can't hate somebody who helps you. If you're around them all the time, and you build a relationship with them, or at the very least have a fundamental, basic understanding of who they are. Then you find it difficult to hate them, because myths have no impact on you, propaganda has no impact on you, because you're seeing the real thing. And that is what is most important about youth centres. It's something that was never really, truly understood.

But for JJ and other true adherents of the youth worker model, it is about putting faith in young people. When I ask him about his reaction to the *Adolescent* drama and my own reflections on middle-class angst, he laughs:

I call that the cyclone of concern. And in the cyclone of concern, the first thing that gets lost is the youth voice. They talk to it, the people who are concerned are not bad people. They have all the best intentions, but they are panicking. And in that panic, they talk to each other. They come to their own conclusions, and they completely miss the point that one of the driving factors behind all of this is a lack of personal agency. Young people have no stake. They have no space. They have no voice. They are not heard. And the decimation of youth services over the past 15 years is a big, big contributing factor to that.

The Warren has recently begun a project to work with young people who are at risk of being radicalised, run by a young man who was himself radicalised as a teenager. 'We have lots of young people who come to The Warren and who were expressing all sorts of disturbing views about things, and we have conversations,' reflects JJ. 'We just have conversations.'

He contrasts this with an approach he sees in many schools where they are identifying young men they think are a problem, putting them all in a room and telling them they can't think this or that: 'It's just made it fucking 10 times worse. You know, it's like confirmation bias. You know, it feeds into the whole conspiracy theory outlook that these bastards are putting in their minds.'

The Warren's approach is fundamentally different:

> It's non-judgemental. We don't tell them how to think. We just begin to build a relationship, and it's about trust. Now that's difficult for some people to hear and they ask us 'shouldn't you be challenging it?' Yes, we will challenge it, but we'll challenge it at a point where we're not going to jeopardise the relationship.

JJ recalls the scene in Michael Moore's *Bowling for Columbine* film, about the two college students who murdered 14 other students in Columbine, Colorado, where Moore asks Marilyn Manson if he would do anything different if he had the chance to talk to those two young men again. Manson pauses and then replies: 'I wouldn't say anything. I'd want to hear what they had to say.'

'It's profundity,' says JJ:

> That simple statement is what we are talking about. All of these sessions, all of these agencies, all of these handbooks and frameworks and guidelines and all of that are nowhere near as effective as a relationship, a positive relationship where the young person feels valued, feels heard and they are given an opportunity just to say their piece.

A report by the Department of Culture, Media and Sport found young people who received youth work support as teenagers were happier, healthier, wealthier and more active in their communities as adults compared with those who did not.[25] With that in mind, and against the backdrop of growing concern about youth radicalisation and extreme violence, we should be re-investing in youth clubs, youth workers and – ultimately – young people themselves.

The challenges facing young men in Britain today are so varied and potentially harmful that there is a strong case for a Minister for Young Men and Boys. At present, issues relating to the radicalisation, misogyny, underachievement and mental health of young men straddle numerous different government departments, and there appears to be no overall strategy. Addressing the issues young men face purely from a law-and-order perspective will not work, just as tackling underachievement at school in the absence of broader measures will not work. A dedicated minister working across government departments, whose role is to think about young people in their entirety, makes complete sense. Young men form a major part of our future society, so engaging in the issues and challenges they face and so helping them fulfil their role as citizens should be a government priority.

12

Living Together ... Well

'Civil war is inevitable.'[1] Elon Musk's post, made during the 2024 riots in the UK, ignited fierce reaction from politicians and the media. Keir Starmer's spokesperson said there was 'no justification' for Musk's comments, and the spat was carried by news outlets across the world, much to the delight of the far right. Many, especially those within the self-defined counter-jihad movement, had long been arguing civil war in Europe was inevitable because Islam was a supremacist religion. There were some who felt that civil war was an unavoidable outcome of Islam existing in Europe, though they thought it regrettable. Then there were some who feared a civil war and thought they had to be prepared for it. A third group, however, not only thought civil war was inevitable but that it should actually be encouraged as this was the only way to expel Muslims from Europe given that liberal society was allowing Islam to take over through immigration and multiculturalism.

While Musk was his usual provocative self, it is the writing of a previously little-known professor at King's College London that has really grabbed the right-wing's attention. A year before the riots, Professor David Betz wrote an article titled 'Civil War Comes to the West' in *Military Strategy Magazine*.[2] Over six pages, Betz, who works in the War Studies department and specialises in civil wars and counter-insurgency policy, explained that many Western countries now have the core components for civil conflict. These include emerging ethnic groups that break the unity of society, a collapse in trust, political polarisation and economic hardship.

'It can be said that a generation ago all Western countries could still be described as to a large degree cohesive nations, each with a greater or lesser sense of common identity and heritage,' he wrote:

> By contrast, all now are incohesive political entities, jigsaw puzzles of competing identity-based tribes, living in large part in virtually segregated 'communities' competing over diminishing societal resources increasingly obviously and violently. Moreover, their economies are mired in a structural malaise leading, inevitably in the view of several knowledgeable observers, to systemic collapse.

He wrote this piece almost a year after disturbances in Leicester between Hindu and Muslim communities in September 2022, which he claimed made his point about the risk of 'intertribal conflict'.

'What this reflects above all is the considerable irrelevance of Britishness as an aspect of the pre-political loyalty of a significant fraction of two of the two largest minorities in Britain,' he added.

Betz's theory really hit the airwaves when he was interviewed by Louise Perry on her *Maiden Mother Matriarch* podcast in February, an episode that has been listened to by over 200,000 people.[3] He went further on this podcast than he had in his original article, claiming the situation was too far gone for the government to do anything about it and that civil war in Britain was likely to happen within the next five years.

His theory was then discussed by Blue Labour advocate Paul Embery, which is where I first came across it.* 'There was a time

---

* Blue Labour is a faction within the Labour Party that promotes blue-collar and culturally conservative values with opposition to current immigration levels and net-zero targets. Its co-founder, Maurice Glasman, has been vocal in his support for Donald Trump and the MAGA movement.

when the question would have seemed so absurd that no serious person would have deemed it worthy of consideration,' Embery wrote on his Substack.[4] 'I have no idea if Professor Betz will be proved correct. I hope not. But having heard him make his case, and considered his status and experience, I no longer think the possibility of civil war in Britain is as fanciful as I once did.'

Since the Louise Perry interview, Betz has been all over the right-wing media. More than half a million people watched his interview with right-wing cultural association the New Culture Forum,[5] and almost 70,000 have listened to him on the Brussels Horizon Podcast. His ideas have been written about in the *European Conservative*[6] and by Tim Stanley in the *Daily Telegraph*.[7] 'Betz sees no solution, so suggests we prepare for anarchy,' concludes Stanley. 'I'm more concerned about fascism. We're not far away from a politician running for office as explicitly anti-Muslim, and to those who say authoritarianism cannot happen here, I reply: lockdown.'

For some, listening to Betz only confirmed what they already knew – principally that Islam is such a threat to Britain that it will eventually lead to conflict. 'My husband, a calm and rational accountant, who hates politics, has been telling me for 10 years that war is inevitable,' wrote one woman on Perry's YouTube channel. 'The only thing worse than a civil war here would be no civil war,' wrote another. 'War is coming, the riots were only a reminder of the anger felt by us English people,' added a third. 'This anger has been brewing for over 20 years.'

'As a 28 year-old fighting age male, I am ready to lay down my life for Mother England and the survival of my folk,' said one of many people clearly longing for the fight.[8]

According to the 2021 census, there are 3.9 million Muslims in Britain, up from 2.7 million in 2011. The largest concentrations of Muslims are found in East London, Birmingham, East Lancashire and West Yorkshire. Nearly 40 per cent of those who live in the east London borough of Tower Hamlets are Muslim, as are 30 per cent in Birmingham, 31 per cent in Bradford and 35 per cent in Blackburn. According to a report published by the Muslim Council of Britain in early 2025,

> the median age of Muslims in the UK is 29 years, which is 15 years less than the British average. Moreover, in 2021, 5% of Muslims were over 65 years of age, compared to 19% overall. 46% of the Muslim population is under the age of 24 years compare [sic] to 29% overall.[9]

While Muslims form 6 per cent of the population overall, they make up 10 per cent of all school-age children (five to 15). In another statistic that might surprise people, Muslims are more geographically dispersed at the regional and local authority level than many other faith communities. At the same time, however, 39 per cent live in the most deprived parts of England and Wales, 61 per cent live in the lowest 40 per cent of areas in the country ranked by deprivation score and just 4 per cent of Muslims live in the least deprived fifth of England and Wales.[10]

Muslims are, however, viewed with suspicion, fear and even hatred by a sizeable section of the British population. HOPE not hate's polling of 22,500 people at the end of 2024 found that 36 per cent of Britons thought that Islam was a threat to the British way of life, with just 24 per cent thinking it was compatible. One in 10 Britons thought that 'almost all Muslims do not want to integrate', while a further 25 per cent believed that 'most Muslims do not want to integrate, although there are some who do'. Of the rest, 11 per cent thought that 'almost all Muslims want to integrate, although there are some who do not'. Two-thirds of those who wanted Britain to be a white, Christian country, as opposed to a multiracial or multi-ethnic country, thought that 'almost all' or 'most' Muslims did not want to integrate. Just under half of Britons, 44 per cent, thought Islam posed a serious threat to Western civilisation, while just 22 per cent thought it did not.

Attitudes towards Muslims are considerably more hostile than towards other religious groups. Analysis in our report 'Fear and HOPE 2024: The Case for Community Resilience' found that attitudes towards Muslims in the UK were almost twice as negative as those towards Hindus, and two and a half times more negative than towards Jewish people.[11]

Working with data scientists at Focaldata, we analysed attitudes towards Islam down to Output Area level. Six of the Output Areas with the highest levels of anti-Islam views were in Tendring, Essex, a local authority within Farage's Clacton constituency. In fact, 27 of the top 50 Output Areas were in Tendring, though according to the census, only 0.4 per cent of the population of Tendring are Muslim.

Very low numbers of Muslims appear to be a common feature of other areas our analysis suggested held high levels of anti-Islam feeling, suggesting that the closer we live together with Muslims and the more interaction there is with them, the less inclined people are to view them as a threat.

In May 2025, HOPE not hate asked those people who believe that Islam is incompatible with the British way of life to explain why. Asked to choose two reasons from a list of seven, 47 per cent said they were concerned about attempts to introduce Islamic legal principles (Sharia law), while 39 per cent felt that Islam was intolerant of free speech and religious criticism. Just over a quarter believed that some Muslims do not want to integrate into British culture, while just under a quarter were opposed to Islamic views on gender equality and women's rights. The least chosen option, at 17 per cent, was concern about the influence of extremist or violent interpretations of Islam.

Another reason for anti-Muslim attitudes is the actions of Islamist extremists and terrorists, and there has been a direct correlation between spikes in anti-Muslim sentiment and terrorist attacks at home and abroad. In our 2017 'Fear & HOPE' report, produced in the aftermath of four terrorist attacks in Britain, 42 per cent of respondents said the attacks had increased their suspicion of Muslims in Britain.[12] Tell Mama, a group that monitor anti-Muslim hate crime, have also found that spikes in abuse and attacks follow trigger events, such as terrorist attacks. In quieter periods, hostility towards Muslims can drop slightly.

Finally, anti-Muslim attitudes have been fostered and encouraged by those in the self-styled counter-jihad movement, who see Islam as such an inherent threat that they actively agitate against it. This has not been helped by lazy or inaccurate portrayals of Muslims in the media. One example of this is an article about Pendle in the *Mail on Sunday* in May 2025 under the headline: 'We Live in Britain's "Valley of Strangers": Inside Muslim-Majority Northern Town Where Locals Say There Is "No Point Speaking English" and Others Say "No One Talks to Each Other"'. The headline and accompanying article are misleading says journalist Taj Ali, who notes that English is the primary language of 87.6 per cent of households in Pendle: 'They're only looking at households where English is not the main language spoken (Less than 13%) but presenting it as though they're talking about all households in the borough.'[13]

Reducing anti-Muslim prejudice is multi-faceted and requires work from everyone. Evidence suggests that engagement with Muslims increases understanding and breaks down barriers, so we must increase and broaden this engagement. Schools have been good at teaching kids about different religions and ethnicities, but we probably need to be more proactive as well and use the kids to reach their parents, who are more likely to hold more hostile views and believe in anti-Muslim tropes.

Sunder Katwala, director of the think tank British Future, is a strong believer in promoting the involvement of Muslims in trusted occupations and British traditions. 'We should project (nationally, regionally, locally and online targeted) Muslim participation alongside others in macrosymbolic things: army, Remembrance, monarchy, local sport, local volunteering and communicate that to the low contact, coastal group in frames they find familiar,' he told me. 'It is a second best to actual contact but has an impact.'

Crucially, the media and politicians need to do more to ensure that British Muslims are not viewed as a monolithic community. There are different strands of Islam, and British Muslims hold a range of opinions on every issue, just like every other community. All too often, divisive figures and even extremists within the Muslim community are treated as 'community leaders' or 'spokespeople' by the media and politicians. While the vast majority of British Muslims identify strongly with the Palestinian cause, a quarter do not. Among the 1,000 Muslims questioned in our large poll of 22,500 people, almost as many Muslims (33 per cent) were supportive of gay couples adopting as the number (35 per cent) who were not.

In early 2020, the Centre for Research and Evidence on Security Threats (CREST), an independent crime consultancy, polled 1,000 Muslims and 1,000 members of the British public and found that Muslims shared many of the same concerns and views as non-Muslims. The poll found that 63 per cent of British Muslims were worried about Islamist extremism and 64 per cent trusted the police – only slightly less than the general population.[14] Jon Clements, who co-authored the report, said the findings 'fly in the face of a number of narratives commonly applied to British Muslims by some politicians, campaign groups and commentators'.[15] 'British Muslims and the general population share similar views on many issues related to policing and the Prevent programme,' he added.*

There have been times when polling has been used to convey a negative impression of Muslims. A poll of 998 British Muslims conducted for the Henry Jackson Society in April 2024 was widely criticised for its selective questioning and presentation of the results. After the *Daily Telegraph*, GB News, the *Jewish Chronicle* and the

---

* Prevent, a key component of the government's counter-extremism strategy, is a programme designed to steer people away from terrorism and extreme political violence.

Spectator all carried the polling results, which appeared to show strong British Muslim support for Hamas, several commentators hit back. Katwala took issue with the wording of some of the questions asked and said it was unfair to make a binary choice between Israel and Hamas rather than asking respondents to express support for Israel or Palestine. 'This survey appeared designed to spin-up support for Hamas as high as it could,' he wrote in the *Eastern Eye*. A similar view was taken by Mohammed Amin, a former tax advisor turned commentator: 'I believe this poll was designed to maximise the scope for finding differences between Muslims and Britons generally, so am not surprised that it found them.'

The reality is that Muslims have the same concerns, frustrations and priorities in life as others in society. In our mega poll, the three key issues identified by Muslim respondents as the most important facing them and their families are the cost-of-living crisis, the NHS and the economy more generally – the same three issues as society at large. Muslims are much more likely to be optimistic than the average person (64 per cent versus 47 per cent) and twice as likely to feel satisfied with how the political system is working in the UK. Engaging with Muslims on bread-and-butter issues, such as the economy, crime and education, rather than just religion or foreign affairs, would not only switch the narrative away from more divisive issues but also help people realise they may have more in common.

Some Muslims do hold negative attitudes on some issues, such as women's rights, homosexuality and Jewish people, and these do need to be addressed and challenged. But let us not delude ourselves into believing they are the only community to have such negative attitudes. While 35 per cent of Muslims in our poll of 22,500 people opposed gay couples adopting children, so did 46 per cent of black British people of Caribbean and African heritage. Among those who identified as Christian, the figure was 27 per cent.

HOPE not hate's Yorkshire organiser Paul Meszaros, who is based in Bradford, says that it is impossible to improve cohesion between

Muslim and non-Muslim communities without addressing other related issues too. 'There is no route to integration and cohesion,' he says:

> There are a multitude of factors that need addressing, like jobs, parks and open spaces, quality of housing and access to good education. Muslims are as aspirational as anyone else and they also get aggrieved at the same things too. Improving the quality of life for Muslims and non-Muslims will go some way to improve cohesion.

The backbench Conservative MP Nick Timothy is currently campaigning to stop what he declares is a new blasphemy law being adopted through the creation of a definition of Islamophobia. While many of those supporting calls for an Islamophobia definition are clear that this will not create a blasphemy law, it is also worth pointing out that many Muslims are driven to finding a workable definition precisely because current legislation does not protect Muslims from often quite vile and threatening abuse. For my part, I would oppose a blasphemy law as we should be able to criticise any religion we want, but there also needs to be a strengthening of the law to protect Muslims (and other religious groups too) from some of the vile abuse they receive, which is clearly intended to whip up hatred and division.

The reality is that the levels of anti-Muslim hate, lack of protection and widespread economic and social inequality facing great swathes of Britain's Muslim communities make some susceptible to more extreme or sectarian solutions and views. The rise of Muslim independent candidates in the 2024 General Election was clearly a consequence of anger at Labour's position on Gaza, but I do not believe it would have had such cut-through if many Muslims had not been feeling increasingly disengaged and ignored by the political system. In much the same way that the EU referendum was the trigger for a seismic shift in political views and allegiances among many white working-class voters in so-called red wall communities, so Gaza was the tipping point for many Muslims.

Integration is, of course, a two-way process, and there is also work to be done by Muslims themselves. 'Muslims need to reach out more, not be so defensive and own our stuff when we see it,' one Muslim community activist told me. 'That doesn't happen enough. Too easy to blame others and not be empathetic enough to how others are feeling. We need to be ready to deal with the things we don't want to hear by listening with compassion and reaching out more not less.'

'We need leadership that encourages that,' she adds.

Another noted that Muslims need to be more relaxed about criticism of their religion and differentiate between those who inadvertently cause offence and those who do so deliberately. Citing the protests outside Batley Grammar School after a teacher showed a caricature of the Prophet Muhammad to pupils during an RE lesson and was driven into hiding by the backlash, this activist told me: 'Things like that really don't help the Muslim community.'

Finally, the government must have meaningful engagement with Muslim community organisations, something they have not had for over 15 years. How can we, as a society, expect Muslims to integrate fully into British society if we have no dialogue with their main community organisations, shut them out of decision making and refuse to elicit their views. Surely it is better to bring Muslims in, listen to their views, challenge them where necessary and ultimately encourage them to fulfil their potential as citizens in society. Keeping Muslim organisations at arm's length only plays into the hands of extremists who argue that Muslims will never be fully accepted into British society. Obviously there have to be red lines that all organisations and leaders – Muslim and non-Muslim alike – must adhere to, such as racism towards other groups or wishing hurt on minorities, but there are also lots of differences and challenges that will probably be better explored if there is at least a dialogue.

* * *

LIVING TOGETHER ... WELL

Faith leaders have often been at the forefront of trying to bring communities together in the face of hate. I saw this first-hand after the murder of soldier Lee Rigby at the hands of two Islamists in May 2013. As the government scrambled to work out a response, hampered by their complete lack of links into communities, faith leaders stepped up and filled the void. Across the country, inter-faith networks spoke with one voice against the horrific murder but also urged unity and calm.

Across the country, as support for the EDL mushroomed and several mosques and other Islamic buildings were attacked, local faith networks came together to show solidarity. HOPE not hate joined with Julie Siddiqi, then of the ISB, and the think-tank British Future, to support a peace vigil in Woolwich nine days after the attack, which was to be attended by leading representatives of the Muslim, Anglican, Catholic, Sikh and Jewish faiths. As an act of solidarity, we started the event at the Greenwich mosque, mingling with surprised worshippers immediately after their 1 p.m. prayers, before making our way up to the barracks to lay wreaths. We also promoted The Big Iftar, where mosques and other Muslim centres opened their doors to the general public during Ramadan, sharing the traditional iftar – fast-breaking meal – with non-Muslims and linked hundreds of HOPE not hate supporters with local Muslim families as part of the related Dine@Mine initiative, giving them an opportunity to spend time with Muslim families over food.

One of the most symbolic moments of opposition to the EDL during this period came in York, where the occupants of a mosque disarmed half-a-dozen EDL supporters protesting outside by offering them tea and biscuits and inviting them inside to play football with fellow worshippers. Imam Abid Salik told reporters:

> We did have a few people who did come to protest but when they came some of the members of the mosque went over and they engaged in a conversation.

Some people went over with cups of tea and biscuits, they were talking for about 30 or 40 minutes and then they came inside, which was a really, really beautiful thing.

News of this incident soon spread, and it quickly gave confidence to others who had felt under attack. Archbishop of York Dr John Sentamu described the mosque's response as 'fantastic', adding: 'Tea, biscuits, and football are a great and typically Yorkshire combination when it comes to disarming hostile and extremist views.' When the EDL held another protest in York a few days later, locals turned up waving teapots at them.

Two years later, after HOPE not hate exposed a plan by Lennon and fellow anti-Islam campaigner Anne Marie Waters to host a Muhammad cartoon competition – which we saw as a deliberate attempt to provoke British Muslims into a violent reaction – we jumped at the chance to support a counter-initiative by Siddiqi called 'Our Cup of Tea'. At its heart was a cuppa and a simple concept: let's meet and talk. Events were held across the country. Jewish and Muslim women came together in north-west London on the eve of the Jewish New Year. 'HOPE not hate' cakes were baked by women at a mosque in Leicester for local police and businesses, and £500 was raised for refugees during a 'tea meeting' organised by The Sheba Project in East London. Former England rugby league player Ikram Butt enjoyed tea with fellow (non-Muslim) fans at an England cricket match against Australia, while ex-Spurs boss Harry Redknapp added his support to the initiative.

While we knew that a simple cup of tea was not going to solve the many contentious issues, the act of people coming together and talking to someone who seemed superficially different from them sent out a powerful and symbolic message of HOPE. For HOPE not hate, we believed that these sorts of community engagements are as much an anti-racist or anti-fascist act as going on a demonstration or leafleting a community. They are about winning hearts and minds, engaging with ordinary people and changing their views through direct engagement.

We used a similar approach in Shrewsbury in 2013, when a planning application to turn a former church into a mosque was met with a barrage of opposition, including an EDL demonstration and threats by far-right activists to burn the building down. Having been brought up in the town, I travelled up and held a local HOPE not hate meeting, where we decided to issue an open letter in support of the Muslim community's right to worship. Within five days, it had been co-signed by 710 people, all but 54 from Shrewsbury. It received considerable attention in the local newspaper, including two front-page stories, and was mentioned on BBC Radio Shropshire. We counterpoised the decency of local people and the Christian tradition of tolerance and acceptance with the violent threats of the far right. The petition was handed in to the leader of Shropshire Council shortly before the vital planning committee meeting, and the mosque was given the go-ahead.

Campaigns like this were a vindication of our approach to community problems. While there is a temptation to fight fire with fire – in this case, organise an anti-fascist demonstration in response to a far-right demonstration – often there are more imaginative and ultimately more successful approaches. These not only bring the majority of local people with you but, most importantly, are more likely to achieve the outcome you want, as they centre your objective. Our approach took the moral high ground by pitting our peaceful and faith-based response against the far right, whose supporters were threatening to burn the place down. Against this stark choice, we gave the Conservative council no option but to overturn their previous objections and pass it.

Perhaps the most consequential inter-faith work I've seen has been led by Peter Adams in Luton. Now director of the St Marys Centre for Peace and Reconciliation, Peter had been taught the virtues of non-violence by Bernard Lafayette, a key associate of Dr Martin Luther King, and had learned much from colleagues working on community mediation in Northern Ireland. Fortunately, he ended up in Luton at a time when the town was being described as the worst place in Britain – a 'hotbed of terrorism' and an incubator of extremism.

Peter played a key role in building community resilience against the EDL in the early years of its existence. He sought to understand the motivations of the EDL leaders and followers, and he cajoled the police and council to take a more nuanced and proactive position towards the group. Working with other faith leaders, he sought to build cross-community resilience and unity. He helped put on numerous cross-faith initiatives, working hard to reduce tensions when they arose and sharing a more hopeful vision of Luton to the outside world. He was vital in reducing tensions in the aftermath of Britain First's impromptu 'Christian patrol' through Bury Park, home to a high concentration of Muslims, in January 2016. He has also never shied away from addressing issues others have ducked. Fearing the issue of on-street grooming by gangs would emerge in Luton, Peter worked with Rehana Faisal, a local Muslim activist, to establish Faiths Against Child Sexual Exploitation, raising awareness around the issue of sexual exploitation in both the Christian and Muslim communities of Luton, often through Sunday schools or madrasa classes.

Inter-faith work should not be contentious, but unfortunately it often is. A combination of faith and political disengagement, cuts, political opposition and a lack of confidence has left inter-faith relations weakened and neglected. Local Government Association analysis has shown that service spending by local authorities in 2022/3 was 42.1 per cent lower than it would have been had the spend moved in line with cost and demand pressures since 2010/11.[16] This equates to councils having made £24.5 billion in service cuts and efficiencies over this period, which of course have had a devastating impact on cohesion budgets and the third sector more generally.

There are other factors too. The Church of England, for so long at the forefront of inter-faith engagement, has withdrawn somewhat as it has become embroiled in sex abuse scandals, as well as balancing the racial/social justice views of the liberally minded church establishment with the growing influence of its evangelical wing. Then there have been growing divisions between minority communities, such as Hindus and Muslims. More recently, the fallout from the Israel–Palestine conflict has ruptured much of what was left of the inter-faith movement, as positions within Jewish and Muslim communities have hardened, and it has become difficult for more moderate voices to be heard.

On a national level, central government's engagement with faith communities and inter-faith networks, which was already fairly limited, virtually ended during the Boris Johnson years. Not only was Johnson not interested in cohesion but in his appointment of Michael Gove as Secretary of State for Levelling Up, Housing and Communities, there was a distinct ideological shift away from inter-faith dialogue and cohesion. Gove took a combative 'drain the swamp' approach as opposed to the more limited 'beat back the crocodiles that come close to the boat' approach of the Theresa May years. Under May, the government's counter-extremist strategy targeted all extremism that looked like – or indeed was developing into – a terrorist threat. Gove took a different view, believing that Prevent's role was to wage an ideological and political war against radical Islam in Britain, hence the notion that the swamp had to be drained.

Gove has been pushing for a more combative approach to tackling Islamism for two decades. In the aftermath of the 7/7 terrorist attacks, Gove wrote *Celsius 7/7*, a book that called for a frontal assault on the ideology behind the terrorist attacks and condemned the liberal society that he accused of allowing extremism to flourish. As a member of Cameron's Extremism Taskforce, he proposed forcing all mosques to sign a charter of non-violence and creating an extra layer of screening for any Muslims taking jobs in the civil service. Fortunately, these suggestions were rejected by Cameron and the police. Baroness Warsi, a former deputy chair of the Conservative Party who served in Cameron's Cabinet with Gove, said in 2017: 'Politically I find his views and what I saw in Government deeply, deeply worrying.'[17]

Under Gove's tenure, the department wound up the Anti-Muslim Hatred Working Group, established under Cameron to address anti-Muslim prejudice in society and improve policies across government, and, with the support of Prime Minister Johnson, ensured that the inquiry into an official Islamophobia definition, set up by May in her final fortnight in office, never got to work. The final nail in this inquiry's coffin was the removal of moderate Leeds Imam Qari Asim as a government advisor in 2022 after he allegedly backed calls for a film about the Prophet Muhammad's daughter to be banned.[18] Qari Asim had been central to governmental engagement with Muslim communities for more than a decade and had fronted up numerous initiatives, led inter-faith dialogue between Jews and Muslims and had been strident in his condemnation of all forms of extremism. He admitted that the wording of his Facebook post about the film was not the best, and anyone who knows him, including civil servants and numerous government ministers who have worked with him, knows that he is not an extremist or an intolerant Islamist, as government briefings tried to suggest. He found out about his sacking through social media.

Several other Muslims involved directly or indirectly in Prevent and other counter-extremism programmes also left their jobs after effectively being frozen out or sidelined. That moderate Muslims, many of them progressive Muslim women, have felt forced to leave their jobs not only reflects badly on where our counter-extremism strategy is going but should act as a warning sign.

In February 2024, the Inter Faith Network announced its closure after Gove's department ended its funding. While the department publicly cited the appointment as trustee of Hassan Joudi, a former deputy secretary general of the Muslim Council of Britain, a body the government refused to engage with, the closure fitted a broader trend of conscious withdrawal from inter-faith and cross-community work.

Inter-faith work can play a vital role in improving community relations, especially at a time of rising sectarianism. But inter-faith work needs to be more than just sandwiches and samosas and offering solidarity in times of need. Inter-faith leaders need to address the difficult issues within their communities and society at large. They also need to be willing to confront fundamentalism within their own religion and act as critical friends to others too.

Faith leaders are in a unique position in their respective communities. The government needs to encourage and support inter-faith networks, while national faith bodies need to arm their local leaders with the tools to confront fear and hate. There will be times when we don't see eye to eye, and there will be people we need to engage with who might have chequered pasts, but the consequence of not doing this work is allowing the peddlers of hate to go unchallenged and unchecked.

Extreme interpretations of religious texts have long existed in the UK, but they currently appear to be on the rise within all religions. Sometimes this manifests in suspicion or antagonism towards another faith, while in other circumstances it might manifest in a sense of religious superiority or supremacism. The conflict in Gaza has certainly increased the influence of hard-line Islamist groups that can point to the indifference shown by Western governments to the suffering of the Palestinians as proof that Muslims can only rely on themselves to solve their own problems. One group that has taken advantage of this anti-Western anger is 5Pillars, a Muslim media operation that advocates a strict interpretation of Islam, including support for a caliphate, Islamic penal codes and jihad.[19] In an illuminating video, aired on 28 August 2024, 5Pillars' editor Roshan Salih and senior correspondent Robert Carter sat down with Dilly Hussain, the group's deputy editor, to discuss Hussain's recent trip to

Afghanistan.[20] Hussain was effusive about his experience, with Carter chipping in to say that '[w]e need someone like the Taliban to come here and shut down [the] education and fix it up'. To them, girls should not be at school.

Salih then added that he doesn't consider Britain home because it is *dar al-kufr* (the Abode of Infidels). Hussain pushed back:

> I think there's enough accommodation in non-Muslim countries, Roshan, let's be frank about it brother. There's enough accommodation, at least in Britain, not France, at least in Britain, where you have enough options and services there where you can kind of live in a Muslim bubble. Let's be honest about it. Alum Rock [Birmingham], possibly London.

Salih was unmoved: 'You turn on the radio in the car and the first thing you hear is Taylor Swift or whatever.'

Hamas's horrendous attack on Israel on 7 October 2023 and the Israeli response in Gaza was met by a huge upsurge in antisemitic and anti-Muslim attacks in the UK. Tell Mama recorded 895 cases in the six weeks that followed the deadly terror attacks, while the Community Security Trust, which protects the Jewish community, recorded 1,563 antisemitic incidents in just 47 days following the start of the conflict. Alongside the threats and attacks, there was an upsurge in conspiratorial antisemitism and the use of antisemitic tropes, especially in relation to supposed Jewish power and influence. It was of no surprise then to find 5Pillars play host on their podcast to several of Britain's most far-right figures, who some would consider to be nazis (i.e. those adhering to some or all of national socialist ideology, as indicated in the definition of 'nazi' at the beginning of this book). Examples of those figures who appeared on the podcast included former BNP leader Nick Griffin and Patriotic Alternative leader Mark Collett, where they were allowed to push their 'anti-Zionist' agenda. Whilst Griffin has in the past denied that he is a Nazi, he has referred to himself as a racist.

5Pillars had previously refrained from engaging in domestic British politics, but that changed in 2024, when the group publicly supported independent Muslim candidates standing in the General Election on a pro-Gaza ticket. Not only were they keen to raise the issue but they also saw it as an opportunity to break the link between the Muslim community and Labour: '4th July is Muslim Independence Day from Labour,' 5Pillars announced in late May.[21] During the election campaign, the group was also highly critical of The Muslim Vote, a pressure group that encouraged Muslims to vote for candidates favourable to Muslim issues, after it promoted four Labour candidates. Following an online campaign initiated by 5Pillars, The Muslim Vote backed down and withdrew its endorsements, much to the delight of Salih and Carter.[22]

Religious nationalism is growing within other faiths too. The three nights of disorder in Leicester between Hindu and Muslim communities in September 2022 was sparked by a march of 300 Hindus through a predominantly Muslim area.

'It's very important for every Hindu to attain [sic] this meeting,' an organiser wrote on a WhatsApp message. 'Otherwise in future, we will have to live in fear.'[23]

News of the march swept through the Muslim community; using WhatsApp to organise, they too began to mobilise to defend their area. Many Muslims later went into a predominantly Hindu area in revenge. It wasn't long before fighting broke out.

The trouble in Leicester highlighted the growing influence in the UK of Hindutva, a modern ethno-nationalist movement that seeks to establish Hindu hegemony in India. Hindutva, the official platform of Prime Minister Narendra Modi and his right-wing Bharatiya Janata Party (BJP), has inspired a rise in hate speech, open calls for violence against minorities and increasingly discriminatory legislation. Hindutva was developed as a political ideology in the 1920s by Vinayak Damodar Savarkar, who argued that Indian Muslims and Christians could not be considered loyal patriots as India was not their 'holy land'. It has drawn comparisons with European fascist and nazi states. Hindutva was popularised by the Rashtriya Swayamsevak Sangh (RSS), a far-right paramilitary organisation founded in 1925 that today has more than four million members and has been accused of inflaming community tensions, stoking riots and carrying out violent attacks on Muslims. The RSS is closely linked with the ruling BJP, and Modi himself has been a lifelong member. The RSS operates several branches in the UK and in 2019 was behind a campaign to persuade British Hindus to vote against the Labour Party because of its position on Kashmir, its strong statements against Prime Minister Modi and the party's close relations with British Muslims.

Christian nationalism is on the rise too – especially within Catholicism – though until recently it has largely gone unnoticed by the progressive and secular worlds. One manifestation of this is known as 'postliberalism' and counts among its adherents US Vice President J. D. Vance. Postliberalism, as the name suggests, stands opposed to liberalism, particularly the focus on individualism and free markets, which it believes has undermined the traditional family, communal bonds and social cohesion.

The most prominent postliberal thinker is the American academic Patrick Deneen, author of *Why Liberalism Failed* and, more recently, *Regime Change*.[24] He has described his work as 'a critique of, not just liberal philosophy, but the way in which liberal philosophy becomes realised'.[25] He believes that people are social beings and need values and community to thrive:

> Liberals have sought the elimination of arbitrary national borders – while ordinary citizens value the nation, their communities, their towns. Liberals have sought to displace the family as the basic unit of society, with catastrophic social consequences on the lives of ordinary people. Liberals have sought to eliminate marriage and birth as basic norms, leaving people increasingly lonely and insecure. Liberals have sought to reject the idea that male and female are sown into the fabric of

our natural reality, increasingly leading to deeply illiberal outcomes (such as allowing biological men to compete in sports against biological women, or forcing people to use 'preferred pronouns' at the risk of jobs and reputations).

In *Regime Change*, Deneen goes further, calling for 'the peaceful but vigorous overthrow of a corrupt and corrupting liberal ruling class and the creation of a postliberal order'. In liberalism's place, he advocates 'aristopopulism', the merging of democracy with a new aristocracy.

'*Regime Change* imagines a pie-in-the-sky blending of working-class populism with a classically educated and conservative new nobility inculcated with the civic virtue needed to assure a politics of the common good,' explains Stephen Schneck, an American political scientist.[26]

More worrying, Schneck adds, Deneen advocates a form of Catholic nationalism that supresses minority rights and freedoms:

> The populist political phenomenon that Americans associate with Trump is actually much bigger than Trump. It's a global movement and, just as it has in the United States, in many countries the new populism has fostered 'religious nationalism' – just another name for integralism. A few examples would be Hindu nationalism in India, Sunni Islam in Turkey, Buddhism in Myanmar, Christianity in Hungary. In each of these countries the integration of religion with the state has come at a cost for believers of minority faiths.

The influence of people like Deneen on Vance was evident during the vice-president's blistering speech at the Munich Security Conference in February 2025, where he said that immigration and liberalism were a threat to Western civilisation.

In addition to postliberalism, we are also seeing the rise of a Christian identity within the far right. Groups like Britain First have long included a Christian theme within their activities, and Stephen Lennon is increasingly using Christian phrases and imagery in his politics and rallies. This adoption of cultural Christianity taps into a long-held view on the far right about defending the Judeo-Christian West from the threat of Islam.

There is a clear sense of unease in Britain today. Economically, socially and politically. A growing number of Britons do not think that multiculturalism is working, and many people believe tensions between communities will get worse over the next few years. However, our polling shows that the British people do want multiculturalism to work, and three-quarters believe the government should be doing more to improve cohesion in society.

As I was finishing this book, I was sent a message from a friend who said we needed to have responses to common anti-Muslim narratives that were circulating online. He attached a post from X that listed some 'facts' about Muslims, such as the Muslim proportion of the prison population, those who had been convicted for 'grooming', terrorist attacks and the level of deformity of Muslim babies born in Bradford. While acknowledging we needed answers to the far-right's narrative on Muslims, I also pointed out that the poster had deliberately selected certain issues to suit his agenda. I likened it to groups that do polling of British Muslims with the aim of eliciting controversial opinions on issues such as Jews, homosexuality or blasphemy.

'Look,' I added, 'I don't disagree with the argument you are making but think we need to step back and really ask ourselves if we want to find a solution, or do we, like the X post, suggest that all these problems are core to Islam. If it's the latter, we might as well take up weapons training and prepare for civil war. If we are genuinely looking for solutions, then we have to work out what these solutions are. And we need to address it like we would any other problem, it's difficult and the answer is multi-faceted. It is carrot and stick. If we expect people to act within accepted values and norms then we also have to ensure that they can live without prejudice and discrimination too, that their kids can flourish to the best of their potential and the social and economic concerns of their communities are addressed.'

'There is no middle ground here,' I concluded. 'We – all of us – either make cohesion work or there will be conflict.'

13

Fool's Gold

On a Friday in early February 2025, a select group of journalists gathered at the Home Office to be given a preview of a video the government was to release a few days later. The short film featured handcuffed men being herded on to a plane to an unknown destination. It was the opening salvo of a government media blitz to show that it was not only tough on illegal immigrants but was succeeding in removing them too. Accompanying the footage, a Home Office press release stated it had 'for the first time' shared images of the inner workings of the removals process. Government adverts began appearing on social media announcing that the government had removed 18,987 foreign nationals from the country since it had come to office, an increase of 24 per cent over the previous year. Not only that, removals of foreign national offenders were up by 21 per cent and illegal working raids up by 38 per cent.

Yvette Cooper, the Home Secretary, insisted that increasing removals was vital for restoring order to the asylum system. Labour had come to power promising to reduce immigration numbers, which had been running at almost a million a year:

To rebuild public confidence in the immigration system, we need to show the rules are respected and enforced. That's why, as part of the government's plan for change, we have put significant additional resource into immigration enforcement and returns, so those who have no right to be here, particularly those who have committed crimes in our country, are removed as swiftly as possible.[1]

Some disagreed with the government's position. In the *Guardian*, Enver Solomon, the chief executive officer of the Refugee Council, wrote: 'Melodramatic footage and maligning narratives that risk punching down on the men, women and children in the boats who are victims of traffickers and smugglers will not give the public confidence that the [asylum] system is working.'[2]

What both sides of the argument could agree on, whether they publicly articulated it or not, was that the video and accompanying social media ads were partly in response to the growing political threat from Farage's Reform UK.

Moral questions aside, the government's approach faces huge hurdles, as the 2025 local elections proved, when Labour lost hundreds of seats in many of its traditional heartlands despite its increasingly tough language on immigration. There is a large gap between rhetoric and reality, and those with the strongest views on immigration simply do not believe the Labour government can bring down the numbers or that it even wants to. Worse still, Starmer risks boxing himself into a corner with his 'Smash the Gangs' pledge, which is proving almost impossible to deliver, in much the same way that Rishi Sunak failed with his 'Stop the Boats' pledge. The more socially liberal wing of the Labour coalition looks on in horror at the government's rhetoric, and many are now voting with their feet and switching allegiances to the Greens and Liberal Democrats.

* * *

There are some people in Britain who simply do not like foreigners, so much so that they will oppose any and all immigration into Britain. In fact, some would prefer those already here to leave and would not even consider the British-born children or grandchildren of immigrants to be properly British. I think this group represents a small minority of British people. In fact, it probably reflects a minority even of those who would register their unhappiness with the government's immigration policies.

Understanding that those who oppose current immigration policy are not one monolithic group is essential if we want to address the immigration issue in a way that meets with the approval of most of the population. This is a lesson for some anti-racists as much as it is politicians and policy makers. Believing those calling for a tightening of immigration policies are racist – and, worse still, condemning them as such – alienates us from many with whom we need to engage and, most fundamentally, ignores the drivers of anti-immigrant views.

HOPE not hate's 'Fear, HOPE and Loss' report, produced in 2018, is one of the most important reports we have ever published.[3] Written by Rosie Carter, the report set out to understand the relationship between a sense of lost hope and abandonment with hostility towards 'the other'. Perhaps unsurprisingly, it found that the communities with the greatest anxiety over immigration and multiculturalism were also the ones that had lost most through industrial and economic decline. Those who were able to move, did, leaving behind older and more resentful people who were ill-equipped to compete in the modern global world. Burnley is a good example. In 1981, the census listed a population of 92,800, but by 2011, during which time the town had lost much of its engineering base, this had contracted to 87,032, a decline of 6.3 per cent. During the same period, the population of the UK as a whole rose from 56,357,500 to 63,285,145, a rise of 8.9 per cent.[4]

Our research allocated all 32,845 Lower Super Output Areas (LSOAs) to one of the five attitudinal tribes we have used in our

'Fear & HOPE' reports over the years and then analysed the 100 LSOAs most closely associated with the most hostile identity tribes (Active Enmity) and the 100 most heavily linked to our most liberal (Confident Multiculturalists).

Our analysis found that most hostile tribes were concentrated in areas with significant socio-economic problems, principally ex-industrial areas and isolated coastal communities, where the population is overwhelmingly white British, work is scarce, precarious, low paid and low skilled. Conversely, the most liberal tribes were concentrated in major cities or in university towns, places where a university education is customary and opportunities abundant.

Of all the 100 areas with the greatest proportional affiliation to the Active Enmity group, 18 sat within the 100 most deprived of 32,844 areas of England, and 99 were in the top 10 per cent most deprived areas in the UK. By contrast, 71 of the 100 areas most closely associated with our Confident Multiculturalist tribe, the most liberal of our six identity tribes, were in the least deprived 20 per cent in terms of income and in the least deprived 10 per cent in terms of employment, and in all areas house prices were far above the local average. These are wealthy areas – not the wealthiest but certainly prosperous places where there are ample opportunities, cultural offerings and prestigious educational institutions.

Perhaps the report's most significant single conclusion was that political parties could not reduce anxiety or even hostility to immigration and multiculturalism by simply cracking down on immigration. Given that the areas with the most hostile attitudes were those with some of the lowest levels of immigration in the country, reducing numbers of immigrants alone would have little impact on these people's lives. As I wrote in the report's introduction:

> Immigration has become a totemic emblem for the many grievances people feel in modern Britain. It is the most visible indicator of a changing Britain. The liberalism, vibrancy and

multiculturalism of our cities is contrasted with the sense of loss and abandonment in our former industrial towns. Immigration is seen as a consequence of globalisation, jobs moving abroad and foreigners coming in and taking our jobs here. And the strong view in many of these communities is that they have been abandoned and left to rot by the political establishment in preference to addressing the needs and wishes of new arrivals in the cities. This sense of abandonment is felt most strongly against Labour, the party which once so many in these communities would look to, but now feel has left them.[5]

Lurid media stories about newcomers getting benefits and services ahead of local British people only increase anger and the sense of grievance. Labour has it worse than other political parties and is more hated precisely because it is seen to have abandoned the very people who once represented it. The report also highlighted the quandary Labour is in. Just as many of the areas identified as the most 'hostile' are disproportionately located in Labour's traditional heartlands, so too are the areas identified as among the most liberal, such as Cambridge and Oxford.

Rosie Carter was also heavily involved in the National Conversation, an initiative we ran with British Future that held more than 130 meetings in 60 towns and cities in an attempt to find a consensus over immigration. 'Over 60 focus groups for the National Conversation taught me a lot,' she wrote,

> but the biggest lesson was that it is not enough to talk about immigration alone. Tackling the underlying mood of anti-immigrant sentiments and anti-Muslim prejudice will also require talking about everything at once, about understanding the grievances people have about their own lives, not just how they feel about other people.
>
> We found that immigration was seen as a national issue, passed through a local lens. Localised pressures or points of

tension could often spill over into anti-migrant sentiment in places with little history of diversity. Sometimes, these were directly related to immigration, such as in neighbourhoods overwhelmed by large numbers of houses of multiple occupancy for a rapidly growing population of migrant workers. But often they were not about migration at all, and instead reflected of [*sic*] broader resentments – about housing, healthcare, or a lack of secure employment.⁶

New analysis by HOPE not hate and our data partners Focaldata reinforces the linkage between anti-immigration views and poverty. In our poll of 22,500 people conducted throughout December 2024 and January 2025, HOPE not hate asked people to choose one of five different possible approaches to immigration: stopping immigration permanently, stopping immigration until the economy improves, only allowing skilled immigrants that benefit the economy, allowing skilled and unskilled immigrants that benefit the economy, or having no restrictions on those who come in. The results were fascinating, with only 11 per cent wanting to stop all immigration permanently, 14 per cent believing we should stop all immigration until the economy improves, 33 per cent thinking we should only allow in skilled immigrants who will help with the economy, 28 per cent believing we should only allow skilled and unskilled immigrants who will help the economy and 14 per cent agreeing with the view that we should allow all types of immigration. What's particularly interesting is that these views have hardly changed since we first asked this question in 2011, shortly after the financial crash and as the new Conservative government was implementing austerity.

Using advanced data analytics, Focaldata has been able to estimate these immigration attitudes down to the 188,802 Output Area levels across England and Wales, within which there are approximately 160 houses. The results clearly show that those areas that support immigration being permanently or temporarily halted have very high levels of deprivation. Over 80 per cent of people in the Output

Area on the Bransholme estate in Hull, considered by some to be the largest council estate in Europe, want to see all immigration into Britain halted. Almost half of the people who live in this area endure multiple levels of deprivation.

An analysis of the 100 Output Areas with the strongest anti-immigrant views found that 70.5 per cent want immigration into the UK halted. Almost the exact same number of people living in these 100 Output Areas, 71 per cent, are suffering from deprivation. Interestingly, 38 out of these 100 areas were in local authorities that experienced disorder in the 2024 riots.

Conversely, only 12.2 per cent of the 100 Output Areas with least deprivation want all immigration to be stopped, either permanently or temporarily.

Stoke-on-Trent has three of the seven Output Areas with the highest support for stopping immigration in the country, with the highest being part of Abbey Hulton, in the east of the city, which is in the most deprived decile in the country.[7] If there was a case study of how attitudes to immigration are linked to deprivation, then this is it.

Go to Wikipedia, and all you can read about Abbey Hulton is that it took its name from an abbey that occupied the site between the thirteenth and sixteenth centuries, with the word 'hulton' derived from the Anglo-Saxon word for 'hill town'. Beyond that, and the fact that local monks raised sheep and operated a tannery there until it was closed in 1538, there is nothing, which of course is deeply unfair to the 7,100 people who live there today. Abbey Hulton is a proud working-class community created in the post-war years as a new estate to take in people while neighbouring areas were cleared for redevelopment. Its council house stock is solidly built, but a lack of upkeep and infrastructure spending means it now looks tired, with paint peeling off and many of the large front-garden fences broken. According to census data, 39 per cent of children in Abbey Hulton are in poverty, and 37.6 per cent of people are projected to be income deprived. Twice as many people are suffering from poor heath in this area as the national average. Most housing in the area is council housing, the area ranks in the bottom 2 per cent nationally for educational attainment and over a third of households suffer from two or more deprivation dimensions, the measurement statisticians use to calculate the extent to which individuals or households experience disadvantage or a lack of resources in key elements of their lives – such as unemployment, health and poor housing.[8] The ward ranks second in the Local Trust's list of the 225 most deprived wards in the country, an index that combines the Index of Multiple Deprivation, a dataset that combines the multiple types of deprivation into a single score, and social infrastructure challenges.[9]

The city as a whole is the UK's 12th most deprived local authority, with over 50 per cent of residents living in areas considered to be among the 20 per cent most deprived areas of the country. The city has the highest rate of infant mortality across England, which is seen as an indicator that reflects the health of the wider population, while over 30 per cent of the LSOAs are in the bottom 10 per cent for deprivation in the country. In 2022, 18 per cent of households containing at least one working-age occupant were considered 'workless households'.

Stoke-on-Trent, which is actually made up of six towns, was once considered the industrial heart of the country. It had coalfields, steelworks and engineering factories. Nicknamed the Potteries, it was famous throughout the world for its ceramics industry and its world-leading brands such as Wedgwood, Royal Doulton, Spode and Minton. At its peak, over 20,000 people worked down the mines, 70,000 in the ceramics industries and 10,000 directly or indirectly through the Shelton Bar steelworks.

By the 1980s, the city had gone into decline. Pits closed as reserves ran out, the steel plants contracted due to cheaper imports and alternative sources of ceramics saw the slow death of the iconic Stoke industry. Today, the city's largest employers are the city council and the hospital, with the biggest private sector employers being Bet365, which employs 5,000 people, and the huge DHL warehouse, which employs 3,000.

'Stoke is the victim of a triple economic crisis and a triple identity crisis,' wrote John Litchfield in an article for Unherd, published in 2019:

> Its pottery, steel and coal-mining industries were among the earliest victims of the de-industrialisation of Britain which began under Margaret Thatcher in the 1980s. The city's public services have been hollowed out by the austerity drive of the past decade. Its town centres, stricken by the collapse of traditional shopping habits, range from the depressed to the derelict.[10]

Economic decline resulted in political upheaval. For many years, Stoke was a Labour city. Indeed, for some time in the early 2000s, the party held every seat on the council. That changed with the emergence of independents and later with the BNP, which at its peak had nine councillors in the city, the second-largest BNP group in the country. It was little wonder that Griffin described Stoke-on-Trent as the BNP's 'jewel in the crown'. Abbey Green, the ward that covers Abbey Hulton, has been represented by two BNP councillors over the years, one of whom later switched allegiance to the City Independents and became the city's mayor. The BNP group quickly collapsed, but the political disenchantment and strong anti-immigrant views of many of the city's inhabitants continued to linger. In the 2014 European elections, 17,165 people in the city voted for UKIP, almost 50 per cent more than voted Labour. In the EU referendum two years later, 69.4 per cent voted to leave, making Stoke-on-Trent the most pro-Leave large town or city in the country.

Just like Burnley, Barking and Dagenham and several other places where support for the BNP – and later UKIP and Reform – has been strong, it is hard to disassociate support for anti-immigration parties within Stoke-on-Trent from its own rapid economic decline. In 2000, Stoke-on-Trent registered as the 34th most deprived local authority in the country but slipped to 18th in 2004 and 16th in 2010.[11] In 2023, 13 years later, the city was the 13th most deprived in the country, and all predictions suggest that it could be as low as the fourth or fifth most deprived when the next national evaluation is done. With such a rapid decline in the city's fortunes, it is hardly surprising that some have a romanticised, nostalgic sense of the past, a time when men walked to work with their neighbours and Stanley Matthews was scoring goals for fun.

The situation in Stoke-on-Trent is mirrored in many other former coalfield communities. The 'State of the Coalfields' report, written by three academics at Sheffield Hallam University for the Coalfields Regeneration Trust, found severe economic and social problems affecting all former coalfield communities.[12] The population in these areas was older and ageing, ill-health was widespread and deprivation was high. Unemployment was higher than the national average, and many of those who were employed were in short-term work or on zero-hour contracts and had long commutes to work. A quite shocking statistic in the report found that 176,000 people in the coalfield communities worked in warehousing jobs in 2022, and warehousing accounted for 30 per cent of all new jobs created in the coalfields in the previous 10 years. For Yorkshire, this figure was 60 per cent.

Compounding this sense of change, a growing number of women have entered the labour market over the last few decades, with many working in more permanent or secure office-based work with local authorities and in the NHS.

The coalfields have lower rates of self-employed people than the national average, a higher proportion of people working part time and lower average wages; only 34 per cent have degrees, almost half the rate of London and 20 per cent lower than the national average. At the same time, the proportion of 16- to 64-year-olds claiming incapacity benefits is 40 per cent higher than the national average and almost twice as high as London. Another report into the coalfield communities, produced by academics at Cambridge, Leeds and Staffordshire, looked at the impact of austerity. The report claimed that:

> public expenditure cuts since 1984 have disproportionately impacted on coalfield and deindustrialised areas of the UK. However, since 2010, austerity has been stepped up with welfare reforms and benefit cuts amounting to £32.6 billion over the period (2010–2021). Coalfield Local Authorities have a combined funding gap in 2025/26 of £447 million.[13]

Easington, in County Durham, is another example of how economic decline has helped shift political attitudes. The constituency, which at its peak was home to a dozen mines, was once as Labour as they came. In 1997, the then Labour MP John Cummings was elected to Parliament with a majority of 30,012 votes, taking 80 per cent of all votes cast. This majority had been slashed to just 6,542 in the 2024 General Election. Reform UK won all but one of the councillors in the Durham County Council election across this constituency, with Labour beating it by just eight votes in one ward. Like Stoke-on-Trent, Easington has struggled in recent years. From a high of a dozen pits, the last closed in 1994, and since then the area has gone into economic decline.

According to the 2021 census, 32.7 per cent of those over 16 have never worked in their lives, 49.8 per cent are economically active – compared to a national average of 57.4 per cent – and almost twice as many people have to commute between 10 and 30 kilometres a day for work as the national average.[14] The number of registered disabled people is 33 per cent higher than nationally, and bad and very bad health is almost twice the average. The constituency is 98 per cent white, with Muslims being the largest minority at just 0.4 per cent. According to the House of Commons library, Easington has the eighth worst employment deprivation of any constituency of the country and is the 19th worst for health deprivation and disability.[15] On the Income Deprivation Affecting Children Index, Easington ranks 35th worst in the country.

When it comes to attitudes, Easington has some of the strongest levels of hostility to immigration and Muslims as well as some of the lowest levels of optimism about the future and their own lives. According to our data analysis, 39 per cent of adults in Easington want to stop immigrants coming into the country, making it the second highest figure for any constituency in the country, behind only Boston and Skegness. Two-thirds of people (67 per cent) believe that Britain should be taking fewer asylum seekers, even if they are fleeing war, famine or persecution, and it ranks 29th in the belief that Islam is incompatible with the British way of life. Perhaps underpinning these views, people generally feel despondent about their futures. Our data analysis suggests that almost 60 per cent are pessimistic about the future and 45 per cent think their lives will be worse than their parents', with 33 per cent thinking they will be better. However, in some parts of the constituency this latter split is 55/25 per cent.

Given the severe economic and social problems many former coalfields face, it is perhaps not surprising that Reform UK polled particularly well in all the areas where there were elections in May 2025. In the nine wards in Ashfield, Nottinghamshire, Reform UK polled 50 per cent, while Labour trailed far back in third place with just 10.7 per cent of the votes.

It might seem obvious to say there is a correlation between deprivation, pessimism and anti-immigrant sentiments, but this simple linkage is all too often ignored by politicians as they attempt to counter the growing hostility towards immigration and multiculturalism from elements of the media and their political rivals. That is not to say that events do not dictate a response, but they risk being done in a knee-jerk or performative way that either comes across as insincere or does little to address the fundamental issues driving people's grievances. Whether it was in response to the wave of unofficial strikes and blockades of power stations and oil refineries in 2009, the election defeat in 2010, the Brexit vote in 2016 or Johnson's capture of the Red Wall in 2019, Labour politicians have repeatedly responded by demanding tougher immigration policies.

We have more recently seen the same again after Labour's 2025 defeat in Runcorn, with some MPs and peers linked to the Blue Labour group demanding tougher action on immigration. Jonathan Hinder, Labour MP for Pendle and Clitheroe, wrote an article in the *Sunday Telegraph* calling for an immediate freeze on immigration,[16] while Lord Glasman, the group's founder and a big supporter of Donald Trump and friend of far-right agitator Steve Bannon, wrote an article in *The Sun* calling for Britain to 'immediately leave the European Court of Human Rights and scrap the domestic Human Rights Act'.[17]

The evidence, of course, offers a different explanation for Labour's defeat in the Runcorn by-election. Three focus groups run for the campaign group 38 Degrees found a prevailing sense of general pessimism about both the government and politics in general, with Reform voters saying they wanted 'to send a clear message to Starmer: you're going down the wrong path' and to deliver 'a bit of a kick up the bum that change is needed'. Perhaps more significantly, the focus groups did not discover immigration to be a major factor behind the Reform victory.

'In contrast to widely held assumptions, cost of living was far more frequently discussed than immigration,' the 38 Degrees press statement continued:

> The cost of living dominated each of the groups, and concerns about immigration came up in the context of pressure on local area public services. When asked about the change participants wanted to see in the coming years, most people focused on having a bit more money in their pockets, while many talked about the NHS. Policing, local services and social care were also

raised. In this section of the discussion, immigration wasn't raised.

In reacting to Reform UK's rise, many people are also failing to comprehend Reform voters' motivations. In early 2025, HOPE not hate and Focaldata analysed the opinions of 4,000 people who said they would vote Reform UK, and while overall Reform UK supporters have far more negative attitudes to immigration than the population as a whole, there are differences among Reform UK voters.

Reform UK, like all political parties, is made up of a broad coalition of voters. Our analysis found five distinct tribes of Reform voters, of which only three have strong anti-immigrant views. Almost all (95 per cent) of the tribe we have called 'Working Right' – who are older, have lower educational qualifications and are more likely to live in rented or council housing, but strongly support workers' rights – think immigration has been bad for Britain. Almost as many (91 per cent) of the Older Authoritarian Right tribe think the same, as do 84 per cent of the Traditional Conservatives tribe. A fourth Reform tribe – Young Radical Men – are slightly less emphatic in their opposition to immigration, with 59 per cent thinking immigration has been bad but 41 per cent believing it has been good for the country. The final group, which we have coined the Moderate Interventionists, actually have a more positive attitude to immigration, with 52 per cent believing immigration has been good for Britain and 48 per cent believing it has been bad. This last group is drawn to Reform because they feel that both of the main two parties have had a chance but have failed, so it is now time to give a new party a try.

It is quite clear that different issues drive different Reform UK voters, and a sole focus on immigration is unlikely to succeed for Labour.

* * *

Between 2020 and 2024, immigration into the UK reached record levels, with net migration hitting 860,000 in the year to December 2023 and 431,000 in 2024, though many of these people came in through programmes allowing immigration from Ukraine and Hong Kong. While most people consider net migration approaching a million a year to be unsustainable, the question is how it is brought down and the narrative that's created around it. And on this latter point a narrative that demonises immigrants and trashes our multicultural society is both morally wrong and politically dangerous.

In May 2025, Starmer gave a speech where he said that the UK risked becoming an 'island of strangers', going on to add that new migrants needed to 'learn the language and integrate' and that high net migration had caused 'incalculable' damage to British society. The reaction was swift and harsh, with many drawing comparisons with Enoch Powell's infamous 'rivers of blood' speech, which imagined a future multicultural Britain where the white population 'found themselves made strangers in their own lands'. Coming a week after atrocious local election results and following several days of harsher immigration rules, Starmer's speech was clearly designed to counter Reform's surge in the polls. Predictably, it backfired, with Labour dropping 3 per cent in the following YouGov poll as more progressive voters deserted the party and with no discernible pick up from Reform voters. Britain's immigration and asylum policy needs to be driven by doing what is right, as opposed to being led by the far right. It needs an honesty, clarity and resilience that it currently lacks, and it needs to trust the public more. The British people have a far more nuanced view on immigration than the media and political narrative would have us believe. Many people are deeply concerned about the apparent ease with which migrants have entered Britain in the last few years – they're understandably bemused that we have had literally no idea of the numbers coming in and are worried by the pressure the current levels of immigration are putting on public services, as well as the difficulties in removing people who should not be here. However, most British people also value the economic, political and cultural contributions immigrants make to the country, whether through the essential roles they play in keeping the NHS and social care sectors working – often by doing the jobs white Britons choose not to do – or their contributions to our music, sport, food and the vibrancy of our towns and cities. In sharp contrast to the binary political debate, most Britons can celebrate our diverse multicultural society while also having some concerns that certain aspects of it are not working. Appreciating this helps us understand our polling, where only one in 10 Britons (11 per cent) want to close the door to immigration permanently, while 75 per cent are happy with varying degrees of immigration. What's particularly interesting is that these views have hardly changed over the 14 years HOPE not hate has conducted regular polling, from our first 'Fear & HOPE' report, conducted in January 2011.[18]

Even when it comes to refugees, probably the group most vilified by the media and the far right, a majority still want Britain to meet its international obligations. In a poll of 3,000 people, commissioned by HOPE not hate in August 2024, before, during and after the riots, we asked people to select groups from a list who should be allowed to live and work in the UK. While 'high-skilled professionals' topped the poll with 86 per cent approval, just ahead of health and social care workers, 70 per cent of people were in favour of 'people fleeing conflict or persecution' being allowed into the country. Those crossing the English Channel in small boats came in last with just 19 per cent support.

Overall, since 2011, attitudes towards immigration have been steadily getting more positive in the UK. In 2011, shortly after the financial crisis and the onset of austerity, 60 per cent of people thought immigration had been bad for the country, with 40 per cent believing it had had a positive impact. Today, 55 per cent now think immigration has been good for Britain and 45 per cent think it has been bad.

While the country is divided over immigration, many people do have very deep anxieties, and it's important we recognise this. All too often, new immigrants, especially asylum seekers housed in hotels, have disproportionately been placed in more deprived communities, many of which are already struggling with above-average levels of unemployment and poor public services. Home Office data, published in 2023, found that the so-called Red Wall areas were housing seven times as many asylum seekers per person as south-east England. This equated to 15.2 asylum seekers per 10,000 people, compared with just 2.1 per 10,000 in the South East. Large numbers of young men having no right to work or any access to meaningful income leaves them with little option but to hang around on the streets or in public spaces. A rapid and unplanned increase in immigration into a local community can understandably cause concern, and at a time when our public services, starved of resources after 15 years of austerity, are already at breaking point, an influx of people into a community can cause resentment and anger. It is not racist to acknowledge these concerns and pressures; the question is how you address them. In fact, it is imperative we do understand people's concerns – real or perceived – because simply dismissing them as racist or as the product of a racist media or political narrative will only push us further away from where ordinary people are, and thus leave the door open for the far right.

The asylum process needs to be quicker, and the best way to 'smash the gangs' is to remove their business model by creating safe asylum passages for people to apply. Newcomers need to be integrated successfully into society, something many Britons do not feel is happening now. At the same time, a majority want cohesion to work, and over two-thirds think the government should be doing more to make it work well. Simultaneously, Britain must continue to honour its obligations to help those fleeing war, persecution and famine. Immigration is a fact of modern life, and our society will suffer – economically, politically and culturally – without it.

According to our own polling, speaking English is considered the most important method to improve cohesion in Britain, yet public funding to help newcomers learn English has been slashed during the years of austerity, and while new funding has been announced by the government, almost half of those who cannot speak English well have actually lived in the country for at least 10 years. Addressing and resourcing this is just as important to helping newcomers.

There is a far more fundamental point that all politicians are afraid to say, which is that we need immigration. The Office of National Statistics (ONS) estimates that the British population will hit 70 million people in 2026, up from 60 million in 2005. At the same time, our population is also aging. In 1972, there were around 7.5 million people aged 65 or over, or 13 per cent of the population. By 2022, this had risen to 12.7 million people, making up 19 per cent of the population. The ONS projections suggest that by 2072 this could rise to 22.1 million people, or 27 per cent of the population. With the numbers of those aged over 80 set to almost triple over the next 40 years, the pressures on public services and public finances will only be met by having greater numbers of working-age people paying into the system. Britain has two simple choices – either for British people to have more children themselves, or to bring in people to fill the necessary roles in our economy. Unsurprisingly, this is a reality the far right conveniently side-step.

Many public services would crumble without overseas workers. NHS data released in 2024 indicates that one in five NHS staff are not UK nationals, almost double the rate it was in 2009. This rises to 30 per cent of nurses and 36 per cent of doctors. While some will accurately point to low pay and poor working conditions driving trained British-born staff out of the profession, as well as a shortage of training places for aspiring doctors and other medical professionals, the fact remains that the NHS currently needs immigration simply to keep its doors open and the lights on. Training new staff and encouraging those who have left to return might appear a sensible policy, but it will take time and money – and is something many people are unwilling to pay for through extra taxes.

In a desperate bid to bring down immigration, the government risks missing its health targets as hospitals, health centres and care homes struggle to staff vacancies, to say nothing of the impact on economic growth of dramatically reduced immigration.

We also have the devastating impact of the climate crisis to factor in. According to the most recent figures available from the International Displacement Monitoring Centre, 75.9 million people had been internally displaced by the end of 2023 because of climate change.[19] The Institute for Economics and Peace predicts that 1.2 billion people could be displaced globally by 2050 due to a rise in extreme weather and natural disasters. Its 2024 report estimates that a quarter of the world's countries face 'high or very high levels of ecological threat', while the number of people facing food insecurity, defined as insufficient or uncertain daily food consumption, could reach 1.7 billion by 2050. This, coupled with an expected 70 per cent increase in sub-Saharan Africa's population during the same period, will only increase pressure on food and water and will almost inevitably see huge new pressures on migration – with many trying to reach Europe.

It is precisely for these reasons that Britain needs a coherent immigration strategy that balances our societal needs and obligations with what is acceptable and manageable to the public. A strategy that is driven by facts and reality, not by fear of the media and political backlash. An economic and industrial strategy to ensure our communities have decently paid jobs and futures, an employment strategy to prevent rogue employers exploiting immigrants at the expense of British workers, a cohesion strategy to ensure that British society can happily absorb newcomers and – in partnership with others – an international climate and aid strategy that seeks to alleviate some of the worst damage of climate change.

To enable a new immigration strategy, we need public support and trust – something that is sorely lacking at the moment. One way to do this is through a consultation with the British public in the form of a Citizens' Assembly, a system whereby a representative group of randomly selected citizens can learn about, deliberate upon and make recommendations on key issues. Citizens' Assemblies are increasingly used in many other countries. In Ireland, Citizens' Assemblies, also known as 'We the Citizens', were established in 2016 and have considered issues ranging from referendums to fixed-term parliaments, population ageing to climate change. Two of the most productive issues they discussed were same-sex marriage and abortion, both topics that have deeply split the country. Bringing people together in order to find a consensus paved the way to real change. 'The deliberations of the assemblies were a vital step on the road to generating support for constitutional change on both issues,' reported an editorial in the *Irish Times*. 'Politicians had shirked dealing honestly with the abortion issue, in particular, for more than four decades and without the assembly's work it is difficult to see how it would have been resolved.'[20]

Some critics have argued that such initiatives allow politicians to abdicate responsibility for making difficult decisions, but it is precisely because politicians seem unable to make firm and considered decisions on deeply moral or contentious issues that a Citizens' Assembly would be helpful. Immigration, I would argue, is an issue where no government in recent times has been able to articulate and carry through a comprehensive and sensible policy that balances the competing risks and advantages. Either governments pander to the right-wing media by solely viewing immigration as a problem – or, as Johnson's government did to its detriment – they talk tough on controlling our borders while allowing record numbers of immigrants into the country without the knowledge of the British people, destroying public trust in the immigration process and the political system more generally.

A public consultation is also backed by many British people. A poll commissioned by HOPE not hate in April 2025 found that 43 per cent believed the public should be consulted directly through a formal process, 23 per cent believed that decisions should be made mainly by experts and civil servants and just 22 per cent thought the decisions should be left to elected representatives and government ministers.

A government-sponsored Citizens' Assembly, backed by active involvement from media outlets, would allow a representative group of people to look at the issue of immigration in its entirety. They could consider the country's economic needs, our moral and legal obligations in helping people fleeing persecution and war, the impact of climate change on world migration patterns, the issues of how best to remove newcomers who commit violent or sexual crimes and how Britain can afford to pay for its increasingly aging population. At the same time, the assembly could also explore how newcomers could be properly integrated into British society, whether through optimal limits to immigration in any given community, and could look at even more sensitive cultural issues relating to people coming from quite different cultural backgrounds. Basically, nothing should be off the table. At each stage, experts can give advice and opinions, and media partners can relay the deliberations to their audiences.

The outcome will quite probably be a compromise, which is why those most pro- and anti-immigration will be hostile to such an initiative, or at least circumspect about it. But unless we find a way to have a proper discussion over the issue and take it out of the hands of politicians who are driven by short-term electoral interests, then immigration will continue to be the toxic and divisive issue it is now.

14

Green Shoots

The sun was shining, and the atmosphere was one of excited nervousness. The buses and shoppers that would normally fill Oxford Street on a Saturday afternoon had given way to hundreds, probably thousands, of people calling for action on climate change. There was a carnival atmosphere as people sang and danced. Ahead of me, some 100 metres down the road, a pink boat was occupying the junction of Oxford Street and Regent Street. It was April 2019, and Extinction Rebellion (XR) were holding 10 days of marches, protests, occupations and rallies throughout London to demand government action to save the planet.

While I strongly care about the climate, I've never really considered myself a climate activist. I eat meat, wear leather shoes and fly for work and holidays. But on that day, that week, I felt I had to do something. I had watched the XR mobilisations around the capital over the preceding few days with the growing belief that now was the time to take a stand. Humans were literally destroying the planet, and something had to change. Issues around the environment and climate change had become an important issue for HOPE not hate, as far-right and populist-right parties led the charge against climate action, and the growing numbers of people being forced to move as a consequence of climate change collided with their growing anti-migrant rhetoric.

XR had been established a year before, in response to the release of a report on global warming by the United Nations Intergovernmental Panel on Climate Change and out of anger that the British government was not doing enough. A more public and disruptive approach was needed to put the issue on the political agenda. The group's demands were simple: the government had to declare an 'emergency' and work with 'other institutions' to make the necessary changes needed, introduce legally binding policies to reduce carbon emissions to net zero by 2025 and create a Citizens' Assembly to 'oversee the changes'.

The police had moments earlier moved in and created a cordon around the pink boat, preventing more people from joining but also stopping the few hundred already there from leaving. I joined a group just down Oxford Street, who were milling around and enjoying the moment. A few people were dancing to the beat of drums; others, like me, were stretching our necks to try to work out what exactly was happening ahead of us. Above, in the sky, a police helicopter was recording proceedings.

A shout went up for us to move to a side street. By now, it was clear the police had had enough and were intent on moving the protestors on. Not wanting to be kettled within a police ring, I moved with the crowd to Henrietta Place, a small road parallel to Oxford Street. There, after a bit more hanging around, people decided to sit down. XR stewards were clearly in contact with others in surrounding streets, and the decision to sit was a calculated move. As we were discussing our next move, word went round to storm the police line ahead of us. Caught up in the excitement, we all moved forward. To my left was a woman and her young child, who seemed no more than four or five years old.

'Stink Rebellion,' the boy bellowed, to the great amusement of those around.

The mother and son were among the first to run forward. The police were initially caught off-guard by the surge, but very quickly they regrouped and, with reinforcements arriving all the time, began to make lines around us. As they encircled us, it was time to take a decision. Move out or stay and risk arrest. Some of the group wanted to stay, even if it meant being arrested, while others were worried about the young kids. Some got out of the encircling police cordon, while others prepared for the worst.

Over those 10 days in April, XR protested outside Downing Street and Parliament, brought London to a standstill, had a die-in at the Natural History Museum, sat on top of trains, marched on Heathrow Airport and even chained themselves to Jeremy Corbyn's house. Despite the widespread disruption they caused and the considerable anger they generated among the right-wing media and government ministers, it appeared as though the public were on their side.

A few days before XR had begun their protests, *Climate Change: The Facts*, presented by Sir David Attenborough, was aired on the crucial 9 p.m. slot on BBC One. 'Right now, we are facing our greatest threat in thousands of years – climate change,' Attenborough told the millions of viewers who tuned in. 'Scientists across the globe are in no doubt that at the current rate of warming, we risk a devastating future. The science is now clear: urgent action is needed.'

Over the course of the 90 minutes, viewers were given a crash course in the science of climate change, narrated by a national institution. Attenborough's softly spoken and impassioned voice only added to the programme's authenticity. I, like millions of others, watched the programme with a sense of rage. The science seemed so clear, yet our political leaders appeared unwilling or incapable of taking the necessary action.

The message from Attenborough's documentary and the XR protests had clearly got through to the general public. A YouGov poll, conducted while the XR protests were happening, found 46 per cent of the public supported the protests while 27 per cent opposed them. In the same poll, a majority of people felt the government was not doing enough to address climate change, while 61 per cent thought a Citizens' Assembly would do a better job of tackling climate change and ecological breakdown than the government.

HOW TO DEFEAT THE FAR RIGHT

A mood of optimism swept through the environmental world. It finally appeared that the public was beginning to wake up to the threat and demanding solutions from their political leaders. In September 2021, Labour threw its weight behind climate action when the then-shadow chancellor Rachel Reeves said she would be Britain's first 'Green Chancellor' as she pledged Labour would invest £28 billion a year in green capital investment, every year, until 2030. Labour's commitment, while ambitious by British standards, was dwarfed by the Inflation Reduction Act, signed into law in August 2022 by the then-US President Joe Biden. The Act was the largest federal climate-change investment in American history, with the capacity to create $3 trillion in climate investments over the next decade and $11 trillion in overall infrastructure investments by 2050. Two months after Biden put pen to paper, the people of Brazil voted out Jair Bolsonaro, who had wreaked havoc on the Amazon rainforest during his four years in office.

That sense of optimism is now long gone. The war in Ukraine pushed energy prices to record levels, and the search for cheaper fuel and the resulting cost-of-living crisis saw country after country jettison green policies amid a surge in fossil-fuel extraction. Oil- and gas-producing countries effectively took over COP (Conference of the Parties) gatherings and scuppered any serious attempts to address climate change.* Then, in November 2024, Donald Trump was re-elected as president of the United States with the promise to 'drill, baby, drill'. In his first 100 days in office, he signed dozens of executive orders to roll back environmental regulations and protections, eased restrictions upon coal plants dumping their toxic ash and mercury, agreed to huge new oil and gas exploration projects and even ordered his Department of Justice to stop individual states pursuing their own climate laws, which he claimed ran counter to his efforts to unleash energy production.

---

* COP is an annual summit held by the United Nations Framework Convention on Climate Change, where representatives from nearly 200 countries gather to discuss and negotiate global climate action.

Here, Reform UK is increasingly vociferous in its opposition to climate action, with Richard Tice, the party's founding leader, even holding climate-denial views. 'The climate has changed for millions and millions of years. That's the reality, way before man-made CO_2 emissions,' he said on *BBC Question Time* in April 2024. More recently, while being interviewed on Sky News, he claimed there was 'no evidence' human activity caused climate change and dismissed academic studies as 'garbage'.[1]

Although Farage has sought to dial down some of the party's past climate-denial views, he has been an outspoken critic of most climate-action measures, especially anything to do with net zero – the aim to balance the amount of greenhouse gas (GHG) that's produced and the amount that's removed from the atmosphere. In 2022, he launched a campaign demanding a net-zero referendum while promoting false claims and framing the debate as one of democratic defiance against elite consensus. A year later, Farage circulated conspiracy theories on X accusing the government of imposing 'climate lockdowns'.[2]

The party's draft manifesto for the 2024 General Election rejected the notion of man-made climate change, but this was later removed after Farage took over the leadership. However, this did not stop him from claiming, just days before the General Election, that carbon dioxide was not a pollutant because it supported plant growth.

Opposition to net zero has become a central plank of Reform UK policy, with Farage describing it as the new Brexit. In addition to opposing initiatives to reduce our carbon footprint, Farage and Tice have been quick to blame climate policy for our economic ills. In the immediate aftermath of the decision to close the blast furnace at the Port Talbot steelworks, Farage took to X and posted: 'It is a disaster that Net Zero is costing 3,000 steel jobs and that we will stop being a primary steel producer.'[3] Tice agreed, blaming 'eco-zealots'.[4]

Support and enthusiasm for climate action has also been undermined by the concerted efforts of fossil-fuel companies and the far right. Several of the big organisations pushing climate-change denial and/or opposing climate action are funded by fossil-fuel companies, or individuals with investments in fossil-fuel industries, or those on the libertarian right who object to any interference in the free market and the ability to make money however they want.

The main climate-sceptic organisation in the UK is the Global Warming Policy Foundation (GWPF), a right-wing think tank set up by the late Conservative chancellor Nigel Lawson in 2009, which claimed to be an 'all-party and non-party think-tank and a registered educational charity which, while open-minded on the contested science of global warming, is deeply concerned about the costs and other implications of many of the policies currently being advocated'.

The GWPF describes its main purpose as being to 'bring reason, integrity and balance to a debate that has become seriously unbalanced, irrationally alarmist, and all too often depressingly intolerant. … Our main focus is to analyse global warming policies and its economic and other implications.'[5]

Its 'open-minded' approach to climate change is highly questionable. Bob Ward, policy and communications director at the Grantham Research Institute on Climate Change and the Environment at the London School of Economics, told the *Guardian* that '[s]ome of those names [on the GWPF's Academic Advisory Council] are straight from the Who's Who of current climate change sceptics'.[6]

The campaigning arm of the GWPF is the Global Warming Policy Forum, and the director of both organisations is Dr Benny Peiser, a German-born climate sceptic. As recently as 2022, Peiser was quoted as saying:

> It's extraordinary that anyone should think there is a climate crisis. Year after year our annual assessment of climate trends document just how little has been changing in the last 30 years. The habitual climate alarmism is mainly driven by scientists' computer modelling, rather than observational evidence.[7]

According to the excellent DeSmog website, which monitors climate deniers and sceptics, the GWPF said in 2015 that 'policies to "stop climate change" are based on climate models that completely failed to predict the lack of warming for the past two decades'.[8] It has also expressed the view that carbon dioxide has been mischaracterised as pollution when in fact it is a 'benefit to the planet'.

One of the main funders of the GWPF is the Sarah Scaife Foundation, which has $30 million worth of shares in energy companies including Exxon and Chevron. Another key funder is DonorsTrust, described by the American publication *Mother Jones* as the 'dark money ATM' of the conservative movement in the US.[9] While DonorsTrust does not formally have a position on climate change, it does fund a number of organisations questioning the link between fossil-fuel emissions and climate change and others blocking attempts to legislate against greenhouse gas emissions.

In October 2021, the GWPF rebranded itself as Net Zero Watch (NZW), a campaign that claims to 'scrutinise' the UK government's net-zero emissions plans and provide a 'clear view of the reality of climate and energy policies'.

Writing on the openDemocracy website, Adam Bychawski claimed that the American Friends of the GWPF received more than $1.3 million from US donors, of which at least $864,884 has been channelled to the UK group. He went on to assert that of the £1.45 million the GWPF has received in charitable donations since 2017, at least 45 per cent has come from the US.[10] In September 2022, NZW published two reports rejecting climate science on the greenhouse effect.

A director of both the GWPF and NZW is Andrea Jenkyns, the former Conservative MP who in May 2025 was elected mayor of Greater Lincolnshire for Reform UK.

Running parallel to NZW has been the Net Zero Scrutiny Group (NZSG), established by former Conservative MP Steve Baker and later joined by Craig Mackinlay, which opposed many of the net-zero pledges made by Johnson's government ahead of the COP26 climate summit in Glasgow.

While the group claims to accept climate science, it is closely linked to the GWPF. Mackinlay employed Harry Wilkinson, the GWPF's head of policy, as his parliamentary aide, and the NZSG used GWPF research and polling in its material. Baker, the group's founder, was a trustee of GWPF until he stepped back following his promotion to a Northern Ireland ministerial job. The NZSG was closely linked to the European Research Group, of which Baker was a key member, the free-market Institute of Economic Affairs and the anti-fuel duty lobbying group FairFuelUK. The head of FairFuelUK is Howard Cox, the Reform UK candidate for London mayor in 2024. Several long-time climate-sceptic Tories are also involved with the NZSG, including former Conservative MP Philip Davies and Lord Lilley. They were two of the five Conservative MPs who voted against the ground-breaking 2008 Climate Change Act. The others were Christopher Chope, Andrew Tyrie (now a peer) and Ann Widdecombe (now with Reform UK).

A more recent arrival on the European climate-denial scene is the Heartland Institute, a Chicago-based free-market think tank that has regularly denied the scientific evidence for man-made climate change. The institute has received at least $676,500 from Exxon Mobil since 1998, but the real figure is actually likely to be far higher as it has stopped publishing its donations. According to the Union of Concerned Scientists: 'Nearly 40% of the total funds that the Heartland Institute has received from ExxonMobil since 1998 were specifically designated for climate change projects.'[11]

An editorial in the *Nature* magazine wrote of the Heartland Institute:

> Despite criticizing climate scientists for being overconfident about their data, models and theories, the Heartland Institute proclaims a conspicuous confidence in single studies and grand interpretations ... [and] makes many bold assertions that are

often questionable or misleading ... Many climate skeptics seem to review scientific data and studies not as scientists but as attorneys, magnifying doubts and treating incomplete explanations as falsehoods rather than signs of progress towards the truth ... The Heartland Institute and its ilk are not trying to build a theory of anything. They have set the bar much lower, and are happy muddying the waters.[12]

Among its more outlandish claims, the Heartland Institute has compared people who believe in global heating to the Unabomber, the US terrorist who killed three people, and its social media account has shared the bizarre 'Great Reset' conspiracy theory, which claims that politicians engineered the COVID-19 virus as a way to destroy capitalism and assert control over people.

The Heartland Institute established a European office in London in December 2024 and has formed close links with several far-right political parties across the continent, including Germany's AfD, the Freedom Party of Austria and Reform UK. Farage spoke at the opening of the Heartland Institute office, while former Prime Minister Liz Truss and several Conservative MPs were also in attendance.[13] The UK operation will be headed up by Lois Perry, leader of UKIP until June 2024, who has described the climate emergency as a 'scam' and has regularly played down the existence of the climate crisis and the threats posed by it.[14]

While climate sceptics and the cost-of-living crisis have been chipping away at support for climate action, there have been mistakes from environmental and climate groups too. The environmental movement has sometimes come across as elitist, lecturing and life-stylist, demanding people fundamentally and radically change their behaviour, not realising that not everyone is able to, or that for some it is a bigger sacrifice than for others. At the same time, the actions and stunts of groups like Just Stop Oil have annoyed many and undermined support for climate action.

HOW TO DEFEAT THE FAR RIGHT

Writing in a special issue of the *HOPE not hate* magazine, back in 2019, Wigan MP Lisa Nandy was critical of some of the climate movement's actions:

> Telling people to get out of their cars is counter-productive in parts of the country where decades of chronic under-investment has left us without public transport. Jobs have disappeared from our towns as successive governments have chosen instead to invest in cities, creating lengthy commutes on public transport for most working-age people in towns like mine.[15]
>
> It is galling to be told by politicians that you should stop eating meat when you and your family are struggling to get by and relying on help from friends and local foodbanks. It is also counter-productive to disrupt the one holiday a family has, one they've saved for all year, instead of targeting the global corporations whose business models rely on frequent air travel and the governments who refuse to tax them.

Instead, she argued that climate action needed to be joined with the fight for social and economic justice: 'Rooting calls for action in the reality of people's lives is essential if the battle against climate change is not to become a battle against each other.'

One of the climate movement's greatest successes was its concerted efforts to win support for climate action in the Conservative Party, which culminated in the Johnson government announcing a Net Zero Strategy in October 2021. Much of this was driven by Johnson himself, but behind the scenes there had been a coordinated effort by some parts of the climate movement to engage with Conservatives. Unfortunately, this consensus began to break down under the leadership of the more economically libertarian Rishi Sunak. Faced with plummeting poll ratings and increasingly fearful of the threat of Reform UK, Sunak gave in to the climate sceptics within his party and began trashing net-zero targets and other climate-action initiatives.

GREEN SHOOTS

Over the course of his first year as leader, Sunak received several open letters from the NZSG, signed by dozens of Conservative MPs and peers, urging a halt to the government's green pledges. In September 2023, it appeared their lobbying had paid off when Sunak announced a U-turn on several key climate targets, delaying both the ending of the sale of new petrol and diesel cars and the phasing out of gas boilers. Sunak then went further, ridiculing Labour for its apparent obsession with the green agenda and even claiming that it wanted to tax meat and force households to have seven bins.[16]

At the 2023 Conservative Party Conference, just a couple of weeks after Sunak's public U-turn, his colleagues went even further, with Transport Minister Mark Harper saying the Tories would stop the 'misuse of 15-minute cities … what is sinister is the idea of local councils deciding how often you can go to the shops'.[17] The idea that local councils were trying to create a system whereby everything residents needed in their daily lives could be accessed within a 15-minute walk or bus ride was indeed sinister, just as it was totally untrue. Layla Moran, the Liberal Democrat MP for Oxford West and Abingdon, took to Twitter/X to hit back at Harper: 'In Oxford we've been descended upon by ultra-right conspiracy theorists purporting to speak for local residents who largely stayed away. It is genuinely chilling to see Government ministers play to this crowd.'[18]

Labour too is backtracking. In February 2024, Labour halved its ambitious promise to spend £28 billion a year on green investment, while in November 2024, five months after coming into power, it announced it was relaxing some of its green targets as the push for economic growth took priority. Now, faced with a growing threat from Reform UK, there are growing calls within the party to jettison its net-zero targets altogether. The day before the 2025 local elections, former Prime Minister Tony Blair called for a net-zero reset,[19] while former Home Secretary Lord Blunkett, speaking to the *Daily Telegraph*, warned that net zero was making Labour toxic among some voters.[20] Though the party itself denies that it has plans to water down its climate policies, pressure is growing.

Refocusing the actions of the climate movement has become an increasing priority for many organisations as the hurdles and opposition to action on climate change become more apparent. Much of this involves finding new approaches to discuss and promote net zero, engaging at a more local level with more lukewarm audiences and rebuilding the climate-action coalition that was once dominant within all political parties.

One organisation that is doing really valuable work is Round Our Way, which, as its website says, 'shares stories about the impact climate change has on our communities and the incredible local people quietly doing something about it'.[21] It seeks to side-step the usual media slanging matches and was 'created for the growing number of us worried that the impact climate change has on families like ours isn't getting the attention it deserves'.

The organisation's co-director and founder is Roger Harding, who, by his own admission, is not your usual climate activist. 'I'm not what you'd call one of life's great nature or conservation people,' he says:

> I was raised in a council house by a single mum, and family finances were often really tight. I've spent my career fighting for people not to have to worry like my mum did, including years working for Shelter campaigning for people struggling to get or hold on to a home, and recently running a charity for working-class young people.
>
> I've come to care about climate change because I've seen families just like mine have their lives made a misery by flooding or put under even more pressure with rising food and energy bills. Those same families are often completely missing from the debate on climate.

GREEN SHOOTS

It is clear that, for Roger, Round Our Way is as much about filling a gap in the climate-action world as it is about delivering on climate action:

> A lot of traditional climate campaigning leaves people feeling the problem is distant in three ways. The first is time. Talk of 2050 or 2100 leaves us thinking this is tomorrow's problem when many of us are focused on getting to the end of the week or month. Second, it feels geographically distant. Talk of the global nature of the problem risks overlooking the impact climate change is having on our local communities right now through flooding and higher prices. Finally, and most worryingly, it feels brand distant. Climate change feels like a problem other people – very middle-class people – worry about, because too often the only people in the news talking about it are posh.

The organisation has been giving a voice to ordinary people in ordinary communities. On its Substack, it takes up stories like kids at Withernsea High School on Humberside who are talking about the loss of local land through soil erosion, and a local football club in North Yorkshire dealing with the impact of flooding, and how a Gloucestershire paramedic is coping with hotter summers and the challenges of overheating. Local people telling real stories about how climate change is affecting our communities.

The British public remains deeply concerned about climate change and its impact on the future. In our poll of 22,500 people conducted over Christmas 2024, 65 per cent agreed that climate change is being caused by human activity, with just 11 per cent disagreeing. When asked if they thought that climate change posed a threat to the future well-being of themselves and their families, 60 per cent agreed and 13 per cent disagreed.

Opinions were more divided when it came to net zero and the economic costs of addressing climate change. In a different poll of

7,000 people, we asked respondents to agree or disagree with the statement that the economic impact of meeting net zero by 2050 is too much to accept and we should have less ambitious targets – 45 per cent agreed and 22 per cent disagreed. However, when we put the same statement against one saying the opposite, things were more balanced – 51 per cent agreed with the statement 'The economic impact of achieving Net Zero by 2050 is too much to accept and we should have less ambitious targets', while 49 per cent backed the statement 'For the future of the planet we have no choice but to move to Net Zero by 2050.'

While opinions overall were almost the same when given starkly opposing statements, there were still big demographic differences in how people thought. Among those over 65, opposition to the 2050 net zero target was at 59 per cent; among those who voted Leave in the EU referendum, it was 62 per cent; and among current Reform voters it was 75 per cent.

The polling did, however, point to an opening for the climate movement on which it could attract mass support, organise on a very local level and highlight the absurdity of Reform's climate policies – and that is cleaning up our rivers, lakes and seas. Four out of five voters (79 per cent) in our 22,500-respondent poll think that cleaning up the pollution in our rivers should be a national priority. Just 4 per cent disagreed. Among those who say they would vote Reform, 82 per cent think cleaning up our rivers is a national priority, with just 4 per cent disagreeing.

The issue was also the most popular when respondents were asked to choose which of the 20 bills in the 2024 King's Speech they most liked. With sewage spillage at record levels, the issue combines outrage at the water companies, which have paid out billions in dividends to their shareholders since privatisation, with disgust that people and their kids have to swim in water with excrement in it, and incomprehension that this issue only ever seems to get worse. Again, the bill to regulate water companies to clean up rivers, lakes and seas in the UK was selected by 59 per cent of current Reform voters – by far the most popular of Labour's King's Speech bills.

Running local campaigns on sewage leaks can unite local communities, show that people power can create change and highlight the shortcomings of Reform's position on climate change. With Reform now in control of nine county councils, one unitary council and two mayoral positions, they too can be the target for action.

The same goes for the issue of flooding, which is becoming an increasing problem across much of the country as the temperature rises. According to the World Weather Attribution, a collective of scientists from several countries, there was a 20 per cent increase in the amount of rainfall between October 2023 and March 2024 because of climate change. The Environment Agency, meanwhile, predicts that climate change could increase the number of properties at risk of surface flooding to around 6.1 million by the middle of the century.[22] This will not only affect residents but farmers and businesses too. With the East Midlands, and Yorkshire and the Humber being most vulnerable to flooding, and these being places where Reform UK has two mayors (Lincolnshire, and Hull and East Yorkshire) and now controls five county councils – Lincolnshire, Derbyshire, Nottinghamshire, West Northamptonshire and North Northamptonshire – plus Doncaster metropolitan council, the opportunities to demand action on flooding and highlight Reform's crazy climate views are immense.

There are other issues too that can jointly mobilise climate activists and working-class communities. One of these can be bus services. A joint study of bus timetables by the University of Leeds and Friends of the Earth found that urban and rural services had decreased by 48 per cent and 52 per cent respectively and in some areas had dropped by as much as 80 per cent.[23] A more recent study, produced by IPPR North* in January 2025, found that people living

---

* IPPR North is a subsidiary of think tank the Institute for Public Policy Research.

in the top 10 per cent most deprived areas have suffered a tenfold greater reduction in the distance travelled by bus per person compared with those living in the top 10 per cent least deprived areas. 'Neglecting England's buses has had serious environmental, social and economic consequences, which have not been felt equally,' said IPPR North's Marcus Johns.[24]

New polling from Persuasion UK, a non-partisan, not-for-profit research initiative that aims to understand what's shaping public opinion on the issues that define British politics, shows that net zero is not the vote-loser for Labour that some would wish us to believe. In a study into the Reform vote, and specifically a group of Labour voters it describes as 'Reform curious', Persuasion UK conclude that while net zero is deeply disliked by the core Reform voter, it is not considered a major issue for those Labour voters who are attracted to Reform. More importantly, Labour risks losing far more votes to the Greens and Lib Dems if it abandons its net-zero policies.

'Core Reform voters now find themselves very hostile to the green transition – but "Reform curious Labour voters" are not,' says Persuasion UK:

> While they care about it much less than the wider Labour vote, they remain broadly sympathetic, in line with the public at large. Hostility to Net Zero is therefore unlikely to win Reform many Labour votes, while diluting ambitions on climate will not help Labour assuage Reform curious voters either (while also posing big risks elsewhere in its coalition).[25]

HOPE not hate's own research has found high levels of support for climate action among one of the five tribes of Reform voters identified in our analysis of 4,000 Reform voters. Called the Older Authoritarian Right, and making up 27 per cent of Reform voters, they are more likely than the general population to prioritise net zero by 2050 and are highly supportive of cleaning up river pollution, introducing renewable energy and even making individual changes like eating less meat to reduce their own carbon footprint. While most Reform voters are strongly opposed to climate action and many in the party leadership peddle climate-denial conspiracies, a chunk of their voters actually do care about the issue, especially anything to do with nature. Rather than dismissing the Reform voter as anti-climate action, we need to identify and engage with the Older Authoritarian Right in the hope of bringing them further on board with climate-action initiatives or, at the very least, driving a wedge between them and Reform UK.

This has all become more important, even essential, now that Reform has won control of nine county councils and one metropolitan council and gained two mayors. In the immediate aftermath of his party's victory, Farage announced that all Reform-led councils would have no engagement with net-zero policies or training. Andrea Jenkyns, the new mayor of Greater Lincolnshire, went even further, telling the media she would explore launching a series of legal challenges to tie the government in knots when it came to climate action.[26] Her particular focus was to block net-zero projects like solar and wind farms, as well as attempts by the Home Office to house asylum seekers in Lincolnshire. She also announced her intention to meet a fracking company to explore the possibility of extracting gas in the county.

Labour also needs to be bolder on climate issues and even defend its own policies. Reform is currently going unchallenged on issues like net zero because too many people within Labour fear it is a vote-loser. The consequence of this is that the only narrative voters are hearing about is from Reform UK. We can hardly be surprised if people start to think net zero is a problem. Nowhere is a more robust position necessary than Lincolnshire, where Reform is threatening to block green projects, putting £1 billion in funding and 12,000 jobs at risk.

I have long been advancing the idea with my colleagues in the climate world that we need to work much closer together against our common enemy. Not only are we stronger if we begin to work together, but Reform taking control of councils gives us every reason to put this into action. We need to hold these councils and their councillors to account when there are floods and other climate-related disasters, expose their ludicrous and dangerous climate policies and build coalitions at a very local level against them.

15

Power to the People

In late January 2025, I attended a coffee morning at the Abram Community Centre, organised by the local MP Josh Simons after he had contacted 1,000 local people inviting them to meet him. Huddled across eight tables, about 100 people sat patiently for Josh to make his way around the room, which he duly did during the two-hour session. It was a fantastic way of engaging with local people and letting them ask the questions that were on their minds. It was also a process that was overwhelmingly appreciated by people who were, at best, lukewarm towards politicians.

'In all the time we had the previous MP I never met them once,' remarked one woman to general nods of agreement from others. 'I might be here to chew his ear off, but at least he's given me that opportunity,' she adds with a dry laugh.

I followed Josh around, listening to his conversations with his constituents, often staying behind to chat to them when he moved on. Not one person raised a national issue, at least within my earshot, but all had a local gripe or two to raise. Wigan borough, in which the town of Abram is situated, had experienced its worst flooding in 30 years on New Year's Eve as 170 centimetres of rain fell in 18 hours, causing the River Mersey to burst its banks in several places. While the Environment Agency later claimed that flood defences saved 21,000 homes, this was little consolation for those affected. And at the coffee morning, held almost a month later, the anger was still palpable.

Most people directed their anger at agencies that seemed more concerned with passing the buck than taking any responsibility. What infuriated them most was a statement by the Environment Agency and the local water company that it would be five years before adequate flood defences could be put in place to prevent a re-occurrence in the future. Even when their local MP announced he had secured a commitment from the government that they would expedite the work to 2027, few believed him. To local people, it just seemed incomprehensible that it would take the authorities several years to act. And it was hard not to sympathise with their anger.

'Britain is broken, nothing seems to work,' noted one woman with a resigned sigh.

It's a phrase I'm increasingly hearing across the country and something I read in the media on an almost daily basis. To be fair, it's a statement that is sometimes hard to dispute. We pay more and more in taxes, but after years of under-investment and poor pay, our public services and infrastructure are in an awful state. In a poll of 3,400 people, conducted in March 2025 by Focaldata for HOPE not hate, 46 per cent of Britons agreed with the statement 'Britain is broken, nothing seems to work.' Among those who said they would vote Reform UK if a general election were held at the time of the poll, this figure rose to 72 per cent.

Many of these same people also believe that Britain is a country in decline and that the political system is not working. In fact, many feel it is actively skewed against them.

A 2025 HOPE not hate poll of almost 23,000 people found a frightening lack of faith in the political process and politicians themselves. Only 5 per cent of Britons strongly agreed that the political system works well in the UK, with a further 17 per cent thinking it works somewhat well. Almost half, 49 per cent, believe it does not work well. Two-thirds of Britons believe the political system is broken, compared to 13 per cent who think it is not. There is an even greater divide when people are asked if politicians listen to people like themselves, with 69 per cent saying they do not and just 10 per cent believing they do.

The overall figures disguise huge differences between various demographic and political groups, with older and wealthier people having more positive views than younger people and those who are economically struggling.

Attitudes towards our politicians, meanwhile, are incredibly poor, with just 4 per cent of Britons saying they trust politicians to tell the truth. Politician was selected as the least trusted profession from a list of 19. Even bankers were trusted by 14 per cent and journalists by 10 per cent. The most trusted professions were doctors, at 65 per cent, and nurses, at 64 per cent.

Part of the explanation for this declining trust in the political system and the politicians engaged in it has been the seismic shocks to society and self-inflicted political scandals that have hit Britain over the last 20 years. The 2008 financial crash, which led to the worst recession since the 1930s and for which no one was held criminally accountable, was followed by the MPs' expenses scandal and then years of austerity and job cuts. We had the societal ruptures of Brexit in the vote itself but also the frustration among Leave voters that Brexit was not being delivered and the anger among Remain voters that our politicians had harmed the British economy. In 2020, Britain shut down during COVID, hitting the poorest hardest and dramatically reducing social contact. Coming out of COVID, we then had Partygate and the appalling behaviour of then-Prime Minister Boris Johnson, and then finally we had Liz Truss's short-lived but destructive tenure in Number 10 that left millions of households facing further mortgage and borrowing costs. All because of the reckless behaviour of politicians.

In June 2024, shortly before the General Election, the British Social Attitudes (BSA) survey reported public confidence in the government and politicians was at its lowest level since the BSA annual study began in 1983. Commenting on these findings, Professor Sir John Curtice, one of the report's authors, said:

> The next government will not simply face the challenge of reviving Britain's stuttering economy and its struggling public services. It will also need to address the concerns of a public that is as doubtful as it has ever been about the trustworthiness and efficacy of the country's system of government.[1]

He added: 'Addressing some of the policy challenges will help in that endeavour. However, it is likely to require much more than that – in particular, a style and manner of governing that persuades people that the government has their interests at heart after all.'

Depressingly, within weeks of taking office in July 2024, the new Labour government was embroiled in its own scandal after it emerged that the prime minister, deputy prime minister and chancellor had all accepted gifts in the form of clothes from a Labour donor. Watching Education Secretary Bridget Phillipson try to explain away the £14,000 she was given for her 40th birthday party was one of the most painful and damaging pieces of television I can remember. The scandal was whipped up, perhaps out of proportion, by the right-wing media and social media personalities, but given their increasing influence it is even more shocking that these Labour politicians did not think of the consequences of their actions before they accepted these kinds of donations.

Attitudes towards the political system correlate with how people feel they are doing. With many people struggling economically and having little hope that things will change for the better, it is perhaps understandable they do not think politics is working. According to our polling, 8 per cent of Britons are financially desperate, unable to afford essentials such as food, rent or the mortgage, while a further 25 per cent are worried about their financial situation – though they are currently keeping up with their essential payments, they fear they might be unable to do so in the future. With new figures suggesting there are 4.5 million children in poverty and changes to disability benefit likely to make three million people worse off, there is little end in sight for those struggling. The economic growth the Labour government is relying on to turn this country's fortunes around seems a distant dream. No wonder most Britons are pessimistic about the future and 43 per cent choose the word 'declining' to describe Britain today when asked to pick three words from a list of 12. The first positive word selected was 'optimistic', which was picked by just 11 per cent of people.

The consequence of this growing dissatisfaction with the political system and politicians, and overall economic pessimism, is that more people are turning their backs on political engagement and democracy itself. An astonishing 40 per cent of Britons in our 23,000-person poll now prefer 'Having a strong and decisive leader who has the authority to override or ignore Parliament' over 'Having a liberal democracy with regular elections and a multi-party system.'

Among some demographic groups, this figure is even. Among people in the West Midlands, the level of support for a strong and decisive leader is at 43 per cent; among those who do not have a degree, it is 44 per cent; and among those who live in council-owned accommodation, it is 51 per cent. Given the size of the polls conducted, the results must be considered robust and the margin of error small. Worse still, at 40 per cent, this is the highest response in favour of a 'strong leader' we have had in six years of asking this question. While it is probably wrong to say that 40 per cent of British people would prefer to live in a dictatorship with no democracy as we know it today, it probably signifies the frustration many people feel about the political system, and their desire for a strong leader who can actually get things done.

In many ways, Reform UK is simply a political articulation of this discontent and disconnect in British politics today. Polling analysis by HOPE not hate in early 2025 found that the growing group of voters who are turning to Reform are doing so precisely because the

Conservatives and Labour have both tried to run the country and failed.

Reform's rise must also be understood in the context of a decline in turnout in elections over the years. The Electoral Reform Society (ERS), in a report on the turnout in the 2024 General Election, states: 'With over 19 million registered voters not turning out [to vote] and an estimated 8.2 million eligible people missing or inaccurately registered almost the same amount of people didn't vote, 27.5 million, as voted at this election, 28.8 million.'[2]

This should send alarm bells ringing among all those who care about the state of our democracy. It is scandalous, as the ERS report continues, that '[o]ne of the key tenets of democracy is that citizens engage in democratic life and by extension take part in voting, however we are seeing unsettling trends of people not turning out to vote and thereby forgoing one of the most fundamental democratic rights'.

The picture at a local level is even more worrying. There were 56 parliamentary constituencies where the turnout in 2024 was less than 50 per cent and, if one takes into account those missing from the electoral register – likely to be disproportionally higher in the lower-turnout constituencies given their demographics – turnout in some places will have been little more than 30 per cent.

Turnout in local elections is even more shocking. In the 2024 local elections, the average turnout hovered around the 35 per cent mark, and in some council wards it was as low as 13 per cent. Even in the metro-mayoral elections, which were created to devolve power to a more local and regional level, there was little interest in voting. In Merseyside, turnout was just 24 per cent, while the West Midlands, East Midlands and South Yorkshire mayoral contests also had turnouts below 30 per cent. When those missing from the electoral register are included, turnout is likely to have hovered around the 20 per cent level.

If turnout in elections reflects the health of a democratic system, then ours is on a life-support machine.

POWER TO THE PEOPLE

Now Reform UK, like UKIP and even the BNP before it, has begun mobilising these non-voters, and only now have other parties begun to get worried. Of course, there are important policy issues and economic and cultural drivers at play, but people's belief that the political system doesn't work, or at least doesn't work for them, is absolutely crucial in understanding the support for Reform. Reform UK voters are even more disengaged from politics than the general public. Just 2 per cent trust politicians to tell the truth, while 72 per cent believe Britain is broken and 50 per cent would support a strong leader over a parliamentary democracy.

Most of HOPE not hate's engagement with the democracy space has come in the form of our numerous voter-registration and turnout campaigns, which we have run annually since 2014. Democracy and participation should be a way for people to feel heard, be included and demand improvements in their lives. The failure to achieve this can easily lead people to look elsewhere – to the extremes – for their political solutions. Unfortunately, changes to registration and voting rules have made participation more difficult, especially for those who arguably need a voice most.

Ahead of the 2014 European elections, HOPE not hate piloted a voter-registration drive to reach new voters. Our 'Campus Callout' saw events taking place at 35 university campuses; a 'Souls to the Polls' initiative engaged with faith communities in Greater Manchester, West Yorkshire and London; and there was also a voter-registration drive among Central and Eastern European communities in London. This has proved to be a basic template for much of our work since. Following the introduction of Individual Electoral Registration, which caused the numbers of people registered to vote in poorer communities and areas with high student populations to plummet, HOPE not hate joined forces with the *Daily Mirror* to promote voter registration in the run-up to the 2015 General Election. Called #NoVoteNoVoice, the centrepiece of the initiative was a two-week bus tour of England and Wales, supported by Unite the Union.

The following year, HOPE not hate linked up with ice-cream makers Ben & Jerry's to run a voter-registration drive to encourage young people to vote in the London mayoral election. The 'Don't Get Frozen Out' campaign saw us touring universities, colleges, local communities and shopping centres across the capital, offering free ice cream to those who registered to vote. To celebrate our partnership, Ben & Jerry's even produced a special ice cream in our honour.

HOPE not hate ran a voter-registration drive in the autumn of 2018 to coincide with the beginning of the college year. The results were staggering. A total of 237,632 people registered to vote during our 'Democracy Week'. The same week in 2017 saw 195,157 registrations, while just 56,586 people registered during the government's own voter-registration drive in early July – and they spent millions. Over the full six-week duration of our campaign, 233,653 more people registered to vote that year compared to the same period in 2017. While we couldn't say that this was all down to us, we were the only non-council operation running voter registration at the time.

I see four key elements to improving the health of our democracy. We need to expand democracy; increase the involvement of people; challenge nefarious actors who seek to undermine democracy and stoke division; and make politics work for us. None of this is rocket science, but none of it is easy to enact, not least because achieving these goals requires upending the status quo and sweeping aside those who have a vested interest in hindering change.

Several organisations have made recommendations to improve our democracy. Some have proposed changing the voting system to a form of proportional representation (PR), whereby numbers of seats are allocated in line with the total numbers of votes received. This is clearly fairer and prevents a situation like we saw in the 2024 General Election, where the combined support for Reform UK and the Greens was at 21 per cent of the total vote, but they received less than 1.5 per cent of the seats. I have long been against PR, believing it creates unstable governments, removes the important link between an MP and their constituents and allows small extremist parties into the political system, where they can wield unfair influence. More recently, however, I've begun to change my mind. Democracy is democracy, and we cannot create systems to suit our own political views and damage those of parties we do not like. In a system where elections are usually decided by a handful of swing seats, and then within them by small groups of swing voters, it is easy to see why most voters believe they are ignored and their support taken for granted. If parties are made to fight for every vote, then they might just be more responsive to the views and wishes of their voters.

Even the argument that our current voting system prevents extremist parties from entering our elected chambers and exerting undue influence no longer holds. We now find ourselves in the unenviable situation where Reform UK could be the largest single party after the next election on just 28 per cent of the vote, depending on how the votes for Labour and the Conservatives are dispersed. It could even win a majority of seats with less than a third of the national vote. That's hardly democratic either. I still worry about losing the connection between the constituent and their MP, but there are different forms of PR that make allowances for this, such as multi-seat constituencies or even keeping the current structure as it is but having an elected second chamber.

Several organisations have been proposing other changes to improve our democratic process. Ahead of the 2024 General Election, the ERS produced a manifesto for Westminster renewal. In addition to moving to some form of PR and an elected second chamber, it also recommended devolving power locally, 'but to do so meaningfully, local and regional government needs to have the right democratic structures, powers and resources and consider how to meaningfully engage citizens in decision-making'.[3] The Local Government Association, which represents all political parties at a local government level, put forward the case for 'civic and democratic engagement', which involves increasing the powers and responsibilities of local government as a way to reinvigorate disillusioned citizens, and the development of 'locally focused devolution agreements that are informed by citizens and are better suited to the strengths, needs and aspirations of local people'.[4]

There are also some practical ways we can encourage greater engagement in our electoral system. Automatic voter registration, whereby councils use existing public data to put adults on the electoral register, would mean millions more people getting a chance to vote in elections. Reducing the voting age to 16, as the government announced it would in July 2025, will introduce the democratic process to people earlier in life and, if combined with democratic and citizenship classes at school, would help bring young people into the electoral process. Weekend voting, or making a general election a public holiday, could also increase turnout by making it easier for people who struggle to fit voting in alongside work, childcare or adult care responsibilities to get to the polls.

There are also things that campaign and community groups could do themselves. I've always thought that the process to register to vote is a very passive action, especially when we rely on local and central government, employers and universities to put our names on the register automatically. In the United States, voter registration is part of the organising process and an opportunity for campaign and community groups to support or oppose a particular policy or candidate. By building voter registration into the process, especially when it is based around a particular policy, you are immediately giving people a reason to vote. You can reward or punish candidates depending on whether they adopt your programme and hold elected politicians accountable if they renege.

While many of us are working tirelessly to improve our democracy, there are others who are trying to subvert it. Protecting our system from nefarious actors – both extremists and state actors – who seek to deliberately undermine trust in our political process by spreading disinformation and deepening distrust between communities should be a core task of the government.

A parliamentary report, published in 2020, concluded that 'Russian influence in the UK is the new normal [and that] the UK is clearly a target for Russian disinformation.' However, it also accused the government of not knowing the true extent of Russia's attempts to tip the scales in the EU referendum and – quite incredibly – doing nothing to actually find out.

What can be proved, though, is that the British far right has sometimes been a useful conduit for Russian state actions. Stephen Lennon has long been a *cause célèbre* for the Russian state media and one outlet for this disinformation. Lennon received disproportionate coverage from Russia Today (later RT) and from state-owned news agency Ruptly between 2015 and 2020. He was regularly interviewed on these channels and his events often live-streamed, so much so that there are 98 videos of Lennon on the Ruptly website from this period. When my colleague Joe Mulhall bumped into the Ruptly journalist who had covered many of Lennon's events at a bar one night, he asked him why Lennon was provided with such coverage. 'I just get told to from Moscow,' the young journalist replied.

Russian media interest in Lennon was part of a wider Russian plan to amplify extremist voices in order to foster division and discontent in Western countries. The most high-profile Russian intervention was during the US Presidential Election campaign in 2016, when multiple means were used to undermine Hillary Clinton's campaign and promote Donald Trump. One part of this clandestine war was the St Petersburg-based Internet Research Agency (IRA), an organisation engaged in online propaganda and influence operations on behalf of the Putin administration, Russian businesses and Russian intelligence. The IRA was the brainchild of Yevgeny Prigozhin, then a close friend of President Putin, who went on to establish the Wagner mercenary group. According to a joint investigation by Bellingcat, The Insider and *Der Spiegel*, Prigozhin's operations were 'tightly integrated with Russia's Defence Ministry and its intelligence arm, the GRU'.[5]

The Russian propaganda operation has been busy in the UK. A report by CREST in December 2017, produced in collaboration with academics at Cardiff University, identified the systematic use of fake social media accounts linked to Russia, which amplified the public impacts of four terrorist attacks that took place in London and Manchester in 2017: 'The evidence is that at least 47 different accounts were used to influence and interfere with public debate following all four attacks. Of these, eight accounts were especially active, posting at least 475 Twitter messages across the four attacks, which were reposted in excess of 153,000 times.'[6]

The report found that many Russian troll accounts positioned themselves as 'breaking news' sites, presumably so they could help shape narratives in the immediate aftermath of terrorist attacks in order to 'try and sow seeds of antagonism and anxiety'. Many were tweeting incessantly with highly opinionated and strongly ideological viewpoints. 'Another day, another Muslim terrorist attack. RETWEET if you think that Islam needs to be banned RIGHT NOW!' was posted immediately after the Manchester Arena bombing and retweeted 3,606 times.

The CREST report also noted that these false accounts were directing messages at 'thought communities' more aligned with their own online identities: 'There are multiple instances of them "@-ing" Tommy [Stephen Lennon], former leader of the English Defence League and Nigel Farage. The purpose being to try and stir and amplify the emotions of these groups and those who follow them, who are already ideologically "primed" for such messages to resonate.'

HOPE not hate's Patrik Hermansson found that one of these Russian accounts belonged to a 'David Jones'. Claiming to be from 'Southampton/Isle of Wight', his pro-Brexit and anti-Muslim Twitter account amassed over 100,000 followers during its four-year existence and tweeted 137,000 times. This account also had dozens of interactions with Lennon on Twitter during 2017 on issues ranging from 'Muslim rape gangs' to the dangers of Islam. The vast majority were retweets, but there were some original tweets as well, similarly tagging Lennon.

Analysis by the Alliance for Securing Democracy (ASD) found that a significant number of the 600 Twitter accounts it analysed, either directly tied to the Russian government or closely aligned with its propaganda, had 'tweeted prolifically in Robinson's [Stephen Lennon's] defence'. Speaking to the *Guardian*, ASD social media analyst Bret Schafer said: 'The clustered focus on the Tommy Robinson case in late May [2018] suggests that Russian-linked accounts saw his arrest as a clear opportunity to amplify political divisions both in the UK and abroad.'[7]

In February 2020, Lennon was invited to Russia by journalist Edvard Chesnokov, who was deputy international editor at *Komsomolskaya Pravda*, one of the most popular newspapers in Russia. Lennon was greeted on his arrival by Alexander Malkevich, a journalist and head of the Foundation for National Values Protection, a Russian not-for-profit NGO, and held a press conference under the theme 'What's Going On with Free Speech in Europe?' Lennon was introduced as a politician and journalist. The EDL founder told the audience that not only had he been jailed for making a video but that he had also been 'illegally' banned from Twitter for 'supposed extremist statements'.

The RIA-FAN news agency reported Lennon as saying that all the problems he was talking about were connected to Muslims: 'This is not just about one-off crimes by individuals but about gangs of migrants raping underage British girls,' said Lennon. 'You can't believe the British media! I've seen their manipulations, how they make up lies about me … that's why I'm here. Because all these issues are relevant in Russia.' Lennon also called for the break-up of the European Union, denied Russian involvement in the Salisbury Novichok poisonings (targeted against former Russian intelligence officer-turned-defector Sergei Skripal) and claimed the EU was destabilising Ukraine and that then-German leader Angela Merkel had plans to lead a NATO invasion of Ukraine.

'We can cooperate to preserve our Christian values, culture and identity,' the Englishman added. 'Russians see Putin as the defender of their country. He is a strong politician. The West doesn't have enough strong men. Western politicians are emasculated.'

Lennon's host Malkevich has a colourful past. As well as being the head of the Foundation for National Values Protection, he had previously been head of USA Really, a Russian propaganda outfit that was sanctioned by the US for election interference after running a troll factory in Russia that disseminated disinformation during the 2016 US Presidential Election. USA Really was linked to, and believed to be funded by, the Russian oligarch and founder of the IRA Yevgeny Prigozhin.

Malkevich would later be involved in a number of other pro-Putin initiatives to undermine democracy and support the involvement of Russian businesses and troops in Central African countries. He's clearly an important cog in Putin's soft-power operations around the world, so for him to be so centrally involved in Lennon's visit to Moscow can only suggest that it was considered to be in Russia's strategic interest to have him there.

Improving democratic structures and making voting easier can only take us some of the way along the journey to a more engaged and responsive political system. Participatory democracy should be more than a single vote every few years. We need to create structures and a mindset where participatory politics creates opportunities for people to be more actively engaged in decision making. This can be done formally, through the creation of consultation processes and even Citizens' Assemblies, but it can also be done organically, through campaign groups and existing networks such as tenants' associations and faith networks.

This will always be more possible at a local level, but the process of mobilising communities around specific issues can still be scaled up if necessary. Often, the best campaigns are those organised and operated from outside formal council or business structures. A great example of this has been the Living Wage Campaign, started originally in East London by The East London Citizens Organisation. Launched in 2001, one of its biggest triumphs was securing an agreement to ensure all those who worked on building and servicing the stadiums for the 2012 London Olympics received a basic living wage. Councils and businesses have also adopted the living wage, which is considerably higher than the minimum wage. All of this was achieved by mobilising communities, bringing unions, campaign groups and faith networks together and old-fashioned organising. According to Citizens UK, the alliance behind the effort, the Living Wage Campaign 'won over £2 billion of additional wages, lifting hundreds of thousands of people out of working poverty'.

To achieve a real increase in participatory democracy, we need nothing less than a democratic revolution. It is part organising, part mindset change. It's convincing ourselves that we can create change if we organise ourselves and mobilise against those standing in the way of the change. This means we – as in the wider progressive movement – need to change the way we operate too, especially if we really want to engage with working-class communities. We need to be better at listening to local people rather than coming into communities with preconceived ideas and telling people what to do. It means embedding ourselves in the communities we want to engage with rather than dropping in from the outside. It means addressing the issues of concern for local communities rather than deciding the issues beforehand. Finally, and perhaps most importantly, it means having a willingness to listen to people who might have different views rather than showing an immediate intolerance to attitudes and opinions with which we might not agree.

HOPE not hate was founded on the view that you need to take people from where they are, not where you are. We have had to listen to people and treat them with respect, even if we didn't always agree with them. We accepted that we had to understand why people might think differently from us, and we learnt quickly that we needed to earn the right to be heard, even if it meant dealing with their issues before we could raise ours. Above all, we found that the best resource for building resilience and challenging hate almost always came from within local communities, so our job was to identify, support and amplify those voices.

Increasing democracy – and participatory democracy at that – is a powerful antidote to the populist far right. It can challenge the widespread perception that current politics has failed, challenge the perception that nothing can change and, when linked to campaigning, can break down perceived barriers and divisions between communities by organising around issues of shared concern.

An emerging concept to challenge far-right populism is democratic populism. One of its leading advocates is Chantal Mouffe, a French-born academic at Westminster University, who has developed a theory of left-wing populism as a response to the failure of the social-democratic project, with its adoption of a centre-right line in its response to the 2008 financial crash and its embrace of austerity. The consequence of this, she has argued, has been its abandonment by its traditional working-class base, which has turned to far-right populism. Adopting a left-populism, she argues, would rebuild the boundary between left and right and offer a counterweight to the appeal of the far right.

Explaining the difference between right-populism and left-populism, Mouffe says that 'the former tends to restrict democracy while the latter works to extend and radicalise democracy. A left-populism is not opposed to democracy and institutions, but instead corresponds to what I call a radical reformism.'[8]

Another person pushing this approach is Ricken Patel, the founder of the online global campaign group Avaaz. 'Democratic Populists respect democracy, listen to all voters (including those who support the other "side"), seek to serve not 51% of people but the large majority of people, and are willing to face conflict with various actors to do it,' he says.

At its core, democratic populism seeks to find issues and causes that overcome the 'us and them' of modern political debate by gaining widespread support, inspiring others to public service and the common good and being willing to face conflict with various actors to do it.

'Democratic Populists tend to be humanists in the sense of having time and consideration for any person,' Patel adds:

> Their sincerity also tends to show up in how they communicate – not so much the robotic press-release speech of traditional politics (largely driven by a desire to avoid offending various groups), and more just being honest and open with people about what they think and feel. This is sometimes easier for Democratic Populists because what they think and feel is often more aligned with most people. They don't tend to hide their true opinions, and voters can tell the difference.[9]

Democratic populism runs counter to our own prejudices, and to the evangelical nature of many activists, whereby we are so convinced of the righteousness of our own beliefs that we lack the empathy or willingness to consider others and compromise, and it also runs counter to vested interests on our own side.

Possible campaigns against water companies over sewage leaks and flooding in areas controlled by Reform councils and mayors, as outlined in the previous chapter, are perfect examples of the type of democratic populist campaign that can bring communities together around a populist goal, and in the process undermine the appeal of Reform.

Back in Abram, Josh Simons has a lot of work to do to ensure the government keep their promise of funding new flood defences in 2027. If he succeeds, then he can show that his intervention can achieve real results for people. If the government reneges on its promise, then he risks being just another failed politician, and his seat at the next election is in real peril.

One of the most vocal people at his coffee morning summed up the challenge he is facing. 'If he,' she said, pointing at the MP, 'achieves that then I will probably vote for him.' But her anger over the issue and her general disdain for a political system that she felt hasn't delivered clearly showed she would be a vocal adversary if he failed. With Reform UK showing a strong second in the Makerfield constituency at the General Election, the stakes are high for Josh Simons.

16

Hope

I'm finishing this book as news comes in about Reform UK's electoral success in the 2025 local elections. The party won 677 out of 1,637 council seats up for election, two mayoral contests, gained control of nine county councils and one unitary authority, and won a parliamentary by-election, beating Labour in their 16th safest seat. And some of its successes were startling. In County Durham, once one of Labour's safest heartlands, Reform won 65 of the 98 seats available, in Doncaster 37 of the 55 available, in Lincolnshire 44 of the 70 and 49 of 62 seats in Staffordshire.

The general public now think Farage is likely to be the British prime minister after the next election, and opinion polls put Reform UK several points ahead of Labour, with the Conservatives floundering badly in third.[1] While the Tories are facing an existential threat to their future, Labour are doubling down on their strong rhetoric on immigration in the hope of attracting back some Reform voters.

As this book goes to print, we are reminded why Reform UK is such a threat and why it needs opposing. During the Hamilton, Larkhall and Stonehouse by-election for the Scottish Parliament in June 2025, the party ran Facebook ads falsely claiming that Scottish Labour leader Anas Sarwar was prioritising Pakistanis over Scots.

Ten days later, former Reform Chairman Zia Yusaf told BBC Radio Four's *Today* programme: 'I want to be crystal clear about what Reform UK's position is which is we will deport everybody who is here in this country illegally which is roughly 1.2 million people.'

Reform UK cheerleader Matt Goodwin was ecstatic, posting on X: 'If you don't think Reform is serious about illegal migration you're not paying attention.'

One only has to look to Trump's America to see the horrific scenes of immigration officers randomly stopping people of colour on the street, whisking those without papers into vans and even leaving young kids on the sidewalk.

Before the next general election, we have the 2026 local elections to deal with, which will be a far bigger test than the 2025 elections. There will be elections for the Scottish Parliament and Welsh Senedd and all-out elections in the 32 London boroughs and Birmingham, Bradford, Sunderland, Sandwell, Barnsley, and St Helens, to name just a few. There will be elections in areas where elections were deferred in 2025 because of local government reorganisation, plus the normal thirds in most metropolitan councils.

It is not just on the electoral front that we are now facing a threat – but on the street and in our communities too. Much of the anger and discontent that contributed to the 2024 riots still exist, and the release of Stephen Lennon from prison could provide an outlet for that anger. And if all this wasn't enough, American tech companies are planning to pressure Trump to force the British government to water down the already weak oversight of social media companies. The race riots in Ballymena, Northern Ireland, of June 2025, where migrants were literally burnt out of their houses and a local mosque was petrol bombed, were a deeply frightening development, much of it cheered on enthusiastically by the British far right.

After years of thinking that there was a British exceptionalism to the growth of far-right populist parties of the likes we have seen across Europe, we could now be just a few years from having a far-right government ourselves.

HOPE

This is the challenge we are facing, and this is the challenge we must overcome. Hopefully this book has explained the threat and given some pointers to what we must do, but time is short, and if we are going to stop the far right – in all its guises – then we need to get ourselves organised now.

In October 2011, I sent an email to our 200,000 supporters offering them the chance to win five pairs of tickets to Billy Bragg's Leftfield in Motion tour. All they had to do was tell us why they supported HOPE not hate. It proved to be one of the most useful, insightful and definitely most thought-provoking exercises we had ever conducted. More than 3,000 people replied, and what they told us was revelatory. We had adopted the 'HOPE not hate' name as a useful campaign slogan, partly to reach women who were often put off by aggressive anti-fascist slogans but also to contrast our message of HOPE with that of the BNP's hate. But for our supporters, the name 'HOPE not hate' meant much more. To them, it was a system of values representing how they wanted to live their lives.

'I love the HOPE not hate campaign because – to hate is to lose all HOPE!' said Mike, from Liverpool.

'I love the HOPE not HATE campaign because I believe that with the light of HOPE we will continue to out shine the negativity of HATE soul by soul by soul by soul by soul … x,' wrote Paulette, from Birmingham.

'The idea of HOPE is something that inspires the good inside each individual, hate in itself is a destructive force which at the end of the day can only lead to our own demise and dismay. Hope is the future, Hope is the fight, Hope is Human,' noted Thomas, from Essex.

'It's the blue sky above the dark clouds, the voice of reason that drowns out mindless prejudice. HOPE represents the big meadow that is more enduring than the odd weed!' added Pauline from Beaconsfield.

Reading these competition entries was revelatory for me, and from that point on I have always tried to think about the importance of values in our mission and message. Now, sitting here today with all that's happening around us, I actually think it is more important than ever. It is the anchor to our mission but also the dream of a better tomorrow.

HOPE not hate came into being in recognition that anti-fascism had to change to meet the threat of the emerging BNP. Now, facing the threats we have before us, it seems appropriate to re-evaluate where we are and consider how we must change to meet these challenges. I hope this book has contributed to this. I don't profess to have all the answers, but I hope I've been honest about where we are and what we need to do. This book is not meant to be a dig at any individual or group, just an honest reflection that if a far-right party is leading in national opinion polls and far-right influencers can put tens of thousands on the streets, our current strategies are clearly not enough.

It is perfectly understandable if some people feel overwhelmed with what is happening here and around the world. I feel the same sometimes, but I also strongly believe the future is not set, and through hard work, innovative campaigning and, above all, a big dollop of HOPE, we can turn things around.

HOPE on its own is not enough. As I have explained throughout the book, economic insecurity and pessimism are driving much of the discontent and fear we are now seeing. The appalling state of our public services and the seeming inability of recent governments to deliver on their campaign promises has undermined trust in the political process and democracy itself. Addressing these issues and giving people the prospect of their kids' lives being better than their own will go some way to reducing this anger and sense of decline. While economic growth is a key priority for the current Labour government, and it recently announced major infrastructure projects like the third runway at Heathrow and airport extensions at both Gatwick and Stanstead, and building a new rail link between Oxford and Cambridge, these are all in the more affluent south-east of England. We also need an industrial strategy that addresses the problems in other parts of the country, especially in the former coalfields and coastal communities, that goes beyond warehousing and offers young people better training and a brighter tomorrow.

Alongside economic growth, the government needs to play a more active role in rebuilding our communities, providing resources and support to expand social capital and rebuild our community and youth service infrastructure. The more cohesive communities are and the more people interact with one another, the more barriers will be broken down and suspicions eased. Cohesion is not just about how different ethnic or religious communities live together but about how we all do, and the government needs to proactively help improve cohesion and not expect it to happen without them. At the same time, the government needs to prepare for crises too, and the HOPE not hate proposal of a Community Resilience Fund, coupled with the restoration of the Tension Monitoring Unit, is much needed.

There is also work for us all to do too. As individuals, we must be better at talking to people who hold different views from our own, and even if we do not necessarily agree with them, we at least need to treat them with respect and hear them out. At the same time, we all need to do more to be better citizens, to look out for our neighbours, get involved in local community initiatives and interact more with others. Building community is a job for us all.

Anti-fascists need to work in the communities most susceptible to the far right, talking about the issues that are important to local people – rather than our own issues – and addressing people where they are, not where we might be. We need to treat people with respect, even if we might disagree with some of their politics, and we need to earn their respect by helping them before expecting them to do something for us. This also requires long-term engagement, not just turning up at election time. We must also understand how important civic pride is to local communities. Celebrating what we have in common – our history, local traditions, the sports clubs we support and the community groups we might be involved in – can be the glue that binds us together.

Progressive groups need to start working better together too. We are each too weak to face the threats we do now alone. We need to pool resources and skillsets, share good practice and help each other in our campaigns. A victory for one must be considered a victory for all. Anti-fascists must work better with poverty campaigners, migrant and asylum groups, climate activists and those working for greater democracy – not least because we are increasingly facing the same political opponent.

Throughout the 21 years since we set up the HOPE not hate campaign, I've always found our strongest assets are in the very communities that are susceptible to far-right narratives. Consider the town crier in the Ribble Valley, or the young mothers in Friar Park. Dee Johnson and her community choir, or the youth and community workers in Burnley, Bradford and Hull who work tirelessly in some of the poorest communities in Britain. We've seen Angela Sinfield and the mothers who took on the groomers and the BNP; and Julie Siddiqi and Peter Adams and their strong inter-faith and community actions, and more recently the ordinary people who came out on to the streets to clean up and rebuild their communities after the riots. Time and again, ordinary people do amazing things to make their communities better. Our job is to identify, support and train these people and amplify their work.

It is not about us – whether that be HOPE not hate, local councils or the government – going into these communities and telling them what to do. These people know their communities better than anyone, and we all need to trust them by giving them the tools to do what they are already doing but on a bigger scale.

In an ever-more dangerous and complex world, one in which we face uncertain economic futures and the ever-increasing threat of climate change, we need something to hold on to, something to motivate us to get out of bed each morning and face down the politics of hate – and that is HOPE.

Yes, we are right to feel angry and even a bit scared at what's happening in the world, but let that anger be our motivator and let us use it to turn HOPE into action. Never underestimate the power of people, because people can do amazing things. Time and again, when given an option, people will usually choose HOPE over hate. It's just that we need to give them the HOPE – offer them a better future and provide them with the skills, resources and confidence to believe that a better tomorrow is possible.

The American environmentalist David Orr once wrote that 'HOPE is a verb with its sleeves rolled up.' Faced with growing threats, I would add that HOPE also has to be our guiding light to a better tomorrow. We can do this if we do it together.

Acknowledgements

I would like to say a massive thank you to everyone who has contributed to this book. It was written in just 15 weeks, but it was 25 years in the making. Over that time, I have worked with dozens of truly wonderful and dedicated people, many – like Ruth Anderson, Rosie Carter, Matthew McGregor, Jemma Levene and Sam Tarry – who have long-since moved on, but all have remained in the HOPE not hate family.

I have drawn heavily on the work of my colleagues over the years and this book is as much a tribute to them as it is my own story. I would particularly like to thank Joe Mulhall and his research team, who have provided much of the material for this book; Georgie Laming and her team, who take on hate through their campaigns and comms; Misbah and the community team who deliver HOPE and build resilience; and Anki, who helps with data and insight. Then there is Matthew Collins, who has quite literally been in the trenches with me since I first met him in 1993. Keeping us all together is Kelly and her operations team, including Mary and the ever-patient Andy Vine.

Managing me is unquestionably a thankless task, so I would like to thank the board members of HOPE not hate Limited and the trustees of the HOPE not hate Charitable Trust – both past and present.

HOPE not hate is more than just the staff who work for it. Rather, it is the hundreds of thousands of people who have supported us over the years, whether that is through activism, funding or just moral support. Without their passion and generosity, HOPE not hate would not have achieved half of what we have done.

The *Daily Mirror* has supported us over the years, as have Unison, the NEU and the TUC. Gordon Brown, who embodies the moral decency that we should all strive for, personally supported us when he was prime minister and continues to work with us today, and of course, my old friend Jon Cruddas, who fought the far right alongside us in Dagenham but has also been a valued sounding board and mentor to me.

A big shout out must go to all those at HarperCollins who approached me with the idea of writing this book and stewarded it through the process. You know who you are.

I have always said that I feel incredibly lucky to get paid for doing a job I like and I'm deeply passionate about. My own motivation, however, is the people I've met in communities around the country, who, mostly in an unpaid capacity, keep the flame of HOPE alive in often quite difficult and even hostile circumstances. The likes of Jason Hunter in Burnley, who has been our number one super-activist since I first met him in 2002; Andy, from Manchester; and Paul Meszaros, from Bradford, who started out on the antifascist journey with me in 1989 and has done truly inspirational work ever since. There is Narmada from Unison, who, through her own experience of growing up amidst the civil war in Sri Lanka, has constantly reminded me of the importance of HOPE in a time of hate. There is Julie Siddiqi, whose positivity and tireless work to bring communities together is a personal inspiration to me, and Peter Adams, who has done amazing work in Luton but also acted as my sounding board for all things community and interfaith.

ACKNOWLEDGEMENTS

An eternal debt goes to all the brave people who have operated inside far right groups for us over the years. I mention a few in this book – Darren Wells, Andy Sykes and Robbie Mullen – but there are dozens more who, at great personal risk to themselves, have given us information from inside often violent and racist groups. This includes Arthur, a young antifascist, who went to over 400 meetings, rallies and gigs during 10 years inside the BNP and helped identify David Copeland, the London nailbomber. We owe these people a great debt.

Finally, I'd like to thank my long-suffering family, who have had to put up with me over all these years, often at great personal risk to themselves.

This book is to you all.

Notes

Prologue

1. '"Hitler Youths" Using Instagram to Recruit Children', *The Times*, 13 September 2020, https://www.thetimes.com/uk/social-media/article/hitler-youths-using-instagram-to-recruit-children-xfgnglklv

1: Eleven Days That Shook Britain

1. https://www.gq-magazine.co.uk/article/southport-riots
2. https://www.thetimes.com/uk/crime/article/who-are-the-far-right-groups-organising-the-southport-stabbing-protests-q22f07q5q
3. J. Mulhall, 'A Post-organisational Far Right?', HOPE not hate, n.d., https://hopenothate.org.uk/research-old/state-of-hate-2018/online-radicalisation/post-organisational-far-right/

2: Local Heroes

1. The *Guardian*, 3 May 2002, https://www.theguardian.com/politics/2002/may/03/localgovernment.uk

3: In the Know

1. 'Archive 2004: The Secret Agent', BBC, 22 October 2009, http://news.bbc.co.uk/panorama/hi/front_page/newsid_8320000/8320387.stm
2. 'Nick Griffin Minder, Joe Owens, Standing as "Independent" in Wavertree', *Searchlight*, 9 June 2024, https://searchlightmagazine.com/2024/06/nick-griffin-minder-joe-owens-standing-as-independent-in-wavertree/

3. C. Seiga, *Killer*, London, John Blake, 2001.
4. 'Susan Hall Is Not Fit to Represent London', HOPE not hate, n.d., https://hopenothate.org.uk/susan-hall-election-hub/
5. M. Townsend, 'Most Londoners Think Tory Mayoral Candidate Susan Hall's Social Media Activity Is Racist, Poll Finds', *The Guardian*, 7 October 2023, https://www.theguardian.com/uk-news/2023/oct/07/most-londoners-think-tory-mayoral-candidate-susan-hall-social-media-activity-is-racist-poll-finds
6. 'Stop Pampering the Left's Attack Dog', *The Critic*, 14 May 2024, https://thecritic.co.uk/stop-pampering-the-lefts-attack-dog/
7. M. Brown, '"Key Architect" of Riots after Southport Attack Jailed for Seven and a Half Years', *The Guardian*, 6 January 2025, https://www.theguardian.com/uk-news/2025/jan/06/key-architect-of-riots-after-southport-attack-jailed-for-seven-and-a-half-years

4: The Battle for Barking and Dagenham

1. F. Elliott, 'Hodge: White Voters Flock to BNP Because of Neglect by Labour', *Independent*, 16 April 2006, https://www.independent.co.uk/news/uk/politics/hodge-white-voters-flock-to-bnp-because-of-neglect-by-labour-358050.html
2. 'BNP at 7% in YouGov Poll for Telegraph', ConservativeHome, 21 April 2006, https://conservativehome.blogs.com/torydiary/2006/04/bnp_at_7_in_you.html
3. L. Brooks, 'Election Voices: "Young People Don't Think Their Vote Will Make a Difference"', *The Guardian*, 6 April 2010, https://www.theguardian.com/politics/2010/apr/06/general-election-2010-young-voices
4. 'BNP Leader Nick Griffin Challenges Unilever over Marmite Image', On Demand News, YouTube, 22 April 2010, https://www.youtube.com/watch?v=OH3CaTtYyBU
5. C. Woodhouse, 'Marmite Launches Legal Action against BNP', *Independent*, 22 April 2010, https://www.independent.co.uk/news/uk/politics/marmite-launches-legal-action-against-bnp-1951308.html

5: When Hate Comes to Town

1. 'Still Rigged: Racism in the UK Labour Market', TUC, 31 August 2022, https://www.tuc.org.uk/research-analysis/reports/still-rigged-racism-uk-labour-market
2. Race inequalities and ethnic disparities in healthcare, British Medical Association, 31 March 2021, https://www.bma.org.uk/advice-and-support/equality-and-diversity-guidance/race-equality-in-medicine/race-inequalities-and-ethnic-disparities-in-healthcare
3. @Nigel_Farage, X, 18 July 2024, https://x.com/Nigel_Farage/status/1814047452212740479

NOTES

4. Lee Anderson, Facebook, 19 July 2024, https://www.facebook.com/LeeAndersoninAshfieldEastwood/photos/disgraceful-scenesimport-a-third-world-culture-then-you-get-third-world-behaviou/1008736060924989/?paipv=0&amp%3Beav=AfbjBexY1dZw5HbT62g5AFkr700hbTfQhv6SkSCngcjjw4F0MdcUYVitqHPbg886hSo&amp%3B_rdr
5. 'Who Do the Online Agitators Think They Are to Pass Judgement on Harehills and the Great City of Leeds?', *Yorkshire Post*, 19 July 2024, https://www.yorkshirepost.co.uk/news/opinion/columnists/who-do-the-online-agitators-think-they-are-to-pass-judgement-on-harehills-and-the-great-city-of-leeds-4709317
6. 'About', Hopeful Towns, n.d., https://www.hopefultowns.co.uk/about
7. 'Understanding Community Resilience in Our Towns', HOPE not hate, August 2020, https://hopenothate.org.uk/wp-content/uploads/2020/09/Understanding-community-resilience-in-our-towns.pdf
8. 'Fear and HOPE 2024: The Case for Community Resilience', HOPE not hate, October 2024, https://hopenothate.org.uk/fear-and-hope-2024/

6: Tackling Taboo Issues

1. H. Dixon, 'Lamborghini Lawyer of Manchester "Victims" Believes Allah Chose Him to "Challenge the Zionist Regime"', *The Telegraph*, 26 July 2024, https://www.telegraph.co.uk/news/2024/07/26/akhmed-yakoob-lawyer-manchester-airport-police/
2. W. Hazell, 'TikTok Lawyer Endorsed by Galloway for Mayoral Election Says He Was Sent by Allah to Fight Zionism', *The Telegraph*, 20 April 2024, https://www.telegraph.co.uk/news/2024/04/20/galloway-west-midlands-mayor-allah-zionism-akhmed-yakoob/

7: Celebrating Modern Britain

1. 'PM's Speech at Munich Security Conference', Gov.uk, 5 February 2011, https://www.gov.uk/government/speeches/pms-speech-at-munich-security-conference
2. N. Clegg, Full Transcript, Nick Clegg Speech on Multiculturalism, Luton, 3 March 2011', *New Statesman*, 3 March 2011, https://www.newstatesman.com/politics/uk-politics/2011/03/open-liberal-violent

8: Kippered

1. International Business Times, 13 March 2015, https://www.ibtimes.co.uk/ukip-leader-nigel-farage-desperate-create-green-unpleasant-land-1491854
2. C. Hope, 'Ukip Already Has Four Seats "In the Bag", Says Leading Expert Matthew Goodwin', *The Telegraph*, 4 March 2015, https://www.telegraph.

co.uk/news/politics/11450075/Ukip-already-has-four-seats-in-the-bag-says-leading-expert-Matthew-Goodwin.html
3. M. Holehouse, 'Revealed: Nigel Farage Planned Aids Comment as Part of "Shock and Awful" TV Debate Strategy', *The Telegraph*, 3 April 2015, https://www.telegraph.co.uk/news/general-election-2015/11514369/Revealed-Nigel-Farage-planned-Aids-comment-as-part-of-shock-and-awful-TV-debate-strategy.html
4. 'Gordon Brown: Lead, Not Leave', People's In, Facebook, 3 June 2016, https://www.facebook.com/watch/?v=1053759234700690
5. D. Boffey and T. Helm, 'Vote Leave Embroiled in Race Row over Turkey Security Threat Claims', *The Guardian*, 22 May 2016, https://www.theguardian.com/politics/2016/may/21/vote-leave-prejudice-turkey-eu-security-threat
6. D. Maddox, '"Wrong and Unfair!" Ukip Accuses Labour of "Cheating" in Target Constituency', *Express*, 1 June 2017, https://www.express.co.uk/news/politics/812058/Election-2017-UK-Ukip-Labour-Left-Hope-Not-Hate-Dagenham-Rainham

9: Hate International

1. '"Mr. Brexit" Nigel Farage Speaks at Donald Trump Rally in Jackson, MS', Right Side Broadcasting Network, YouTube, 25 August 2016, https://www.youtube.com/watch?v=oj4K9fr_WgY
2. P. Hermansson, 'My Time Undercover with the Alt-Right', *New York Times*, 27 September 2017, https://www.nytimes.com/2017/09/27/opinion/alt-right-neo-nazis.html; B. Lindquist and P. Hermansson (dirs), *Undercover in the Alt-right*, Sveriges Television, Silverfish Media, 2018, https://www.imdb.com/title/tt8836342/
3. https://www.routledge.com/The-International-Alt-Right-Fascism-for-the-21st-Century/Hermansson-Lawrence-Mulhall-Murdoch/p/book/9781138363861?srsltid=AfmBOor0lYCHh0cYfmM2Sho2tNEC9t_Np0Ok-TgSyOvM3cXNkykX6cva
4. S. Murdoch, 'Defend Europe Extremists Charter Ship from Convicted Fraudster', HOPE not hate, 17 July 2017, https://hopenothate.org.uk/2017/07/17/defend-europe-extremists-charter-ship-convicted-fraudster/
5. M. Townsend, 'Far-Right Activist Posted to Serve on Trident Submarine', *The Guardian*, 24 August 2019, https://www.theguardian.com/world/2019/aug/24/far-right-groups-infiltrated-uk-nuclear-submarine-crew
6. 'Exclusive: Could *The Telegraph* Be Bought by a Political Extremist?', *The News Agents*, 22 February 2024, https://podcasts.apple.com/gb/podcast/exclusive-could-the-telegraph-be-bought-by-a/id1640878689?i=1000646416938
7. 'Alliance for Responsible Citizenship', Legatum, n.d., https://www.legatum.com/portfolio/alliance-for-responsible-citizenship/

NOTES

8. *Undercover: Exposing the Far Right*, Channel 4, 21 October 2024, https://www.channel4.com/programmes/undercover-exposing-the-far-right
9. 'History of the Pioneer Fund', HOPE not hate, 16 October 2024, https://investigations.hopenothate.org.uk/history-pioneer-fund/
10. 'Jared Taylor', Southern Poverty Law Center, n.d., https://www.splcenter.org/resources/extremist-files/jared-taylor/
11. H. Shukman and P. Hermansson, 'Race Science Inc.', HOPE not hate, 16 October 2024, https://investigations.hopenothate.org.uk/race-science-inc/
12. Ibid.
13. Ibid.
14. D. Miller, 'Beyond the Iron Gates: How Nazi-Satanists Infiltrated the UK Underground', The Quietus, 27 November 2018, https://thequietus.com/opinion-and-essays/black-sky-thinking/ona-fascism-nazis-folk-horror-underground-occult/
15. Shukman and Hermansson, 'Race Science Inc.'

10: Civic Pride

1. 'Community Britain', Co-operative Party, n.d., https://party.coop/community/
2. B. Flatman, 'UK Nightlife Faces Extinction by 2029 if Venue Closures Persist, Warns Industry Body', Building Design, 3 January 2025, https://www.bdonline.co.uk/news/uk-nightlife-faces-extinction-by-2029-if-venue-closures-persist-warns-industry-body/5133603.article
3. 'New UK Government "Must Address Play Crisis" as a Third of Children in Britain Do Not Have Access to Any Nearby Playgrounds', Fields in Trust, 6 June 2024, https://fieldsintrust.org/about-us/news/new-uk-government-must-address-play-crisis-as-a-third-of-children-in-britain-do-not-have-access-to-any-nearby-playgrounds
4. 'Online Nation: 2024 Report', Ofcom, 28 November 2024, https://www.ofcom.org.uk/siteassets/resources/documents/research-and-data/online-research/online-nation/2024/online-nation-2024-report.pdf?v=386238
5. H. Paylor and A. Baker, 'The Long Shadow of the Cost of Living Emergency', Carnegie UK, 26 April 2023, https://carnegieuk.org/publication/the-long-shadow-of-the-cost-of-living-emergency/
6. 'Understanding Community Resilience in Our Towns', https://www.belongnetwork.co.uk/resources/understanding-community-resilience-in-our-towns/
7. 'Building Back Resilient: Strengthening Communities through the COVID-19 Recovery', Hopeful Towns, 1 November 2021, https://hopenothate.org.uk/2021/11/01/building-back-resilient-strengthening-communities-through-the-covid-19-recovery/
8. 'Loss on the Terraces: Football, Towns and Local Identity', Hopeful Towns, 20 October 2020, https://hopenothate.org.uk/2020/10/20/loss-on-the-terraces-football-towns-and-local-identity/

9. P. Heatherington, 'Ghost Towns', *The Guardian*, 7 November 2001, https://www.theguardian.com/society/2001/nov/07/housingpolicy.guardiansocietysupplement

11: Young Angry Men

1. I. Youngs, 'Adolescence Hard to Watch as a Dad, Starmer Tells Creators', BBC, 31 March 2025, https://www.bbc.co.uk/news/articles/cx28neprdppo
2. H. Green and D. Guinness, Adolescence Is a Powerful Wake-Up Call about What's Happening to Our Sons Online', *Big Issue*, 23 March 2025, https://www.bigissue.com/opinion/adolescence-misogyny-masculinity-boys-wake-up-call/
3. Jacqueline Jenkinson, 'The 1919 Race Riots in Britain: Their Background and Consequences', PhD diss., University of Edinburgh, 1987.
4. G. Pearson, '"Paki-Bashing" in a North East Lancashire Cotton Town: A Case Study and Its History', in G. Mungham and G. Pearson (eds), *Working Class Youth Culture*, London, Routledge, 1976, https://www.taylorfrancis.com/chapters/edit/10.4324/9781003460251-4/paki-bashing-north-east-lancashire-cotton-town-geoff-pearson
5. 'The Manosphere', HOPE not hate, n.d., https://hopenothate.org.uk/2019/02/18/state-of-hate-2019-manosphere-explained/
6. 'Andrew Tate', HOPE not hate, n.d., https://hopenothate.org.uk/andrew-tate/
7. 'Andrew Tate Banned from Social Media Platforms after HOPE not hate Campaign', HOPE not hate, 23 August 2022, https://hopenothate.org.uk/2022/08/23/andrew-tate-banned-from-major-social-media-platforms-after-hope-not-hate-campaign/
8. 'State of Hate 2024: Pessimism, Decline and a Rising Radical Right', HOPE not hate, 2024, https://hopenothate.org.uk/state-of-hate-2024/
9. A. McDonnell, 'How Britain Voted in the 2024 General Election', YouGov, 8 July 2024, https://yougov.co.uk/politics/articles/49978-how-britain-voted-in-the-2024-general-election
10. 'State of Hate 2025: Reform Rising and Racist Riots', HOPE not hate, 2025, https://hopenothate.org.uk/state-of-hate-2025/
11. A. Deo, 'Plugged In but Disconnected: Young People and Hateful Attitudes', HOPE not hate, July 2024, https://hopenothate.org.uk/plugged-in/
12. 'Youth Radicalisation: A New Frontier in Terrorism and Security', Vision of Humanity, 20 March 2025, https://www.visionofhumanity.org/youth-radicalisation-a-new-frontier-in-terrorism-and-security/
13. 'Social Media Algorithms Amplify Misogynistic Content to Teens', UCL News, 5 February 2024, https://www.ucl.ac.uk/news/2024/feb/social-media-algorithms-amplify-misogynistic-content-teens
14. D. Lawrence, 'Luke Hunter: Profile of a Nazi Terror Propagandist', HOPE not hate, 23 December 2020, https://hopenothate.org.uk/2020/12/23/luke-hunter-profile-of-a-nazi-terror-propagandist/

NOTES

15. 'State of Hate 2021: Backlash, Conspiracies & Confrontation', HOPE not hate, 2021, p. 64, https://hopenothate.org.uk/wp-content/uploads/2021/02/state-of-hate-2021-v21Oct.pdf
16. J. Stone, 'Priti Patel Says Fans Have Right to Boo England Team for "Gesture Politics" of Taking the Knee', *Independent*, 14 June 2021, https://www.independent.co.uk/news/uk/politics/priti-patel-taking-knee-boo-england-b1865409.html
17. 'The Forgotten: How White Working-Class Pupils Have Been Let Down, and How to Change It', House of Commons Education Committee, 22 June 2021, https://publications.parliament.uk/pa/cm5802/cmselect/cmeduc/85/8502.htm
18. K. Malik, 'Being White Won't Hold Boys Back: Being Working Class Just Might', *The Guardian*, 18 October 2020, https://www.theguardian.com/commentisfree/2020/oct/18/being-white-wont-hold-boys-back-being-working-class-just-might
19. A. Deo, 'Plugged In but Disconnected: Young People and Hateful Attitudes', HOPE not hate, July 2024, https://hopenothate.org.uk/plugged-in/
20. P. Hermansson, 'The Rapewaffen Telegram Channel', HOPE not hate, 23 June 2020, https://hopenothate.org.uk/tag/rapewaffen/
21. P. Hermansson, 'State of Hate 2025: The Online Exploitation Cult Grooming Teenagers to Violence', HOPE not hate, 2025, https://hopenothate.org.uk/state-of-hate-2025-764/
22. 'Britain's Lost Generation: Government Cuts Have Shattered Council Youth Services and Left Vulnerable Youngsters Exposed', Unison, June 2024, https://www.unison.org.uk/content/uploads/2024/06/youth-services-final-FINAL.pdf
23. 'Almost a Billion-Pound Decline in Funding for Youth Services Revealed by YMCA', YMCA, 23 January 2020, https://www.ymcadlg.org/almost-a-billion-pound-decline-in-funding-for-youth-services-revealed-by-ymca/
24. G. Kumah, 'YMCA Calls for Urgent Action to Reverse Decline in Youth Services Funding', YMCA, 28 January 2025, https://ymca.org.uk/ymca-calls-for-urgent-action-to-reverse-decline-in-youth-services-funding/
25. 'Youth Provision and Life Outcomes Research', Department for Culture, Media and Sport, 29 February 2024, https://www.gov.uk/government/publications/youth-provision-and-life-outcomes-research

12: Living Together ... Well

1. @elonmusk, X, 4 August 2024, https://x.com/elonmusk/status/1819933223536742771?lang=en
2. D. Betz, 'Civil War Comes to the West', *Military Strategy Magazine* 9, no. 1 (Summer 2023): 20–6, https://www.militarystrategymagazine.com/article/civil-war-comes-to-the-west/

3. 'The Coming British Civil War: David Betz', Maiden Mother Matriarch, YouTube, 12 February 2025, https://www.youtube.com/watch?v=Gid48FgiHho
4. P. Embery, 'Is Britain Heading for Civil War?', Substack, 4 March 2025, https://substack.com/home/post/p-158333279
5. 'Britain's Civil War Will Be Ethnic: Islamists Have Already Started It; Prof. David Betz', New Culture Forum, YouTube, 7 April 2025, https://www.youtube.com/watch?v=IJZ_puCwuAA
6. R. Dreher, 'Is Civil War Coming to Europe?', *European Conservative*, 14 April 2025, https://europeanconservative.com/articles/commentary/is-civil-war-coming-to-europe/
7. T. Stanley, 'Britain Is Lurching towards Civil War, and Nobody Knows How to Stop It', *The Telegraph*, 3 April 2025, https://www.telegraph.co.uk/news/2025/04/03/civil-war-is-coming-to-britain/
8. 'The Coming British Civil War: David Betz', Maiden Mother Matriarch, YouTube, 12 February 2025, https://www.youtube.com/watch?v=Gid48FgiHho
9. 'British Muslims in Numbers: Census Report Summary March 2025', Muslim Council of Britain, March 2025, https://mcb.org.uk/wp-content/uploads/2025/03/Census-Report-Summary-2025-.pdf
10. A. Mohdin, 'Census Says 39% of Muslims Live in Most Deprived Areas of England and Wales', *The Guardian*, 30 November 2022, https://www.theguardian.com/world/2022/nov/30/census-says-39-of-muslims-live-in-most-deprived-areas-of-england-and-wales
11. A. Deo and M. Malik, 'Fear & Hope 2024: The Case for Community Resilience', HOPE not hate, October 2024, https://hopenothate.org.uk/wp-content/uploads/2024/10/FINAL-FEAR-AND-HOPE-291024.pdf
12. R. Carter and N. Lowles, 'Fear and HOPE 2017: Race, Faith and Belonging in Today's England', HOPE not hate, 2017, https://hopenothate.org.uk/wp-content/uploads/2017/08/fear-and-hope-4-2017-08.pdf
13. @Taj_Ali1, X, 18 May 2025, https://x.com/Taj_Ali1/status/1924200286374994195
14. J. Clements and D. Forman, 'Listening to British Muslims on Policing, Extremism and Prevent', Crest Advisory, 2 March 2020, https://www.crestadvisory.com/post/executive-summary-listening-to-british-muslims-on-policing-extremism-and-prevent
15. L. Dearden, 'British Muslims Are Concerned about Islamist Extremism and Do Trust the Police, Survey Finds', *Independent*, 2 March 2020, https://www.independent.co.uk/news/uk/home-news/muslims-uk-views-extremism-police-prevent-survey-crest-a9370081.html
16. 'Further Funding Cuts for Councils Would Be Disastrous: Urgent Funding and Reform Is Needed', Local Government Association, 13 September 2024, https://www.local.gov.uk/about/news/further-funding-cuts-councils-would-be-disastrous-urgent-funding-and-reform-needed

NOTES

17. R. Merrick, 'Michael Gove Has Same "Crazy" Anti-Muslim Policies as Donald Trump, Former Tory Chairwoman Says', *Independent*, 25 March 2017, https://www.independent.co.uk/news/uk/politics/michael-gove-donald-trump-baroness-warsi-anti-muslim-crazy-tory-chairwoman-a7649411.html
18. 'Qari Asim: Imam Removed as Government Adviser over Film Protests', BBC, 13 June 2022, https://www.bbc.co.uk/news/uk-england-leeds-61771695
19. '5Pillars UK: What Are British Islamists Thinking?', Sara Khan, 20 November 2017, https://www.sarakhan.co.uk/blog/5pillars-uk-what-are-british-islamists-thinking/
20. 'British Islamist Roshan Salih, Editor Of 5Pillars: I Do Not See Britain as Home, It Is the "Abode of Infidels"; I Am Supportive of Taliban, Wish Them a Lot of Success; Muslims in Britain Should Withdraw Their Children from School, Especially the Girls', MEMRI TV, 28 August 2024, https://www.memri.org/tv/british-islamist-roshan-salih-editor-5pillars-britain-not-home-abode-infidels-support-taliban-girls-school
21. 'July 4th Is Muslim Independence Day … from Labour', 5Pillars UK, 30 May 2024, https://5pillarsuk.com/2024/05/30/july-4th-is-muslim-independence-day-from-labour/
22. 'The Muslim Vote Pledges Not to Endorse Any Labour or Tory Candidates', 5Pillars UK, 8 June 2024, https://5pillarsuk.com/2024/06/08/the-muslim-vote-pledges-not-to-endorse-any-labour-or-tory-candidates/
23. Y. Koshy, 'What the Unrest in Leicester Revealed about Britain – and Modi's India', *The Guardian*, 8 February 2024, https://www.theguardian.com/uk-news/2024/feb/08/unrest-leicester-muslim-hindu-revealed-britain-modi-india-2022
24. P. Deneen, 'Revitalizing the American Republic', Postliberal Order, 25 November 2024, https://www.postliberalorder.com/p/revitalizing-the-virtues-of-the-american
25. E. Oldfield, 'Patrick Deneen on the Failure of Liberalism and the Importance of Relational Living', Theos, 14 June 2023, https://www.theosthinktank.co.uk/comment/2023/06/14/patrick-deneen-on-the-failure-of-liberalism-and-the-importance-of-relational-living
26. S. Schneck, '"Regime Change" Argues for a Controversial Postliberal Future', National Catholic Reporter, 29 September 2023, https://www.ncronline.org/culture/book-reviews/regime-change-argues-controversial-postliberal-future

13: Fool's Gold

1. 'Home Office Smashes Targets with Mass Surge in Migrant Removals', Home Office, 10 February 2025, https://www.gov.uk/government/news/home-office-smashes-targets-with-mass-surge-in-migrant-removals

2. E. Solomon, 'Lights, Camera, and a New Low: Why Is the Government Making Deportation TV', 10 February 2025, https://www.theguardian.com/commentisfree/2025/feb/10/immigration-asylum-labour-deportation-flights
3. R. Carter, 'Fear, HOPE & Loss: Understanding the Drivers of HOPE and hate', Hopeful Towns, September 2018, https://www.hopefultowns.co.uk/_files/ugd/078118_61e4a6ea0b3a4090babb963af01c3752.pdf
4. 'Burnley', Citypopulation.de, n.d., https://citypopulation.de/en/uk/admin/lancashire/E07000117__burnley/
5. Carter, 'Fear, HOPE & Loss'.
6. 'Understanding Community Resilience in Our Towns', August 2020, https://hopenothate.org.uk/wp-content/uploads/2020/09/Understanding-community-resilience-in-our-towns.pdf
7. 'Area Profile: Abbey Hulton', ONS, n.d., https://www.ons.gov.uk/visualisations/customprofiles/build/#E05014555
8. '"Left Behind" Neighbourhoods', Local Trust, n.d., https://localtrust.org.uk/policy/left-behind-neighbourhoods/
9. 'Index of Multiple Deprivation', Geographic Data Service, n.d., https://data.cdrc.ac.uk/dataset/index-multiple-deprivation-imd
10. J. Lichfield, 'Stoke: The City That Britain Forgot', Unherd, 20 November 2019, https://unherd.com/2019/11/stoke-the-city-that-britain-forgot/
11. 'The English Indices of Deprivation 2010 Stoke-on-Trent: Summary', Gov.uk, March 2011, https://webapps.stoke.gov.uk/uploadedfiles/Indices%20of%20Deprivation%202010%20-%20Summary.pdf
12. S. Fothergill, T. Gore and D. Leather, 'The State of the Coalfields 2024: Economic and Social Conditions in the Former Coalfields of England, Scotland and Wales', Sheffield Hallam University, Centre for Regional Economic and Social Research, 19 April 2024, https://www.shu.ac.uk/centre-regional-economic-social-research/publications/state-of-the-coalfields-2024
13. D. Eherington, M. Gray and L. Buckner, 'Still Digging Deeper: The Impact of Austerity on Inequalities and Deprivation in the Coalfied Areas', University of Staffordshire, n.d., https://eprints.staffs.ac.uk/8893/
14. 'Area Profile', ONS, n.d., https://www.ons.gov.uk/visualisations/customprofiles/build/#E14001211
15. B. Francis-Devine, 'Constituency Data: Indices of Deprivation', House of Commons Library, 4 July 2024, https://commonslibrary.parliament.uk/constituency-data-indices-of-deprivation/
16. D. Penna, '"Hyper-Liberal" Labour Ignoring Working-Class Immigration Concerns, Says Red Wall MP', *The Telegraph*, 4 May 2025, https://www.telegraph.co.uk/politics/2025/05/04/hyper-liberal-labour-ignoring-immigration-concerns/
17. M. Glasman, 'Labour Faces the Same Fate as the Tories after Reform Surge – Unless It Does Five Things', *The Sun*, 3 May 2025, https://www.thesun.co.uk/news/politics/34783180/maurice-glasman-keir-starmer-election/

NOTES

18. 'Fear and HOPE: The New Politics of Identity', HOPE not hate, 14 March 2011, https://hopenothate.org.uk/2011/03/14/fear-and-hope-the-new-politics-of-identity/
19. '2024 Global Report on Internal Displacement', Internal Displacement Monitoring Centre, 2024, https://www.internal-displacement.org/global-report/grid2024/
20. F. O'Toole, 'Lead Role on History's Stage', *Irish Times*, 15 November 2003, https://www.irishtimes.com/opinion/editorial/the-irish-times-view-on-citizens-assemblies-out-sourcing-political-decisions-1.392488

14: Green Shoots

1. Left Foot Forward, 17 February 2025, https://leftfootforward.org/2025/02/reforms-richard-tice-calls-man-made-climate-change-absolute-garbage-in-embarrassing-interview/
2. @Nigel_Farage, X, 13 June 2023, https://x.com/Nigel_Farage/status/1668555766670802944
3. @Nigel_Farage, X, 19 January 2024, https://x.com/Nigel_Farage/status/1748312917945065768
4. @TiceRichard, X, 21 January 2024, https://x.com/TiceRichard/status/1749054301811445944
5. The Global Warming Policy Foundation, https://thegwpf.org/images/stories/gwpf-reports/accounts.pdf
6. C. Davies and S. Goldenberg, 'The Voices of Climate Change Sceptics', *The Guardian*, 24 November 2009, https://www.theguardian.com/environment/2009/nov/24/voices-of-climate-change-denial
7. H. Horton, 'Tory MP Steve Baker Shares Paper Denying Climate Crisis', *The Guardian*, 15 April 2022, https://www.theguardian.com/politics/2022/apr/15/tory-mp-steve-baker-shares-paper-denying-climate-crisis
8. 'Global Warming Policy Foundation (GWPF)', DeSmog, n.d., https://www.desmog.com/global-warming-policy-foundation/
9. A. Kroll, 'Exposed: The Dark-Money ATM of the Conservative Movement', *Mother Jones*, 5 February 2013, https://www.motherjones.com/politics/2013/02/donors-trust-donor-capital-fund-dark-money-koch-bradley-devos/
10. A. Bychawski, 'Exclusive: Influential UK Net-Zero Sceptics Funded by US Oil "Dark Money"', openDemocracy, 4 May 2022, https://www.opendemocracy.net/en/dark-money-investigations/global-warming-policy-foundation-net-zero-watch-koch-brothers/
11. 'Smoke, Mirrors & Hot Air', Union of Concerned Scientists, January 2007, http://www.ucsusa.org/sites/default/files/legacy/assets/documents/global_warming/exxon_report.pdf
12. 'Heart of the Matter', *Nature* 475 (2011): 423–4, https://www.nature.com/articles/475423b

13. H. Horton and B. Quinn, 'Farage and Truss Attend UK Launch of US Climate Denial Group', *The Guardian*, 15 January 2025, https://www.theguardian.com/environment/2025/jan/15/farage-and-truss-attend-uk-launch-of-us-climate-denial-group-heartland
14. @LoisPerry26, Twitter/X, 13 December 2021, https://x.com/LoisPerry26/status/1470540869140889608
15. 'Extreme Weather. Extreme Denial. Extreme Politics', HOPE not hate, n.d., https://hopenothate.org.uk/climate-change-far-right/yes-we-need-climate-action-but-it-needs-to-be-rooted-in-peoples-daily-reality/
16. 'From the Editor: "A Meat Tax Was Never a Policy in the First Place: It's Like Saying I Have Cancelled My Plans to Stop Eating Steak"', *Farmers Guardian*, 25 September 2023, https://www.farmersguardian.com:8443/blog/4128741/editor-meat-tax-policy-saying-cancelled-plans-stop-eating-steak
17. M. Silva, '15 Minute Cities: How They Got Caught in Conspiracy Theories', BBC, 3 October 2023, https://www.bbc.co.uk/news/uk-politics-66990302
18. @LaylaMoran, Twitter/X, 2 Octobe 2023, https://x.com/LaylaMoran/status/1708868459008761881
19. B. Wheeler, 'Blair Says Current Net Zero Policies "Doomed to Fail"', BBC, 29 April 2025, https://www.bbc.co.uk/news/articles/cpvrwyp0jx3o
20. D. Penna, 'Lord Blunkett: Net Zero Push Risks Making Labour Toxic to Voters', *The Telegraph*, 4 May 2025, https://www.telegraph.co.uk/politics/2025/05/04/lord-blunkett-net-zero-push-risks-labour-toxic-voters/
21. 'Telling Everyday Stories of Climate Impacts', Round Our Way, n.d., https://www.roundourway.org/
22. M. Poynting, 'One in Four Properties at Flood Risk by 2050: Report', BBC, 17 December 2024, https://www.bbc.co.uk/news/articles/c99x4599gr7o
23. N. Jobe, 'Bus Services Cut by More than 80% in Parts of England and Wales since 2008, Finds Study', *The Guardian*, 28 November 2023, https://www.theguardian.com/uk-news/2023/nov/28/bus-services-cut-by-more-than-80-perent-in-parts-of-england-and-wales-since-2008-finds-study
24. 'Revealed: Bus Cuts Hit Deprived Areas the Hardest', IPPR, 7 January 2025, https://www.ippr.org/media-office/revealed-bus-cuts-hit-deprived-areas-the-hardest
25. S. Akehurst, 'Getting to Know "Reform Curious Labour Voters"', Persuasion UK, April 2025, https://cdn.persuasionuk.org/reform_labour_final_report_cc3c7c1dd2.pdf
26. D. Maddox, 'Downing Street Fury at Farage Plot to Tie Up Starmer Government in Legal Challenges', *Independent*, 4 May 2025, https://www.independent.co.uk/news/uk/politics/nigel-farage-reform-diversity-jenkyns-b2744343.html

NOTES

15: Power to the People

1. 'Trust and Confidence in Britain's System of Government at Record Low', National Centre for Social Research, 12 June 2024, https://natcen.ac.uk/news/trust-and-confidence-britains-system-government-record-low
2. T. Ridley-Castle, 'This Year's General Election Left Millions of Voices Unheard', Electoral Reform Society, 19 December 2024, https://electoral-reform.org.uk/this-years-general-election-left-millions-of-voices-unheard/
3. 'Manifesto for Democracy 2024', Electoral Reform Society, 12 June 2024, https://electoral-reform.org.uk/latest-news-and-research/parliamentary-briefings/manifesto-for-democracy-2024/
4. 'The Case for Civic and Democratic Engagement', Local Government Association, n.d., https://www.local.gov.uk/topics/devolution/devolution-online-hub/public-service-reform-tools/engaging-citizens-devolution-0
5. 'Putin Chef's Kisses of Death: Russia's Shadow Army's State-Run Structure Exposed', Bellingcat, 14 August 2020, https://www.bellingcat.com/news/uk-and-europe/2020/08/14/pmc-structure-exposed/
6. M. Innes, 'Russian Influence and Interference Measures following the 2017 UK Terrorist Attacks', CREST, 18 December 2017, https://crestresearch.ac.uk/resources/russian-influence-uk-terrorist-attacks/
7. J. Halliday et al., 'Revealed: The Hidden Global Network behind Tommy Robinson', *The Guardian*, 7 December 2018, https://www.theguardian.com/uk-news/2018/dec/07/tommy-robinson-global-support-brexit-march
8. G. Le Dem, 'Chantal Mouffe: "We Urgently Need to Promote a Left-Populism"', Verso blog, 4 August 2017, https://www.versobooks.com/en-gb/blogs/news/3341-chantal-mouffe-we-urgently-need-to-promote-a-left-populism
9. 'Democratic Populism and Human Politics', Ricken Patel, 31 January 2025, https://www.rickenpatel.net/post/democratic-populism-and-human-politics

16: Hope

1. 'Which of the Following Do You Think Is Most Likely to Be Prime Minister after the Next General Election?', YouGov, 16 May 2025, https://yougov.co.uk/topics/politics/survey-results/daily/2025/05/16/c6e51/1

For more unmissable reads,
sign up to the HarperNorth newsletter at
www.harpernorth.co.uk

or find us on X at
@HarperNorthUK